Managing
Today's University

Frederick E. Balderston

MANAGING

TODAY'S

UNIVERSITY

 Jossey-Bass Publishers
San Francisco · Washington · London · 1974

MANAGING TODAY'S UNIVERSITY
by Frederick E. Balderston

Copyright © 1974 by: Jossey-Bass, Inc., Publishers
615 Montgomery Street
San Francisco, California 94111
&
Jossey-Bass Limited
3 Henrietta Street
London WC2E 8LU

Library of Congress Catalogue Card Number LC 74-9111

International Standard Book Number ISBN 0-87589-236-1

Manufactured in the United States of America

JACKET DESIGN BY WILLI BAUM

FIRST EDITION

Code 7428

The Jossey-Bass
Series in Higher Education

Preface

Universities are remarkably flexible and resilient organizations. But conflicting demands on their resources and financial stringency have produced serious new stresses within them. In the past, these institutions were capable of growing in many directions without having to assess mission or scope and without being specifically accountable—financially or otherwise—to funding agencies, the tax-paying public, faculty, or students. That period has ended, and universities increasingly are being asked to justify themselves. Accountability is difficult to achieve. The problems of identifying and measuring the components of such complex organizations or of analyzing and evaluating their performances are enormous, and these problems are complicated by uncertainties about how to identify and demonstrate the quality and quantity of education, research, and public service. Each year large numbers of graduates receive degrees, research is conducted in many fields and through many organizational arrangements, and public service programs are engineered. But the task of justifying the continued investment in higher education is formidable.

In *Managing the University* I have brought together a variety of ideas about how universities can solve these problems. I have gleaned the ideas from a background as a student and teacher of economics and management in several universities; as a research administrator; as a vice-president of the University of California; as a member of the Technical Advisory Committee to the Carnegie Commission on Higher Education and of the Board of Directors of the National Center for Higher Education Management Systems at WICHE; and as codirector of the Ford Foundation Program for Research in University Administration of the University of California, from 1968 to 1973.

The guiding purpose of the Ford Foundation program was to develop and test, in empirical applications, new techniques to analyze university problems and new models of educational resource allocation in order to assist university decision-makers and others concerned with university management to understand the basic functions of these complex systems and to utilize effectively the tools of modern management. To attain this objective, the program was funded in May 1968 for a three-year period, and in August 1971 for a two-year continuation. Charles J. Hitch, president of the University of California, served with me as co-principal investigator. Roy Radner, professor of economics and statistics, University of California, Berkeley, was closely affiliated with the program as research advisor, critic, and graduate student advisor.

Policy guidance and in-house research direction were provided by a research directorate composed at various times of Robert M. Oliver, professor in the department of industrial engineering and operations research and chairman of the Operations Research Center, University of California, Berkeley; Stephen A. Hoenack, director of the Management Information Division, Office of Management Planning and Information Services, University of Minnesota; George B. Weathersby, lecturer, Graduate School of Education, Harvard University; and Frank A. Schmidtlein, currently with the Center for Research and Development in Higher Education, University of California, Berkeley.

The program personnel consisted primarily of doctoral students at the University of California, Berkeley, whose dissertation topics fitted into the scheme of the program. They included Jane W. Bolce, David W. Breneman, Sharon Bush, Daryl Carlson, Michael Cooper, Jonathan Halpern, Philip Held, Stephen Hoenack, David Hopkins, Jeffrey Morris, Hannah Kreplin, Lucian Pugliaresi, Ralph Purves, Robert Sanderson, Frank Schmidtlein, Gary Wagner,

Thomas Walsh, George B. Weathersby, Paul Wing, Donald Winkler, and David Wise. Among the senior researchers who contributed to the work of the program for varying periods were David Barththolomew, Arthur Geoffrion, Ferdinand Leimkuhler, and Kneale Marshall.

The program offices were located in close proximity to the Berkeley campus and the offices of the president of the University of California, the Carnegie Commission on Higher Education, and the Center for Research and Development in Higher Education. Interaction with members of all of these groups greatly aided program personnel by permitting them to become involved with ongoing problems of university administration, both at the single and at the multicampus level, and by providing contact with other research groups concerned with similar problems of investigation and analysis. To all the above, the program is indebted.

An advisory committee of people in key academic and administrative positions reviewed the work of the program and provided proposals for future research. The committee members, who met annually in Berkeley with the co-principal investigators and the research directorate of the program, included William J. Baumol, professor of economics at Princeton University; Robert L. Clodius, then vice-president of the University of Wisconsin; Alain Enthoven, then vice-president of Litton Industries, Inc., Richard W. Judy, professor of political economy at the University of Toronto; Benjamin Lawrence, director of the National Center for Higher Education Management Systems at the Western Interstate Commission on Higher Education; Jacob Marschak, professor in the Western Management Science Institute, University of California, Los Angeles; James G. March, David Jacks professor of higher education, Stanford University; Chester O. McCorkle, Jr., vice-president of the University of California; Joseph A. Pechman, director of economic studies, The Brookings Institution; and Roy Radner, professor of economics and statistics, University of California, Berkeley.

Ford Foundation support of the program is gratefully acknowledged. Concepts, techniques, and findings from the program have, hopefully, had some effect on the perspectives of planning and decision in the University of California. More than forty technical reports from the program have been distributed to interested universities, agencies, and individuals. These reports are listed in Appendix B. In many ways, the most important outcome of the program has been that a number of the young people who were affiliated with it have gone on to make important contributions in universities and national organizations. Our understanding of the complex organization of universities is still incomplete) and, given the dynamics of universities, it is likely to remain so). Nonetheless, many problem areas have proved susceptible to analysis through the Ford program. I hope that analysis will facilitate better understanding and consequently better management of large university systems.

I am indebted to colleagues in The Netherlands, where I was a visiting professor in the faculty of economics of the University of Amsterdam while on sabbatical leave from Berkeley during the spring of 1973, and in particular to Herman J. Hopman of the administration of the University of Amsterdam and George Verberg of the Planninggroup Postsecondary Education in the Ministry of Education, The Hague.

Special thanks are due to Susan Price and Breena Ahoy for expert typing, to Ikuku Workman for typing and drafting, to Carol Talpers for her skill, patience, and candor as an editor, and to my family for their patience.

Managing the University is written for those who share a special concern for the enduring qualities of universities and their contributions to society—citizens and trustees, students and faculty members, legislators and commission members, devoted alumni and energetic critics—as well as for administrators, budget analysts, economists, and planners who have specific professional and technical concerns with the subject. Reference is made where necessary to technical contributions and sources, but my intent has been to make the discussion accessible to the broadly interested reader.

Briefly, to outline the organization of topics and the rationale for this organization, Chapter One provides an initial definition of management-as-process and the reasons why management of universities has become an important issue. It offers some definition of the characteristics of the university and the nature of managerial decision-making in the university context as it is examined and illustrated throughout the book. Then, it sets a general analytical frame for what is to follow and shows why the university is inherently complex, based on my paper "Complementarity, Independence, and Substitution in University Resource Allocation and Operation" (1973). After a brief discussion of mission and scope, attention is given to the major processes of instruction and research, to the several types of university resources, and to the sources of funding. At every stage of concern—funding, resource inputs, activities, and goals or purposes—the university must deal with arrays of elements rather than single components; and the concepts of *complementarity, independence,* and *substitution* are introduced to suggest a framework that can be applied later to the issues of organization and resource analysis.

Chapter Two identifies the values that condition and motivate the behavior of persons in the university and characterize its philosophical commitments as an institution. Even though it is uncomfortable to do so from a strictly analytic standpoint, I believe it is important to present early in the book some notion of the gestalt of the university as a distinctive social organization, one that is and needs to be perceived as different from a church, an army division, a governmental agency, or a business corporation (even though it shares some of the attributes of each of these). This chapter seeks to define university values and atmosphere. Chapter One, then, demonstrates the structural complexity of the university that requires analytic subtlety, while Chapter Two identifies the moral requirements of the university's operation that require insight and patient nurturing. The apposition between these structural and evaluative issues recurs in the succeeding chapters.

Chapters Three and Four together show the structural frame of constituencies of the university (not clearly divisible as external or internal) that promote divergent interests and participate in the university's apparatus of influence and authority, and then outlines the academic organization of the university, showing how various units of university structure are arranged and linked with each other. Chapter Four completes this analysis by focusing on administrative services, representational entities, and the presidency.

Chapter Five, describes an imperative function of university management by illustrating the need for policy analyses at three levels of institutional choice—the procedural, substantive, and constitutional. In this chapter I suggest that some of our unfulfilled hopes for planning, programming, and budgeting systems may be achieved through decision-making by policy analysis. Such analysis requires however an appreciation of all the material in Chapters Six through Ten.

Chapter Six defines the market environments to which the university relates and analyzes the university's major transactional relations with its environment. These relations provide indicators of institutional opportunity, obligation, and evaluation, as illustrated by the fact that the university operates in a series of competitive environments with other institutions that provide evaluative signals for it.

At this point we are ready to examine the patterns of university costs, explain the techniques needed to measure and understand costs, and show what forces cause financial crisis. Chapters Seven, Eight, and Nine are the expository heart of the economics of university management. They discuss, in turn, cost analysis, resource allocation, and the varieties of financial stress. Chapter Eight is substantially based on my paper for the annual meeting of the American Council on Education in 1971 that appeared in the ACE proceedings volume, *Universal Higher Education.*

Chapter Ten takes up the need for information for decisions, the data sources and systems for extracting and focusing such information, and the design options for data systems of the kinds that are now necessary. It stems from my essay on the design and uses of information systems in *Evaluating Institutions for Accountability,* edited by Howard R. Bowen (*New Directions for Institutional Research,* No. 1, Spring 1974).

Chapter Eleven, the concluding chapter, provides an integration of this managerial perspective for the contemporary university by discussing issues and strategies for guiding the university towards survival, stability, and excellence on both short-range and long-term bases.

Berkeley, California   FREDERICK E. BALDERSTON
September 1974

Contents

Managing
Today's University

Chapter 1

Organizing for Management

The significant universities of the western world vary greatly in age, size, legal form of organization, institutional style, and mode of financing. Yet they have in common the coupling of teaching and research, the offering of a diversity of programs up to the most advanced stages of systematic learning, and the implicit commitment to humane ideals and scholarly interests that cross the boundaries of governments. They are (mostly, but not entirely) focused on the young and paid for by the old, through government. They are supposed to endure forever, and they make their budgets one uncertain year at a time.

Today, universities in all parts of the United States and in much of the rest of the world have other features in common. Their sponsors consider them too important to leave alone, in a world where knowledge counts, too costly to forget about, and yet dangerous to tinker with. Universities thus face new requirements for planning, new accommodations to coordination and control, and demands for explicit, rational management.

Need for Management

Historically, the university has been an institution, not an enterprise or a service agency. It makes strong claims for loyalty and

1

effort on those involved with it, and it defends a distinctive, autonomous place in society and the right to choose its members, settle its aims, and operate in its own way. Now the university has become a mixture of institution, enterprise, and agency. This is partly because it has assembled a large and confusing range of activities and operations, but partly also because the major parties at interest want to view it in different ways: the faculty and students, as an institution; the trustees and some administrators, as an enterprise; and the governmental sponsors, as an agency. Conflicts of purpose, law, motivation, and style flow from these different views.

University budgets have risen in the past two decades at a much faster rate than GNP. This growth is the result of enrollment expansion, program elaboration, productivity problems, new responsibilities, and inflation. Universities have put accelerating pressure on their sponsors, and now they must face counterpressures —both for planning and control and for severe budgetary constraint. Many universities are having to stabilize or even retrench in their activities and budgets after getting accustomed to the euphoria of growth and a rising internal standard of living.

Inescapably, the focus of this book, therefore, is on the allocation of scarce resources in universities, and on the analytics of choice as to organization, effectiveness, priority, and decision: in short, ways of *Managing Today's University*. Management has its politics, psychology, and art as well as its economics, technology, and science, and neither the reader nor the author should forget this. As a teacher and administrator, and a true believer in the university and what it seeks to do, I am only too aware of the paradox of this book: new approaches to management are very much needed and are on the way, yet management is counter to the university tradition. To some of the important audiences, it is a term conveying insult and provocation. And, indeed, it is a risk, for some of its systematic devices could deliver the university to its enemies or could damage its capacity to evoke the imagination, the stamina, and the free commitment that are essential for original learning. Thus, the obligation is to create, present, and use approaches to management in universities that will enhance their viability and effectiveness and will serve sensitively and not impair the work of the scholar and student. The use requires wisdom in the particular case, and all that can be done in exposition of approaches to management for universities is to show that the analytic devices presented are designed to take into account essential features of motivation and commitment that make the difference in the quality, as well as the quantity, of the work that scholars and students do.

Everyone involved in university management must give equal attention to processes, mechanisms, and consequences. The crucial—and the most puzzling and mysterious—of the processes are those of learning, seasoning of character, creative new work at the edges of knowledge and imagination, and responsible advocacy of values. There are many supporting processes too—for communication, for delivering intricate arrays and combinations of services, for evaluating and keeping track of where ideas, people, and resources are, and for decision.

The mechanisms and structures of the university—its physical facilities and organization—are ways to make the processes operate. Both the physical structures and the organizational mechanisms are largely given at any particular time in the history of the institution. Their sizes, shapes, and conditions are endowments of capability and also barriers to easy and rapid change. Change is costly and requires both design and investment.

Universities are more attuned to their processes and their mechanisms than they are to consequences. They customarily have much more exact measures of activity or size than they have of consequences or results. It is easier to get them to say how many students they have than what the students have learned and how they have changed. It is easier to count the books written than to say which are of value. Even the moral commitments of universities are largely to process and mechanism and not to consequences or to agreed goals: the process of free inquiry and exchange of ideas; the mechanisms for fair assessment and for resolving conflicts. But as to philosophical ends, universities are designed to house enduring disagreements without breaking apart.

Universities may be a prototype of the postindustrial organization. Partly this is because they live on and for knowledge, and knowledge is the matrix for the future society. But it may be, also, that the university at its best offers an interesting and sensitive balance between individuality and collective interdependence;

between felt commitment and formal authority; between creativity and production; and even between the frivolous and the serious, the sacred and the profane. Other organizations, if they are to advance the human condition, may in the future have to become more like universities than the other way round. The topics covered here, then, may be of some interest for comparative organization.

I have said that the processes, mechanisms, and consequences of university operations require equal attention. Where, then, is the focus of decision-making and of management in this intricate institutional context? Part of the answer is that resources are scarce relative to hopes and needs; either explicit institutional decisions are made about the use of resources, or the pattern of usage is determined by the ways whereby hundreds or thousands of individuals press their claims on each other and on the institution. Increasing weight is now given to explicit decisions about the allocation of resources, and the good sense with which these decisions can be made is one significant issue to which the book is addressed. The other part of the answer is that universities are complex, bureaucratic, and on many matters voluntaristic and consultative. We cannot, therefore, examine the issues as if there were one decision-maker or one manager. Rather, proposals and counterproposals, weighing of possibilities, and consultation with those who legally or functionally have a role in the decision—all these contribute to the important official determinations. In short, we deal with the operation and design of a *managerial process* and not the question of coaching a single executive to do the right thing.

This perspective draws directly from the work of Barnard (1938) and Simon (1947) and their successors in the modern theory of the properties and behavior of formal organizations. According to that theory, authority does not necessarily proceed from the top down, but, to the extent that one person is willing to have his span of actions limited or directed by another, is conferred by subordinates on their superiors (Barnard, 1938). Goals are worked out by numerous accommodations in the organization rather than, as may appear, being adopted and announced from on high. A rough equilibrium or balance between what its participants of all types deliver to it and what they get from it is necessary for the survival of the organization (Barnard, 1938; Simon, 1947). Thus, the boundaries of the organization are not limited by its legal definition but by the functional ways in which various classes of participants are involved in it.

Within every organization, an informal organization is intertwined with the formal structure (Barnard, 1938; Simon, 1947). Decision-makers strive for effective participation and are activated by their identification with the organization, as well as by the desire for pay and status. But decision-makers are limited by incomplete information and by difficulties of calculating how to be rational. They function according to concepts of "bounded rationality" (Simon, 1947). The direction of organizations, according to the theory, is imparted by the concern of its executives for adjusting and focusing its procedures and mechanisms, by their concern for the selection of key personnel, and by their success in locating the strategic kernel of the often ill-defined major choices affecting the long-range future of the organization (Barnard, 1938).

This approach to managment-as-process fits the university. Because we do not accept at face value the legal or official conventions of who does what according to title or position but are interested in the functioning of this managerial process, we shall have to accept a complication of this approach: namely, that there are many contributors to the managerial process, differently situated in the university—some with administrative titles and others without. And so we must understand and organize the process; we can no longer simply distribute titles and choose individuals for them. Perhaps it is not a forlorn hope that this functional view will soften the antagonism of the academic reader toward the notion of managing a university, for it will be shown that the skilled and active participation of students and faculty, as individuals and as groups, is crucial to the effective conduct of the institution. Managing can no more be left to administrators than, in the famous aphorism, war can be left to the generals.

It is, however, true—and it will be shown as each topic is treated why it increasingly has to be true—that the trend is toward processes of decision that are explicit and systematic, not implicit, diffuse, and atomistic. In the past, many important questions were buried by collegial consensus-making or were left to happenstance. Such questions require examination of goals, clarifying information, consideration of elements that are difficult to reconcile, and courageous choices among alternatives. All the institutions of contemporary American society face new pressures to "show cause" and to engage in explicit reexamination of what they are doing and of the consequences of their actions. Corporations are required to respond to new legal standards related to environmental concerns; employers and trade unions must show affirmative action as well as nondiscrimination in employment; charitable foundations must demonstrate that they are following explicit standards of deportment; courts and law enforcement agencies must conform to explicit standards of individual justice; even political organizations and politicians must observe a heightened morality. Contemporary society has an increased awareness of interdependence, and all types of institutions and organizations are now obliged to deal with additional dimensions of their behavior and its consequences and to function in a more explicit and justifiable manner. Universities cannot expect to be an exception.

Universities are increasingly impacted in superstructures of several kinds, including superboards and coordinating agencies, interinstitutional agreements, and complex relationships with agencies at several levels of government. The management of relations with these superstructures occupies an increasingly important place in the university administrator's agenda. I will show how universities can fulfill their missions more effectively than before by responding in creative ways to these new pressures for explicitness.

Universities are only a part of the large array of types of institutions in higher education, or, more fashionably, postsecondary education. But universities are the oldest type, are the most clearly different from the secondary schools, and are the most complicated in organization and function. Thus, analysis of university management will offer many clues to the management, also, of educational institutions having a more truncated scope and mission.

Elements of University Management

The first task in developing an appreciation of the managerial process is to examine the main features of university operations and determine the degree of complexity inherent in these and the connections between them. There are several essential domains of analysis: funding (the acquisition of financial balances with which to defray the costs of resource-inputs); resource-inputs (personnel, raw materials and supplies, and the services of capital goods); processes or activities (which use resource-inputs to produce outputs); and goals (indicators of achievement or welfare of the institution).

Each of these domains is composed of numerous elements or components. Thus we have to talk about multiple sources of funding; multiple resource-inputs; multiple activities and outputs; and multiple goals. Furthermore, the linkages between a funding element, a resource-input, an activity, and a goal involve combinations and interdependencies. We must examine the aspects of complementarity, independence, and substitution in these relationships. These relationships are important to the decision-maker. For example, if two types of resources are substitutes for each other when used in a given process, it may be possible to economize by using more of one resource and less of the other to keep the process operating at the same level as before; but if two resources are strictly complementary, a decrease in the use of one cannot be offset by an increase in the use of the other. Considerations of complementarity and substitution will be discussed in connection with funding, programs, and purposes.

The concepts of complementarity, independence, and substituition can be defined with the help of Figure 1. Suppose that to hire work-study students (resource-input R—2) it is necessary to pay 30 percent of the wages from institutional funds (F-1), while special federal funds (F-2) pay the rest. The two sources of funding are *complementary* in this use, for the institution can hire an additional work-study employee by "matching" 30 percent of its own funds with 70 percent federal funds; but if institutional funds are tight and the institution has to save money by dropping a work-study student, it can save the 30 percent it previously paid out of institutional funds; but it also has to give up the 70 percent it was previously able to get in federal funds.

An example of *independence* is a gift made by an alumnus (F-3) for a guest lectureship (R-3) with the restriction that it can be used only for that purpose.

Two funds are *substitutes* if they may be used in varying

proportions to pay for the same resource. For example, a university may ordinarily charge part of the salary of a faculty member (R-1) to his research grants (F-3); but if these run out and are no longer available, it is necessary to pick up the cost from institutional funds (F-1).

Correspondingly, some activity (say, A-1) may be enlarged or reduced simply by changing the amount of only one independent input (say, R-2). Another (say, A-2) may require two resource-inputs (R-1 and R-4) in fixed proportions. Still another (A-3) may be carried on by assigning either faculty (R-1) or administrative personnel (R-5) in various possible proportions. To evaluate these relationships of complementarity, independence, and substitution, it is always necessary to look backward in the flow of operations: from goals to activities and outputs; from activities to resource-inputs; from resources to the sources of funding.

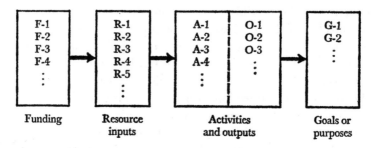

Funding   Resource   Activities   Goals or
                   inputs   and outputs   purposes

FIGURE 1

By looking *forward* as the arrows point in Figure 1, we detect another aspect of interdependence. A particular resource such as faculty (R-1) may be allocated in part to the activity of supervising dissertation research (A-4), which produces contributions to two goals (G-1, educated people, and G-2, new knowledge). According to this example, each unit of R-1 that is used up in A-3 has inherent joint consequences in contributing to both G-1 and G-2. If one of these goals, say G-1, is favored by a constituency that is concerned about goal attainment but the contribution to new knowledge is not, the fact that both goals receive some contribution means that the constituency is partly dissatisfied with the manner in which the resource is employed to produce the goal consequences in which that constituency is interested. Instances of this kind of interdependence, or "jointness," are widespread in universities. As we shall see in Chapter Seven they complicate considerably the task of cost analysis.

Guiding the affairs of a university would not be an onerous task if the fundamentals of the structure were simple: one funding source, from which only one type of resource-input would need to be purchased from a perfect market, then used for a single productive activity to produce a single output, which would then contribute to a single, well-defined goal, the achievement of which would induce the sponsors of the university to provide continued or expanded funding. But the actual situation is not simple. The general goals of a university are shrouded in vagueness. By common consent, there are several goals, but there is not consensus among those concerned with universities about the relative importance of the goals, the interdependencies among them, or ways of measuring attainment of them.

A university contains a great array of processes and activities, each of which produces one or more types of results or outputs. Some outputs contribute to a single goal and others to the attainment of two or more goals. Classification and analysis of the processes and identification of the ways in which one process is needed for the performance of another are technical tasks, and there has been progress with them. But choosing priorities among these processes, assigning responsibilities for them to units of organization, and adding or dropping academic programs—all involve decisions that arouse questions of institutional purpose, power, and function.

Processes and activities absorb resources. We now have better ways to trace resource use and impute costs to ongoing programs and activities. But in the short run, the capital plant of a university (its buildings, land, library collection, and major equipment) and its roster of professors and senior administrative personnel are fixed in supply. They also are arrays of heterogeneous, differentiated, and specialized resources. One task of management is to finance and allocate variable inputs and supplies so that the plant and faculty can function well. Another is to foster the quality of plant and faculty and find financing. Another and much more difficult task is to arrange reassignments of the largely fixed resources toward expanding uses and needs and away from lower-priority needs. And finally, management must supervise new investment in capital facilities and in long-term employment commitments of academic and administrative staff, shaping long-term change in institutional programs and institutional, mission.

A university has multiple sources and types of funding. For all major universities, the most important source is government. However, this is not a single source, and funding is not in a single, undifferentiated bloc without conditions on use or purpose. Numerous levels of government and particular agencies may be sources of financing, each willing to supply funds only for specific uses and under specified conditions. Government (in the United States, state governments, in most of Europe, the national ministries of education) allocates to public universities their operating support under stated conditions of use in specific resource-input or program categories. American private universities assemble their general university funds from a combination of endowment income (to the extent not earmarked for special purposes), student tuitions, and current gifts from alumni and other donors.

The money for resource-inputs is in part drawn from general university funds. Thus, a unit increase in use of any given resource may be a competitive claim on this funding pool. The size of the claim is determined by the unit price the institution pays for that input. But there is an important class of funding cases in which an increment of funding is strictly tied to the resources needed for one subset of processes or activities, which contributes to one specific part of the goal domain and may not be used for any others. The earmarked funding is independent of general funds, and a client— the funding source—is supporting the resource-inputs and the subset of activities because of the client's interest in a specific output or a specific one of the set of university goals. In this case, an increase of general university funds has no positive effect, and a decrease no negative effect, either on the willingness of the client to supply earmarked funds or on the results obtained from the activities supported from the earmarked funds.

Acquisition of funds is a complicated institutional task involving a great many actors and, for the different types of funds, differing sequences of negotiations and decisions. To assure that financial resources are accounted for and that legal and other conditions on their use are met, their stewardship involves other people and decision sequences. Still another group of people and other procedures determine the allocation of funds (where choices can be made by decision-makers within the university) among activities, units of organization, and uses. And still another group, using its procedures of decision, manages funds acquired and allocated to assure that desired effects are achieved from the processes and activities supported.

In dealing with the relationships between funds, resources, activities and their outputs, and goals, the central administration is not so much running the show as guiding and monitoring a series of decision sequences and operations. It is no wonder that the crazy-quilt pattern is baffling to outside observers; its inherent complexity is usually not well understood even by those whose professional lives are at stake.

Some universities live in absolute poverty, threatened with closure because their funds are insufficient to deal with the immediate consequences of fixed commitments. But no university is absolutely rich, in the sense that some source of funds, without conditions, is freely available for every conceivable activity or recommended change of commitments. A university can only be well off relative to its commitments and mission. Now we turn to examination of a university's mission and scope.

Mission and Scope. The mission of the university is traditionally defined as "teaching, research, and public service." The full-scale university offers curricula leading to the most advanced academic degrees. It also offers curricula leading to less advanced degrees in a variety of fields, and in these areas faces direct competition, as well as some complementary relationships, with other types of institutions. Universities may also offer nondegree instruction—short courses, certificate programs, and informal education for specialized, often very advanced clienteles—and these (often classified under the head of *public service* because they do not entail formal academic degrees) compete with many alternative methods, varying from nation to nation and from field to field, of updating and upgrading professional knowledge or providing intellectual stimulus not related to occupation.

A university without research may have the name but fails the definition as conclusively as would the university without students. Systematic inquiry by individuals or groups of scholars, leading to new findings in each field represented in the institution, is a function having a proper claim on a university's resources—a claim that the institution properly presses on its sponsors. The processes of instruction and the processes of research are in some ways distinct, and they compete for space, personnel, and other resources. Universities, and particularly their academic spokesmen, claim that strong complementary linkages exist between instruction and research. Few people argue that the functions of teaching and research must inevitably and always be closely coupled. The able high school teacher of mathematics or history should certainly have ample background, skills in organization and exposition, and empathy with students. But he or she is not obliged to publish as an original scholar. The industrial or governmental chemist is expected to perform research tasks, and he may publish in the technical literature. But he is not expected to teach. The link between teaching and research is, however, an article of faith in the universities, and we shall see why when the topic of jointness is discussed later in this chapter.

Public service—in a sense different from the provision of education to students for their useful lives and different from the provision to the world generally of the results of scholarly inquiry—is an arguable element of university mission. Public service contributions of a university assist local, regional, or national constituencies by providing them with information, help, enlightenment, or amusement. In the United States, the Morrill Act of 1863 (establishing land-grant institutions) added public service to the university agenda. The university may have programs of applied research and problem-solving for public agencies and for significant clienteles. It may disseminate useful information to professional and lay clienteles, operate educational radio stations, sponsor cultural events for the university community and a wider public, operate hospitals and clinics, maintain park space and museums, and offer harmless amusements and ritual occurrences.

Some of these activities are spin-offs from teaching and research commitments, others are important to the community and to constituency clienteles, and still others are part of the university's marketing effort and its attempt to preserve relations with supporting clienteles. These activities add to administrative and organizational complexity, and many of them come into question if they do not make a contribution to the university's resources or at least appear to break even.

A most important task of university management is to guide the institution's definition of its mission and scope, determining changes in the array of programs and in their scale and quality. For institutions that are affected by state or national schemes of planning, coordination, and control, this guidance includes negotiation with the superstructure.

The campus administration, like Janus, must look in two directions: to the relations of the university with its external environments (for sources of students, external resource markets, clientele relationships, and funds), and to its internal relations with the ongoing institutional processes and constituencies. (Thus, the frequently heard accusation that a college president is two-faced is functionally accurate!)

When interpreting a university's mission, the administration must look to two levels—the global image of the campus, and the valuation of particular degree programs and their impact on the occupational and academic marketplaces.

The global image of a campus conveys signals of its quality and distinctiveness. Its academic programs and departments contribute to this positively if they are of recognized quality and negatively if they are recognized to be poorer than the general impression of that campus. They contribute to its distinctiveness if they are part of an image of specialized strengths (for example, Massachusetts Institute of Technology's programs in physics, computer science, and electrical engineering) or convey independent distinction (for example, Cornell University's medical school, which is separated both geographically and functionally from the Ithaca campus).

Doctoral and professional degree recipients go to distinct and segmented career destinations. They are hired for specialized jobs for which their advanced training is essential. Only a few employers may have needs for some specialists such as biophysicists. A law degree, however, may serve as background for many other jobs besides those in a law firm. Those who make hiring decisions at these career destinations evaluate a campus as a source for the specialties in which they are hiring. There may, however, be some (positive or negative) halo effect on the general reputation of the campus in other areas than those from which graduates are being recruited.

Academic Programs. The design of academic programs is determined by what the bodies of knowledge are held to be, by what are defined as the professions, and by what sampling of these the university and its sponsors are willing to provide. A given university at a given time contains only a sampling of the known span of academic programs.

The bodies of knowledge, once thought by the Encyclopedists to be capable of definitive classification and integrated mastery, expand over time in number and subdivide into specialties and subspecialties as far as ingenuity and the search for differentiation of the intellectual product can take them. To be a useful point of definition for an academic program, a body of knowledge has to be institutionalized, with an identifiable company of scholars sharing interests and findings in it, an apparatus of publication, agreed standards of scholarship, and some basis for recognizing who the scholars are and what they have to know. Intellectual and academic history gives the broad groupings: humane letters, fine arts, languages; mathematics, philosophy, history; the social sciences; the life sciences; and the physical sciences. Within each of these, subdivision and specialization continue, and hybrids develop.

Intellectual and academic history also provide the list of the traditional learned professions: law, medicine, and theology. Modern professions for which systematic education is all or part of the process of licensing have followed: dentistry; engineering (and its subdivisions); architecture and urban planning; and education. In fields such as business and public administration, librarianship, and social work, systematic education has been invented so that the trained professional can compete advantageously with those who have learned what they know by on-the-job experience in the field; licensing may or may not be a general condition of employment.

The ministries of education in the countries of Europe, and the National Center for Educational Statistics of the U. S. Department of Health, Education, and Welfare, gather and publish statistics of enrollment and degrees granted. To do this, they adopt descriptive classifications of disciplines and professions. State coordinating agencies and such organizations as the National Center for Higher Education Management Systems (NCHEMS) have developed academic program classification structures for use in planning and educational program costing. The most detailed of these classifications schemes define the array of programs that a university could offer. As new fields emerge from the research process or from the development of newly defined professions, the classification schemes must include them. In the United States, many disciplines and professions serve as accrediting bodies. Each professional organization develops, for its own purposes, specifications of the educational content and the staffing and resource standards that need to be met by an institution seeking certification. Academic institutions in the United States are to a great extent in business for themselves (although state coordinating agencies are now constraining them increasingly), and accrediting organizations provide a means of enforcing some conventions of respectability and quality control. (In other nations, where the ministry of education has power to approve initiation and monitor the conduct of academic programs and is usually the main or sole source of funding, the ministry does the accrediting.) A university typically has internal mechanisms for approval of each degree program. These enable it to control certification of students' achievements and to identify officially approved programs to which institutional resources may properly be committed.

The decision to have a particular degree program is distinct from the question of how to organize and manage it. Each program leading to a degree is, crudely put, a product, and each student who completes that program is a unit of product. Responsibility for each program may be assigned to any of a great variety of organizations: schools and colleges, departments within colleges, and committees that administer degrees. The design of such structures and assignment of responsibilities within them are discussed in Chapters Three and Four.

A university is defined by the span of academic programs it offers. Some of these programs should lead to academic degrees at the most advanced level of scholarship or graduate professional learning, with concomitant research commitments. If very few fields are represented, the institution has insufficient variety to be thought of as a university even though it may have high academic distinction. Some of the institutes of technology in the United States have broadened their offerings to include management studies, social sciences, and other fields and professions. Some, such as Carnegie-Mellon University (formerly Carnegie Institute of Technology) have changed to the university name, while others cling to the old title.

Handelshögskolan in Stockholm (The Stockholm School of Economics) and the Economische Hogeschool at Tilburg, The Netherlands, continue in the continental tradition of the independent higher technical school. In 1972, the well-known Nederlandse Economische Hogeschool in Rotterdam became part of the new Erasmus University, which also has a new medical faculty and is developing additional faculties. In France, L'École Polytechnique and other *grands écoles* operate entirely outside the traditional French universities, training the most elite cadres for French government and industry. These independent technical schools, and some remaining independent medical colleges and professional schools in the United States, have the advantage of simplicity of institutional design, but they may suffer isolation from the wider intellectual developments in academia.

I have discussed the functions and programs of the university. The name *university* conveys academic status too, and a potential mandate to claim more functions. Portland State University in Oregon and Northern Illinois University are examples of state-sponsored colleges that got both the name and the university mandate during the expansion of the 1960s. In California, the legislature changed the name of the California State College system in 1972 to the California State University and College system. State colleges such as San Francisco State (eighteen thousand students) and San Jose State (twenty-two thousand students) were renamed California State Universities at San Francisco and at San Jose. For these two large and diversified institutions with quite strong faculties in many areas, it was undoubtedly a welcome step. In other states and in better academic times, renaming has gone in tandem with the initiation of doctoral programs, programs in the prestigious graduate professions, and a substantial research program. It is not at all clear that these functions can be accorded to the California State Universities in present fiscal and market circumstances.

Program and Purposes. A university is located in the markets for reputation, faculty, and students. It may be visible or obscure, strong in all fields or variable in reputation from field to field. The same institutionalizing forces that define each body of knowledge— existence of a body of scholars, standards of judgment, and media of publication and communication—serve as the main source of current judgment of a university's prestige in each field, largely via the visibility and reputations of its senior faculty. Changes in the reputation of a department are noted first by the cognoscenti and then, with successive time-lags, by the wider group of academics, graduate students, impinging professional clienteles, and other publics.

The chief academic administrators of a campus are interested in how successfully the graduates from each degree program are placed and how well each program is regarded by those at the career destinations and those who are knowledgeable about program quality at other institutions. Thus, each degree program contributes to the institution two components: a largely independent impact on a clientele community; and a (generally mild) impact on the reputation of the campus. Each degree program is seen by the campus-level administrator as independent of the others or as complementary to them. Only if a program actively detracts from the perceived acceptability of the campus and its other degree programs (because, for example, of very much lower perceived quality than the average on the campus) would the administrator draw the inference that reduction or elimination of that program would improve the status of the campus. There are other reasons why a given program might be viewed as incompatible with the intentions and market-locus of a campus: (1) the program might violate an image of highly-defined specialization in degree markets that the campus is seeking to build; (2) the program might require a student clientele that is seen as incompatible with the students normally enrolled on the campus.

A comprehensive university that has a reasonably wide range of degree programs and deals with both undergraduate and graduate students is unlikely to perceive incompatibility restraints of either of the above types. Thus, in evaluating what happens to degree-recipents and how well they are regarded, degree programs are either independent of or complementary with one another. They are very unlikely to be competitors. Any campus can identify new degree programs that it does not yet offer, and these, too, are likely to satisfy the criterion of nonsubstitution with existing ones, Thus, from the standpoint of relations with degree-recipient markets, a campus that is already comprehensive has no incentives to avoid additional programs (the case of independence) and may have active incentives to initiate them (to achieve complementarity). All of the above reasoning concentrates on the interdependencies among programs in the institution's evaluation of the worth to it of the various types of graduates it turns out.

The campus administrator's interpretation of the program aspect of the goal domain, then, is measured by the acceptability and placement success of graduates in specific programs and by the academic reputation and quality of these programs. In general, these goal valuations are either independent or complementary. A university administration typically has no direct incentives, with respect to its goal valuations, to reduce or eliminate an existing program because of its negative impact on another part of the goal domain. In principle, a university has an incentive to expand—to offer new programs that will add new elements to its goal performance but will not penalize the valuation placed on its existing programs and their rates of operation.

The prowess and reputation for basic research of the faculty in a particular discipline has several consequences. First, it adds to the global eminence of the institution. Second, it increases the value and prospects for placement of the recipients of advanced professional and scholarly degrees in that discipline, both because of the reputation effect and because those faculty who are eminent in research are influential among their peers, nationally and internationally. Third, a good reputation attracts better students, from a wider market; and it is often said with considerable truth that the outstanding graduate was very probably an outstanding student when admitted to his degree program. Fourth, there is a funding market for support of basic research. The outstanding researcher in a field with an active funding market may thus attract funds for part or all of the costs of his research activities, or may even be a nucleating agent in attracting funds for the support of junior faculty and graduate students. Finally, an eminent research faculty is, by definition, at the most important frontier of its field. It thus contributes to the atmosphere of intellectual striving and excitement in its own specialty and more broadly on the campus.

The university administration views applied research and service activity somewhat differently. These activities provide a service or problem-solving capability for a clientele group. In scholarly fields where basic research dominates reputation and prestige, there is not likely to be a positive linkage from the applied research and service activity to the attracting power of the institution for scholars or for outstanding students. The attitude of the university administration is likely to be "why not," if the clientele organization is willing to provide full funding. Such funding is thought to be independent of any other funding and not available unless the applied program or service activity is undertaken. Furthermore, an additional external clientele is pleased and (hopefully) no other clientele is offended. And finally, the added resources bought with the earmarked funding may contribute to other purposes if used in joint-output processes, and the overheads of the institution can be spread over the additional activity.

Nevertheless, problems may arise from the accumulation of applied research and service functions. Within the institution, those committed to basic scholarship may complain that too much energy is devoted to applied research and may seek control over the funding and resources for high-level purposes. The consequent conflict with the faculty and research cadres who are devoted to the applied research or service activity may become an administrative problem. And if the proponents of basic scholarship are successful, the external clientele may be disappointed by the diversion of attention from its perceived needs and interests. The external clientele may impose conditions—tight control of the earmarked funds or security classification of research results and clearance for the personnel in-volved—that conflict with policy standards of the institution. Those devoted to basic scholarship may also argue that the applied activity is prestige-diminishing and thus devalues other areas of goal perfor-mance. Finally, although the applied activity may have been thought to be manageable with no increase of overheads, an accumulation of it expands the burdens on support administrators and adds to the complexity of the institution's management tasks.

The charters, origins, and specific histories of some univer-sities determine the numbers and qualifications of the students they enroll. Some institutions have more latitude in managing their location in the markets for students. Others must accept enrollment, in numbers and conventionally-defined qualifications, according to rules set by governmental sponsors.

I have already mentioned the power of good academic reputa-tion in attracting outstanding students. The administration is in-terested in admission policies for several other reasons. There are well-known correlations between the high school achievement level of a student and the educational level, income, and assets of his or her parents. A private college or university that must charge tuition and that regards tuition as a major source of funds for general insti-tutional purposes has an interest in pursuing a selective admission policy. Lower-income students cost the institution money in financial aid that offsets tuition income, and less-qualified students cost it added academic resources or have less prospect of success in grad-uate school or in occupational placement. A private university expects to make money on its undergraduates and to use the surplus for its graduate programs. Yet private colleges and universities devoted increased resources, in the 1960s, to the education of minority members and economically disadvantaged students. Often this was stimulated by the liberal social views of faculty and middle-class students. In broad public policy terms, it is a good thing that many private universities and colleges broadened their admissions policies. But for the top administrators this caused problems of varying acuteness. Internal stresses were temporarily heightened by the presence of a new student constituency, and many conservative alumni and donor clienteles were disgruntled.

Administrators of a state-supported university always have

had to pursue an admissions policy that takes cues from the political context. The link between admissions policy and tuition income has been weakened or broken. Selective admission still enhances institutional prestige and the academic performance and career success of graduates. But state institutions must now justify denial of admission to a resident of the state. Admissions policy has to be supported by political bargains. If a public university is to exercise some selectivity in admissions policy, it must do so under the shelter of such political bargains. These bargains call for budgetary support of each state institution, in return for which it provides its share of access to educational opportunity. These shares are allocated among the state university, the comprehensive colleges, and the community colleges by means of admissions eligibility rules. Even while it sings the virtues of its academic prestige and tries to demonstrate the worth of that prestige to the political power structure and general citizenry of the state, the administrative leadership of a high-quality state university has to pursue a less selective admission policy than its counterparts among private universities. And it seeks in various ways to avoid the elitist label. Politically, the greatest enemy of the high-quality public university is the right-wing populist politician, who attracts away the support of the conservative establishment while, at the same time, denying the university support on egalitarian grounds! And the administration of a high-quality public university may also face significant problems in the goal domain, of justifying graduate programs which fail to meet the manpower needs of the state or which have high loss rates of mobile graduates who go to jobs outside the state.

It is an important task of university management to guide the institution to a desired place in the markets for reputation, faculty, and students. If some elements of these possible areas of choice are foreclosed by limitations of charter, resources, or rules of the superstructure, these become givens, and management must guide the institution within these fixed constraints.

Summary

We have now completed an examination of the multiple character of funding, processes and outputs, and institutional goals. The links among these, in the form of complementarity, independence, and substitution, provide an initial perspective of the managerial process. In Chapters Three and Four, these concepts are applied to an analysis of the university's units of organization. Jointness and interdependence reappear as crucial issues in the analysis of costs (Chapter Seven), financial stress (Chapter Eight), and the budgetary mechanism (Chapter Nine).

Before we can proceed further, however, it is necessary to examine the values or norms of behavior that impress themselves on the members of a university community and give a university its special character. This is a different dimensional view of normative issues than the one just discussed, but it is no less essential, for it is concerned with the individual and group values that make possible a university's scheme of largely voluntaristic learning and that determine the atmosphere of the institution.

Chapter 2

Values of the University

The informing values of a university are drawn from the surrounding society. These values condition important aspects of the behavior of the members of the university community, stimulating them toward the hard efforts of learning and producing feelings of identification that bind them together in subtle ways. Let us start by examining the ways people behave in a university when they are together in small or large groups—the kinds of audiences found on a campus.

Audiences

Members of a university find many scheduled occasions to attend. The desired behaviors of both performer and audience are different at a public lecture, an official exercise, a tutorial session, a political rally, a seminar, or a football game. Each type of occasion reflects a facet of the essential institution. Big-time spectating is not unique, of course, to universities, but athletic entertainments are a traditional indulgence in Anglo-American universities. (Some continental universities have practically no mass entertainments, which may be a handicap to them.) These are occasions for the display of enthusiasm. And often they serve as the one common ground for very different constituencies, from the sentimental alumnus to the undergraduate. Recently, the potency of the university's athletic attractions appears to have declined somewhat, and cultural events now claim larger audiences. Universities are justified in serving as patrons of concerts, plays, art exhibits, films, and public lectures. These stimulate the aesthetic appreciation of students, and they are generally significant as psychic income to the kinds of people who collect in and around universities. They promote shared interest in a civilized life.[1]

The university makes specific moral demands of both the performer and the scholarly audience at scheduled academic occasions—such as public lectures or colloquia or course meetings—when a sholar is to present his findings and ideas. The presenter is obligated to state his views and findings fairly and fully, to give credit to sources, and, as an advocate, to accept fair questions and critique. (It also helps if the speaker is interesting.) The audience has an obligation to hear him out and to distinguish between the courtesy it owes the presenter and the critical response it should make to the ideas presented.

Underlying all of this are presumptions of the lecturer's competence to speak and the audience's obligation to be instructed (although not necessarily, of course, to be persuaded) by what he has to say. The purpose fails if the audience is put to sleep, and it also fails if the speaker is a demagogic success. If the occasion breaks down and the audience will not permit the speaker to go on, this is not merely a discourtesy to him but an affront to the standards of academic life. In the recent period of heightened political and moral passions, such breakdowns sometimes occurred, both in sponsored public lectures and—very occasionally—in academic courses offered for credit, when the speaker was an object of rage or when part of the audience was determined to take over the occasion to provoke a confrontation with the university. Prudent presidents have sometimes canceled commencement exercises or have decided not to invite some lecturers when there were risks of such disruptions.

[1] One critical reader (Sara Balderston) points out that these cultural and aesthetic activities are worthwhile for their own sake.

Universities rediscovered, in the 1960s, that they are vulnerable institutions. The disintegration of moral consent to let ideas take their chances was a frightening experience, and it demonstrated clearly how dependent a university is on felt restraints, not on pure bureaucratic authority. As the police are well aware, a few policemen at a big gathering can control the aberrant behavior of a few individuals only if the crowd is overwhelmingly interested in allowing them to do so. And, of course, increasing the number of police or the amount of force they use may be no solution at all.

In the conduct of academic occasions, the university lives by a different and more subtle standard than that guaranteed by the First Amendment. Members of the audience are obligated to restrain or at least postpone their free speech rights, so that the purpose of the occasion can be served. The speaker is obligated to conform with standards of academic conduct, in the content of what he says and the way he says it. And if he does not, he has breached these standards even if he is completely within First Amendment rights.

When civility fell off in the universities, administrators had to develop explicit distinctions between the kinds of academic occasions, the kinds of speakers, the kinds of eligible sponsoring organizations, and the kinds of eligible participants in the audience. They had to do this not only in the interest of elementary physical control (which was sometimes impossible to guarantee anyhow) but in order to preserve the moral imperatives of academic conduct and to make these credible and enforceable in the university community. Administrators faced two other problems not unique to universities—they had to defend their institutions from external interventions and from internal misappropriations.

One distinction that could be drawn fairly easily was between a scheduled meeting of an academic course for credit and any other campus gathering. For the latter, decisions had to be made about the eligibility of sponsoring organizations to obtain university facilities for a meeting. There was no longer any institutional guarantee that speakers had academic cachet and sanction or that audiences would be critical and respectful. The only remaining restraint—eligibility of the sponsoring organization to use university facilities—was confined to a few sanctions on the public responsibility of the sponsor and to questions of the schedule for facilities and events.

This very limited regulation of public political and ideological events was, paradoxically, both a retreat and a liberating change for American universities. Previously, they tried to keep more than a shadow of *in loco parentis* over the character and content of these events and the behavior of those who attended them. Previously, the institution guaranteed the academic responsibility and respectability of the event. If the event was to be politically partisan or ideological, a tax-supported university might have to deny permission to hold it, because the institution was supposed (often required, by constitution or statute) to hold free from partisan or religious influence, and the institution was responsible for content and conduct. Once it became established that there ought to be other kinds of public events and that these should not be held to academic standards, the university could more easily permit them because it no longer took responsibility for the qualifications of the speaker or the content of speech.

Freedom to Teach and Freedom to Learn

As the university abandoned most forms of institutional control over general public events, it had to regulate more specifically the character of formal instruction. Traditionally, the university controls the appointment of instructors and assignment of their academic duties, and it controls the admission of students and their access to facilities, courses, and activities. A person unconnected with the university could properly be barred from an academic event, and attendance at the meetings of a course could also be restricted to those students and staff having specific permission. These restraints could be invoked to protect the academic freedom of the instructor and to establish eligibility based on the competence of the participant as one present to learn. A test of these academic principles came when, in the turmoil of the 1960s, groups of students sought the right to initiate courses and choose their own instructors, and when some regularly appointed instructors gave over the meetings of their courses to guest lecturers.

A student proposed course can be a good thing, but universities had to assert institutional control. They could not escape from institutional responsibility for the content and character of instruction and for the certification of what is learned. The guest lecturer in a course with a regular instructor, however, is a more delicate matter, because denial of permission might be construed as denial of the instructor's freedom to choose how to present ideas. Doctors teach medical students by having them look at and talk with hospital patients. Why shouldn't law professors teach law students by having them talk with criminals, or political scientists by having their students hear a celebrated revolutionary?

When this problem arose in the University of California, institutional control was asserted on these three points: The regular instructor is to retain the right and obligation to certify the content of the academic offering and the performance of students. The guest lecturer (if not academically certified) is to be present only as an incidental, illustrative case in point for the students, and nothing more. And the topic presented, with the guest lecturer presented as clinical material, is to be pertinent to the purposes of the course.

These distinctions were drawn both to justify the university to the world external to it and to preserve it from internal manipulation. If the university resisted the efforts of politicians to make or veto academic appointments on political criteria irrelevant to academic qualification, it had to show that it had criteria of its own to control such appointments and duties, whether for pay or not. If the university drew a distinction between the strictly scholarly occasion and the nonacademic event and insisted, on free-speech grounds, that it ought to permit criticized public events to occur while disclaiming responsibility for their content, it also had to show that academic occasions followed rules of competence, qualification, and pertinence for academic purposes.

Because the judgments of content and competence to teach are so difficult and dangerous to make, universities surround them with institutional procedures and mechanisms instead of making institutional policy. Responsibility for the design of instructional offerings is lodged in colleges and departments, and the assignment of teaching responsibilities is generally made as an administrative act within these groups. The individual instructor, therefore, has assurance that the main point of review for his work as a teacher is a group of similarly trained academic specialists who have the institutional responsibility for the conduct of that area of specialization. An issue of the freedom of the teacher to teach may then arise within such a group of specialists. For such cases, the university has institutional avenues of appeal, in which a broader group of academics sorts out the elements of the controversy and makes recommendations. The university administration, by both of these devices, seeks to assure that conflicts are channeled through institutional mechanisms, not made into contests that pit the academics on one side and the administrators on the other side of a discretionary decision.

The case of William Schockley at Stanford University illustrates another way in which the freedom to teach can be a controversial issue. Schockley, a co-winner of the Nobel Prize for his work on the transistor, has become very publicly outspoken concerning the genetic (and inferentially, the racial) basis of intelligence. He announced that he wanted to teach a course on this subject; the response of the Stanford administration was that it would seek the advice of a faculty panel on the question of his academic competence to do so, because the subject was outside the field of his past scholarly work. Schockley's request was in due course denied.

Recent controversies in the United States have also stimulated the effort to define general codes of faculty conduct. The American Association of University Professors designed such a code; the Carnegie Commission on the Future of Higher Education, in its report, *Dissent and Disruption* (1971), discussed the need for codes of both faculty and student conduct and provided a model code of faculty conduct. Numerous individual universities have struggled to define explicit standards. These are intended to serve as a general and credible guide for academic conduct in all areas of specialization, while the special obligations and hazards of proper performance are spelled out through the case-by-case decisions of groups of specialists in their influence on each other.

Administrators find themselves very directly involved, however, when asserted definitions of competence differ from conventional, specialized, academic judgment. As Black students became more numerous and more assertively self-conscious on university campuses, demands were made both to provide courses in Black literature, Black history, and other areas of special interest and to assure that these were staffed by Black instructors. More recently, the same issue has arisen in connection with women's history, the psychology of women, and similar courses. Three distinct claims are made: that the subject ought to be taught; that the teacher must be qualified by categorical condition (race or sex) and not merely by academic background; and that student admission to the course ought to be based on categorical condition, not merely on curricular eligibility or interest.

The first claim necessitates a resource-priority decision. It also raises questions about whether a valid body of knowledge is available. Those who have a strong interest are not content to leave the judgment on this to the academic specialists normally concerned with the curricular area in question; the advocates want the offering, whether or not the specialists say that there is something valid to be taught.

The second claim raises the question of whether academic preparation is as relevant as outlook and personal experience. If it becomes an issue between the academic department that would normally pass on the qualifications of the teacher and the administrators who are trying to cope with interest-group pressure, the issue may be resolved in an ideal way: to find for appointment a teacher who meets both the criterion of academic competence and background and the criterion of category. But this ideal solution, or a compromise facsimile of it, may fail if the specialists balk or if the proponents of the new course demand exclusive control over the nominations for appointment. The proponents may make these demands to secure patronage control of employment or to enforce an ideological orientation. And, because American university faculties are mostly White and mostly male, the denial of the demands can escalate these conflicts to issues of institutional racism or institutional sexism.

The third issue—admission to the course based on a criterion of categorical condition—raises another painful problem. Universities are accustomed to invoking criteria of academic eligibility for course enrollment. They may also use rationing, not only of the total number of students on a campus at each degree level, but in each major, school, or college; and the rationing may extend to a limitation on enrollment in a particular course because the institution or, with its consent, the instructor, wants to insure a particular style of learning in that course. But here is a request, or a demand, for self-segregation of students by race or sex, and for the exclusion of those not meeting the criterion. Not only is this an additional basis of rationing; it is one that collides with principles (and probably with laws) of nondiscrimination. Once again, the prudent and wise administrator can use a mechanism that will avoid the risks of a purely administrative determination, but the outcome cannot, for reasons both of law and of general university policy, be *de jure* recognition of a discriminatory criterion of eligibility to attend a course.

If the university can make a showing of sympathetic response to novel requests or demands, and if its processes show an adequately self-critical willingness to examine whether, by inadvertence or otherwise, a valid area of study has been overlooked, then it will be on better ground to try experiments with promising possibilities, or to explain why budgetary difficulties prevent an ideal response, as they often do, or to deny—as sometimes must be done—the academic validity of the proposals or demands.

The existing units of organization may not be adaptable to new areas of curricular interest, yet may oppose the development of particular offerings or of entire new programs or academic departments. By disciplinary and professional definitions, units of organization emerge rather slowly and in an evolutionary manner. It is fitting that they do so, for a unit of academic organization can be adequately defined and developed only after a significant period of systematic scholarly work and the emergence of a body of knowledge and some criteria of competence.

But student interest and public interest in areas of study may rise and fall in a faddish and mercurial fashion. Witness the sudden interest in the study of ecology and environmental quality, the rapid growth (and incipient decline) of specialties in space science, the swings of interest in Zen, and the attempts to develop the integrated study of the language, culture, social structure, and politics of particular areas of the world. In these situations, university administration becomes an exercise in balancing the risks of very long-term resource commitment, of incomplete specification of the course or program as a field of proper academic interest, of insistent but possibly temporary bursts of enrollment demand, and (in some cases) of temporary external funding—enough to start but not to sustain a new area of study.

Recent American history provides an example of the broad problem of conflict between academic freedom and political accountability. In May 1970, at the time of the United States invasion of Cambodia, large numbers of students and faculty were greatly disturbed. Several universities closed down altogether or waived the requirements for final examinations. Most remained open, and there were movements for reconstitution of the university—putting aside academic business-as-usual, in academic courses and in institutional process, so that (it was urged) the university could devote itself as an institution to opposing the war. But if universities had acceded to a test of moral or ideological relevance at that time of crisis, how could they have resisted successfully the ideological and political intrusions of outside interest groups on other, unwelcome occasions? Thus, universities struggled to draw boundary distinctions that would make it possible for students and staff to express their concerns as citizens but would hold the institutions clear from endorsement of particular positions and from the accusation that academic facilities and operations had been given over, wholesale, to a partisan cause.

Over the centuries, universities in many societies have faced such crises of purpose and character. Sometimes they have collapsed from within. More frequently, if the surrounding society goes through a major convulsion, the universities are overwhelmed—physically destroyed or converted into barracks for revolutionary cadres or made symbols of the victor's interests. The German universities during the rise of Hitler, the Cuban universities subjected to *Fidelista* zeal, the Greek universities after the colonels' coup—all became chattels of the state and objects of control and "purification."

Even during calmer times when no convulsive social movement threatens to penetrate every area of academic discourse, inflaming issues can arise as test cases in almost any field and are not by any means confined to the social sciences, where questions of values are endemic. Nuclear chemists and engineers become embroiled in controversies over reactor safety; biologists and agronomists make farmers angry about pesticides and environmental quality;

English professors lock horns with official doctrine about obscenity; educational psychologists and statisticians arouse passions over the question of racial and genetic versus environmental sources of difference in human intelligence; gynecologists unsettle the Church and traditional morality over questions of contraception and abortion. In the best of circumstances, universities are protected constitutionally from external pressures and by internal regulation from the harassment of those who take intellectual positions unpopular with the academic community or the general public. But a university's academic and administrative leadership is hard put to deal wisely with the *ad hoc* crisis, which is often a confusing mixture of personalities, factions, interest-group pressure, and elements of principle. The private university does not have to face the bludgeon of budget cuts in such controversies; this gives it more time to cope or to let controversy burn out, but time is not immunity.

Freedom to Inquire

A university exists, in large measure, to support, facilitate, and give recognition to new scholarship. As an institution, it does not endorse the product even though it is morally bound to defend the responsible process that gave rise to that product, to the scholar whose work it is, and to the full publication of the results.

Traditionally, academic scholarship has been an individualistic activity: on a topic chosen by the scholar, pursued alone, and (eventually) published in the author's name alone, with praise or blame to him. Although universities did not become the major locus of original scholarship until the nineteenth century, their libraries, laboratories, and ability to underwrite groups of specialists have now become indispensable to systematic scholarship.

Recognition of the merit of the work comes from the scholar's professional peers, partly within but even more outside his own university. The university uses these signals to gauge the worth of his originality. It is one of the paradoxes of academic life that the scholar's competitors are his judges, his colleagues, and his friends.

Productive scholars drive themselves hard, make heavy demands for personal autonomy, and would probably not be able to gain remotely comparable satisfaction from any other career. Thus, it is easy to see why the scholar needs the university, as patron and facilitator. But why does the university need the research scholar? Three reasons are often given. Research and the researcher are necessary for good teaching; society needs new knowledge; and the university gains prominence through the reputations of its research scholars.

The student is able to learn what he should in a subject only if, as the conceptions of what is known change, he has access to the current and emerging state of knowledge. As science accumulates and as societies change, the materials and ideas to be taught need continually to be refreshed. Keeping this obligation for currency is a major demand on the scholar as teacher, and it is easier to meet if the teacher is stretching his own intellectual bounds, is in a group of colleagues whose joint command of their field is current, and is in the wider network of scholarship in the field. Further, advanced students become socialized to the scholarly role and need apprenticeship in research in order to gain facility for later original work of their own. (Teachers of less advanced students need skills of systematic exposition and the ability to reach into the mental set and motivation of the student; and for this aspect of the teacher's work, it is not so clear that the scholar's originality is a crucial factor.)

Universities assert that society needs new knowledge and make their claims for institutional resources partly on this basis. As the tempo of new discovery and accretion of knowledge has increased during the last two or three generations, large-scale commitments have become more necessary for good fundamental scholarship in most fields, not just in the laboratory sciences and science-based professions. Many scholars believe that freedom to inquire means, among other things, adequate financial and psychic support. And societies express needs for applied research on a large scale and have become dependent on organized expertise to support a moving technology and to solve problems.

The process of inquiring involves some of the standards of behavior that exist for the scholar (and that are, for the most part, self-enforced) and that are important aspects of the policy of a university. Each field of academic interest develops its own canons of method, rigor, and style of reporting, and the scholar generally has to conform to these canons. The scholar participates in his field in two ways: as part of the receptive and critical audience for new work, wherever and by whomever it is done; and by contributing to the flow of new findings.

The object is to serve the truth, and the scholar is thus engaged with new problems and unresolved issues. Each field has understood standards of care and competence for the assembling of data or the investigation of sources, and for the construction of theory or interpretation. The scholar is bound to fair disclosure of sources and methods. Once a piece of work is completed, the scholar is also obliged to report it to his peers, and in this capacity he is an advocate for the truth as he sees it. In many areas of science, time priority is important in the announcement of results; this pressure creates temptations to publish prematurely or to over-claim results, and it is a duty (in principle) to resist these temptations.

The critical interaction among scholars in a field is (once again, in principle) exploratory dialogue, in which ideas are tested powerfully for their merit but the opposing scholar is not under attack *ad hominem*. Many scholars are tough controversialists, and in every field there have been bitter disputes and personal feuds, natural enough because scholars care about their work and have their share of human failings, but deplorable nonetheless when they poison the atmosphere of inquiry. Even though scholars in many fields are aligned in schools of thought expressing common sympathies and views about the problems of their fields, it is wrong to judge work too kindly from a friend or too harshly from an opponent, or to make judgments that are biased by chauvinism or irrelevant loyalties or enmities or on the basis of rank or prestige. His own time is usually the scholar's scarcest resource, yet he has some positive obligation to offer criticism, referee others' work in progress, and share his own ongoing work with other scholars who are, at the same time, his competitors.

Like any statements of an ideal, these add up to a counsel of perfection, and the men and women in a scholarly field may all have their occasions of falling short. In the short run, visibility and good reputation among peers matter a great deal, not only to nourish the scholar's ego but also to advance his case for pay, rank, and resources. Yet the moral satisfactions of doing work of enduring quality and serving the company of scholars can be enjoyed by those of quite modest achievement. A good university is a moral community. These observations may help to indicate why, and they may convey why the creative scholar is a character model as well as an intellectual resource to students.

Atmosphere for Learning

These guiding principles operate in universities in many different societies, although the surrounding social and cultural environment may be so hostile to them that their implementation is made very difficult. Universities are organized, operated, and financed according to a wide variety of patterns and styles that affect these values. Thus, there are some essentials of the atmosphere for learning that need to be fostered if the university is to work, and there are some restraints on the manner of its organization that need to be observed in its design and operation. Three prime enemies of these values are disinterest, isolation, and intolerant zeal.

If there is a low ratio of those interested in these academic values to the total number of persons in a university, the values that take great effort are frustrated and the inducements to learn and to be creative become insufficient. This is one reason why universities that have an option to do so are selective in the admission of their students and why all universities select faculty with great care. Universities that cannot be selective in admissions often seek to defend the ratio of the interested by early screening or other forms of discouragement. Unless there is great care in organization, sheer numbers can also overwhelm the spirit of learning by conveying to the student the sensation that his mind and his interests are not significant.

A university is a place for judgments: Is this a good book, a good paper or thesis, a good idea, a good course, a good student or professor. Making these judgments is hard work and requires both energy and reasonable cohesion in the groups of people who share concern about the judgments to be made. Communication within these groups, and across groups where there are wider concerns, is an essential energy-using feature of the university. Communication by the scholar with the wider community of his peers is equally necessary to good work. Thus, the isolation of one person from another within the university handicaps its internal function, and isolation from the wider community of knowledge prevents the sharing and recognition of good new work.

There are interesting problems of balance between cohesion and individuality within a university, and between the claims of the university on the energy of its members for its internal needs and the claims on them for interaction with peers in their disciplines elsewhere.

Time and the materials of scholarship have to be rationed. The feeling that there is not enough time to make good on the claims of students and colleagues can drive scholars into isolation so that, in the short run, they can at least get the satisfactions of creative work. Thus, a precarious feature of the equilibrium of a university is that if its problems of numbers, conflict, or poverty become severe, its members may withdraw from interaction and thus worsen the general situation of the institution.

The moral authority of scholarship flows from the successful engagement of student and scholar in the processes of learning. This is different from politics and different from bureaucratic organization. It has to be voluntary. The patterns of academic and administrative organization and the exercise of authority and administrative control need to be carefully designed for a university because some of the methods that are feasible for other types of organization will frustrate the essential operation of a university. What is workable in the particular case is determined by the expectations that the members of a university draw from the surrounding culture and by the specific history of the institution. The search for efficiency, important as it is, has many subtle perils.

There are those who deny, because they believe so strongly in collegiality and consent, that a university can or should be tended and managed as an organization. Some managerial techniques would damage both individual autonomy and collegial cohesion to the point where the essentials of the university would be lost. But rationing and choices are vital because time and other resources can never be enough. Discerning and sophisticated forms of administration are required.

The same qualities that make it possible for a university to foster individual autonomy and to preserve numerous arenas of exploration and disagreement make it vulnerable to intolerant zeal or intransigence. The demands for easy movement of persons and their fair access to university facilities make police controls and security repugnant—and also increase the exposure to risk. The quickness to defend liberty of ideas makes a university community an easy forum for some kinds of demagoguery, particularly when the surrounding society has heavy conflicts. The necessity for collegial forums of decision makes their conversion to political misuse a serious hazard. The underlying voluntarism of the institution makes it difficult for it to apply sanctions unless the authoritative basis for them, and procedural fairness, are very widely supported by the university population.

Summary

Those who are concerned for the university need to find ways to overcome these hazards—disinterest, isolation, and intransigence—and also to care for its moral condition and to foster the atmosphere for learning. If that atmosphere is good, students and scholars are thus induced by it to great effort. If for any reason that atmosphere is dissipated, a university is reduced to a collection of buildings and paper and meaningless routines.

Chapter 3

Constituencies and Academic Organization

In Chapter One I described the main features of management-as-process in the university and showed how the concepts of complementarity, independence, and substitution can be used to analyze relationships between the components—funding, resource-inputs, activities and outputs, and goals. Chapter Two dealt with the values that define the university as a special institution and guide the behavior of its members.

A university, like any other complex organization, has a system of influence within it and between it and its environment; to accomplish its work it is divided into numerous organizational units. This chapter is devoted to the constituencies of the university— the claimants for attention and influence—and to the division of academic work into appropriate units of organization. In Chapter Four, I deal with other organizational units and with the coordinating tasks of the presidency.

Constituencies

As I use the term, a *constituency* is a set of participants who have similar roles with respect to the university and some solidarity and group interest concerning what it should do for the institution and what the institution should be or should do for it. An individual participant in the university may belong to only one constituency. Many individuals belong to more than one because they operate in several roles, and they may be subject to cross-pressures when conflicts arise between constituencies.

Internal Constituencies. Students, faculty, administrative and technical staffs, and governing board are the internal constituency groups of the university. Some organizational units exist to consolidate the functions, voice, and influence of each group. Others are working teams, committees, and other organizational devices for cutting across constituencies, so that members of the different groups will be brought together and will work together. Each internal constituency has connections with counterparts elsewhere in academia: students with student and youth organizations; faculty members with scholarly and professional organizations, in their own fields and also with broader representative organizations (for example, the American Association of University Professors, and more recently, in some universities, trade unions); and senior and technical administrators with professional organizations in their fields (for example, the National Association of College and University Business Officers, for business managers, accountants, and budget managers). The professional organizations for faculty, and particularly for administrators, are much more highly developed in the United States, reflecting the American taste for voluntary organizations, than in Europe. Student organizations, often connected with political and ideological causes in the wider community, are traditionally more in evidence in the countries of Europe.

An internal constituency may also have strong connections to forces outside academic life. Members of the maintenance or clerical staff may belong to conventional trade unions. Trustees are nearly always part time and may have representational or ex officio roles (for example, the governor or the speaker of the state assembly as an ex officio member of the governing board) as well as individual concerns and interests. Indeed, one way to view the board of trustees of a university is to regard it as an assemblage of representational links between the institution and those parts of the surroundings that it has to take seriously.

External Constituencies. Numerous external constituencies

impinge on the university. We have already mentioned the markets for reputation. In each field, the faculty members draw important signals and stimuli from the scholarly organizations that operate in their discipline or professional area. Because the influence of these judgments extends into the modes of decision-making used by expert panels in federal research agencies and foundations, each group of scientists in a university that relies on extramural funding has vital concerns with the mechanisms of judgment and decision. Each disciplinary group of scholars is a major influence in the markets for faculty appointment and advancement. Each university operates in markets for students, who may be attracted or who (in the case of state universities) have rights of eligibility. These impinging market relationships are discussed in Chapter Six.

There are also significant *institutional,* as against disciplinary or small-group, relationships with funding sources: with state governments, for base budgets of state universities, and in some states for various forms of assistance programs to private universities; with major foundations and private donors with whom the governing board and university president negotiate; and with alumni organizations, which in many American private—and some public—universities now raise current funds through solicitations on such a large scale that they are indispensable to the institution.

The alumni constituency is valuable not only for current giving but for its substantive interest in the university. Some universities now cultivate intellectual, cultural, and public service involvement of alumni well beyond the traditional provision of athletics, alumni magazines, and reunions as stimuli of nostalgic loyalty. To the extent that a university seeks to measure its impact on the lives of former students and retain some educational influence and interest among them, these relationships with former students at the institution could take many significant new forms, including seminars and short courses to up-date professional knowledge and periodic alumni conferences on broad topics of cultural and social concern.

The immediately surrounding local community of a university, and to some extent a wider hinterland of academic, service, and other involvements, constitute another constituency. Many American university campuses were early established on isolated rural sites where land was cheap and the students could be far from city distractions. Now bigger local communities exist around these institutions. The universities and their employees and students are both a purchasing power asset and a source of demand for the full range of community services. These relationships create intricate questions of power, priority, and finance as town and gown share concerns about such matters as land use, housing, the local school system, and police and fire protection.

Some universities—originally located in the less dense parts of cities that have since become huge metropolitan complexes with a decaying central core—find they are caught up in difficult problems of urban change, development, and survival. Columbia and the universities of Chicago and Pennsylvania are the most prominent American private university examples, but many other institutions now have or will soon have a similar agenda of community interaction, involvement, and conflict. The management of these relationships becomes a major institutional priority.

Defects of Internal/External Dichotomy. This description implies that, for each of a large number of market and constituency relationships, the legal or corporate boundary of the university fails to indicate the system of actual behavior. The university, like any other complex institution of contemporary society, both gives and receives a variety of impulses and influences. Which of these will penetrate most forcibly into the affairs of the institution, and which ones it has the greatest need to influence, formally or informally, shifts with the saliency of the different environmental pressures and with the institution's own agenda of priorities. In the effort to retain its integrity as an academic institution, the university cannot ignore this wide range of involvements. Nor can it allow a rising faction that has a particular constituency linkage to overbalance the university's basic functions.

Each of these constituencies is a force to be reckoned with: as a possible source of revenue or claimant for expense; as a participant in institutional process; as a stimulus, goad, opportunity, and source of influence. There are many forms and intensities of influence in the university, and to these we now turn.

Apparatus of Influence and Authority

The lawyer would begin a discussion of authority with an examination of a university's articles of incorporation, the powers accorded such corporations in the relevant jurisdictions, and the duties, entitlements and rights of recourse of trustees, administrators, faculty, and students. This legal framework matters. The university corporation serves as a legal device to own assets and do financial and educational business. The private university, granted corporate status and tax exemption by government, and not much subject to statutory or bureaucratic control, has been in business for itself and has prized its independence. This autonomy is traditionally viewed as a strong enabling influence toward the decentralization and differentiation of higher education.

Organizing the state-supported university as a quasi-independent (sometimes constitutionally protected) corporation helps to put some distance between the university and the pressures of partisan politics and governmental bureaucracy. The state-organized American universities, like the universities of other countries, receive most of their basic operating funds from one government entity, the state government, through one sequence of decisions. In the universities, as in life, power tends to follow money. The corporate form and governing board serve as interposition devices. The development of a variety of other funding sources for parts of the span of university activities has diffused power, because there are different sequences of decision for federal research and categorical funds and still different sequences of decisions for foundation research grants. The university orporation is a creature capable of receiving and administering this diversified series of funding commitments.

Those who want to do something in a university can often find several candidate funding sources. However, money implies influence—often not nearly as much as the decision-makers in the funding source feel they should have, but at least enough influence to assure that the funded activity or function will be pursued by those concerned.

In Chapter Two, we looked at the ethical conditions of university operation. Whether or not these norms are written into the formal policies and regulations of the institution, they are a source of natural authority in the university at its best. Appeal to these norms can successfully block external political power, purely administrative authority, or interest-group maneuvers either within or from outside the immediate boundaries of the institution. In fact, the wise exercise of other forms of authority strengthens these moral demands on the scholar and the student and heightens their incentives to serve the cause of learning and contribute to the long-range vitality of the university.

This is why administrators, who are responsible for husbanding the university's resources and seeing to the effectiveness of its bureaucratic organization, need to work within complicated mechanisms of consultation concerning academic matters and due process for the protection of individuals. These are not a luxury but a long-range necessity if the moral conditions of a university are to be binding. But the administrator who is balancing among claims or defending the resource base or the political and community support of the institution can seldom count on others involved in these consultative processes to feel the same urgency he does about taking timely actions to avoid future catastrophes. Faculty and students are ordinarily concerned with "doing their (academic) thing" here and now and are usually not aware of the combined influence of constituency forces and financial pressures. (Michael Cohen and James March [1974] concoct the delightful phrase "organized anarchy" to describe this. See, especially, their Chapter 9.)

Faculty and students feel a moral right to be consulted about significant questions, and there are many vetoes against overt actions lying around the institution, ready to be invoked through consultative mechanisms. Thus, a discretionary decision may produce an institutional crisis. The main protection against crisis—and, perhaps fortunately, it is a substantial protection—is the normal passivity and and preoccupation of the main internal constituencies. In this milieu, one important, ongoing task of administrative management is that of tending the structure: seeing to it that the elements of the organization interact with each other satisfactorily in the flow of work, that each of them holds within its set of functions and performs effectively, that the procedures for dealing with all sorts of problems are understood and effectively used, and that the energies and resources of the institution are applied to keep the institution in reasonable balance through time.

Both formal authority and informal influence are widely diffused in a university, as compared with other types of formal organizations. Most university presidents would probably give a double "Amen" to the famous and rather plaintive comment of Alfred P. Sloan, Jr., that most of his creative time as president of General Motors was taken up with seeing that the many committees of the corporation were addressing significant problems and moving along with them. The university president's most authoritative leverage on the institution is in seeing to choices of key personnel—where the power of appointment is usually shared not only with the governing board but with consultative and advisory groups that exert influence on the selection of a panel of acceptable choices—and in the work of modifying, as occasion requires, the institution's procedures, policy standards, and organizational form. Exceptions that the structure has not successfully resolved come to the president's desk, and these make case law and serve as a signal of the balance of pressures and priorities in the institution.

Initiatives about the direction of the university may come from many sources both within and external to the university, but the greatest creative burden of the senior administration is its responsibility to form and crystallize the main direction of the institution. Even though symbolic and substantive spokesmanship is essential, the dominant issue is usually to find and support mechanisms—for defining the thrust of change in the institution, obtaining the resources, and making the course of development acceptable.

The university president has genuine, discretionary latitude over a very small fraction of all that is done and all the dollars that are used. Much of his small discretionary margin is taken up with response to conflicting pressures and claims—an essential feature of the task of maintaining viable power to act in the politics of large-scale bureaucratic organization. For the rest—a tiny fraction of all the resources and energies absorbed—truly significant impact on the institution comes about only if the discretionary choices have an amplified effect far exceeding the size of the action or the money allocation. If the officer having the greatest formal authority works in a limited area of discretion, hedged in by many claims and pressures, then the president's role is much like that of all the other administrators in a university, except that he lives with the added risk of being the most obvious target if things go wrong.

A major university has many sources of funding for particular activities and many types of environmental contacts. Negotiation for funds is widely shared among key faculty, administrators, and often trustees. Within limits, fund-getting and information-getting are institutionalized and can be managed. But responsible negotiators for funds and seekers of significant information can demand and get considerable authority to do their work properly. Clark Kerr (1963) emphasized this pluralistic aspect of the distribution of authority in the *multiversity*.

The productivity of the fund-getters, including the president, ought to be evaluated relative to the difficulty of the problem of extracting from the environment what the institution (or a unit within it) feels is needed; but their credibility within the institution usually depends on the absolute level of performance. Some presidents, in fortunate times, have become famous as expansionists and organization builders who secured large private gifts or large capital and operating budgets from public sources. In more normal circumstances, some added funds secured by the president or the governing board can relieve institutional tensions and provide reinforcement of a university's creative thrust in new directions. But the most difficult task—and now, unfortunately, a necessary one for major universities —is to maintain credibility for the top level of authority when the best that can be managed is dignified retreat from the agenda of previous hopes and commitments.

The leverage accorded by ability to make the fund-base grow is now much reduced by bleak economic conditions. But the monitoring and managing of the allocation processes of the institution is important at all times. Also important is the function of getting and interpreting for the institution the significant types of information about environments in which the institution must operate. Most important of all, in view of the significant constraints from superstructure, are negotiations with superstructure and enforcement within the institution of the best bargains that can be achieved. Presidents, of public universities in particular, are finding their skills and energies heavily absorbed in negotiating university relations with coordinating agencies, political authorities in state government, and major Federal agencies from which decisions and commitments have to be extracted. The president's authority within the university must then be used to enforce the negotiated agreements and may be challenged by those adversely affected by them.

This discussion cannot ignore the fact that formal authority, from the governing board on down, is curiously constrained in its impact on the most fundamental processes of learning—those involving scholars and scholars, scholars and students, and students and students. Most of the apparatus of formal authority sets frameworks, establishes schedules, allocates enabling resources, records (fragments of) the record of results, and monitors the general trend of performance. The actual conduct of learning is, of course, much affected by all this. But there is so much swing between minimum and maximum performance that the individuals in a university retain very significant autonomy. This gives them many vetoes over the official intentions of authority in the most important aspect of the university. The formal apparatus does bear on the selection of those who will come into the academic process. But once these choices are made, the largest differences in results come not from the enabling framework but from the capacities, motivations, and incentives of individual scholars and students. They have the ultimate authority in a university, because they determine whether great things will happen in the processes of learning.

The criteria for results, looked at this way, are very imperfectly formulated, and the gauges of quality entail highly specialized and very personal academic judgments. The processes of learning are not well understood. But it may also be true that university administrators are reluctant to move toward systematic measures of accountability for what is learned and discovered because they have so little power to affect the outcomes of these processes.

Units of Academic Organization

The two basic units of operating academic organization are conventionally the school or college and, within a school or college, its divisions or academic departments. A professor is said to hold appointment "in the department of biochemistry" or "the law school," implying (correctly) that for—budget, personnel administration, and academic duties—this is the professor's main point of supervision and locus of activity. In the areas of professional education—law, sometimes engineering, business administration—the professional school may be organized into divisions or committee groups within a single academic department that includes all academic personnel of the school, and these divisions or committees may not have the formal powers of budget allocation and personnel supervision that an academic department has.

In a campus organized according to classically defined scholarly disciplines, each academic department is a collectivity of faculty expertise with (in the pure case) an exclusive mandate to control what is offered to any student on the campus in that field. No department can poach on another's territory. Even though students' choices of majors and electives determine the enrollment distribution, the departments are not permitted to be direct substitutes of one another in the academic content of what they offer. They are all independent or complementary in the supply of course offerings, by type of content. It would be a violation of this principle, for example, to have two departments of mathematics competing with each other and offering identical courses.

The Induced Course-Load Matrix illustrates how one academic department interacts with another in the operation of curricula. This technique was developed at the University of California for analysis of resource-absorption in academic programs, and it has been used as a major element of the NCHEMS/WICHE Resource Requirements Prediction Model (RRPM). Academic operations are defined in a Leontief $N \times N$ input-output matrix. From historical course enrollment statistics of the student majors in a given field, the proportions of academic work they take both in their major fields and in every other field are derived. These fractional coefficients are either zero or positive, and they are ordinarily assumed to be invariate with respect to changes in the number of majors in the field. (This assumption of constant coefficients can be relaxed just as it can in input-output economics, but at the cost of substantially increasing the complexity of an academic operations resource-absorption model.)

Using this matrix of coefficients and the distribution of FTE (full-time equivalent) student enrollment by major, the analyst can quickly compute the total amount of instructional load in each field that is generated by student majors from that and every other field. The sum of these components for any one field is its total instructional work load.

If all off-diagonal coefficients were zero, no interdependencies among academic areas would need to be considered by the institutional administrators. Doubling enrollment in a major would affect only the number of classes, faculty, and other resources in that academic area; and eliminating that major entirely would eliminate the work load for that field but leave all others unaffected. Typically, of course, the historical enrollment distributions, and the curriculum requirements that are legislated by faculties and approved in an institution, do show substantial cross-relations between fields. Thus, the chief academic administrator of a campus, implicitly viewing these interdependencies as a fact, sees them as implying independence (zero coefficients) or complementation (positive coefficients) among programs. If it is suggested that a given academic area be dropped, and if it has a history of substantial cross-relations with other academic areas, the costs of reorganization, redesign of curricula in the remaining fields, and dislocation of student and faculty preferences are likely to be substantial. Such consolidations often require complex sequences of administration—faculty study, debate, and negotiation, the costly process known as academic reform.

The above holds when a campus is committed to the organizing principle of distinguishing each academic discipline, establishing an academic department for it, and giving that department exclusive mandate, not only to administer a program for degree majors in that field but also to provide instruction in that field (service course load) for students in other majors who have requirements or elective interests in the field in question.

There are two important dimensional alternatives to this principle of academic design—the professional schools and the decentralized collegiate organization. The professional schools often claim their expertise not in a scholarly discipline but in the design of a curriculum to fit students for a professional vocation and the inculcation of students with the mores and attitudes of that profession. Some of the intellectual content may overlap with one or another of the basic scholarly disciplines. The faculty of the professional school may then have to decide whether to send its students to the academic discipline departments for background courses or to assign some faculty of the professional school to especially designed courses within the school. Organization of a campus into decentralized colleges strikes even more deeply at the fundamental principle of complementation because each college may seek a faculty and offer a set of courses or seminars chosen to be consistent with its style and mission. Course offerings in one college on the campus may then overlap with those in another. College-initiated courses also compete with those offered by specialists in a field to the campus as a whole. Adams and Michaelsen (1971) discuss this problem in their study of the University of California, Santa Cruz.

The departmental organization in a particular university often has specific institutional history to account for seeming irrationalities: finer breakdown into small departmental units, or even partially parallel and competing departments if there is a history of ideological schism or a conflict of leadership personalities.

There is also a problem of scale. Academic departments, measured by the number of faculty slots, can vary within one campus from one professor (a distinguished isolate, or a tenured survivor of a past phaseout decision) to more than one hundred. Really large academic departments cannot operate internally by the consensual and collegial styles that are traditionally congenial to academic life. They have to develop internal committee systems and bureaucratic structures for the large mass of work entailed in personnel administration, scheduling, and student contact (Dressel, 1970).

In a well-known study of PhD programs at the University of California, Berkeley, David Breneman (1971) developed the concept of the academic department as a *prestige-maximizing firm* and sought to explain, in these terms, differences between departments in rates of persistence to the degree, aspirations for eminence, and other factors. From this point of view, the faculty members of a department gain reputation in two ways: through the recognition accorded their individual research by peers in the discipline, and by sharing the collective reputation and visibility of the department. Graduate students who attain the PhD are the proteges of one or two individual faculty members, who vouch for them at the time of job placement, and of the departmental PhD program. A conventionally prestige-increasing PhD placement is one in a university academic department of high reputation or a prized research appointment. There are also prestige-neutral appointments (in middling institutions and in most industrial or government jobs) and prestige-reducing appointments (in teaching or professional posts that add no luster to the department). Breneman's hypothesis, generally confirmed through systematic interviews and other qualitative evidence, includes the inference that a department interested in prestige-maximizing tightens its passing standard for PhDs if it fears that, on completion, some candidates could be placed only in prestige-reducing positions.

In these aspects of a department's operation, its faculty members are bound together in a calculus of mutuality in which the good of one contributes to the good of all, and all have incentives to enforce on themselves and on their advanced graduate students the highest (conventionally defined) academic standards, both for research and for graduate teaching.

In any university, however, an academic department has many other duties and responsibilities, and these must be shared by its members. Unless there are separate graduate and undergraduate faculties—which in American universities is rare—a department administers a program for undergraduate degree majors and often one for terminal master's degree candidates who will go into purely teaching jobs or into professional employment. The department's roster of courses is partly for these students and partly for students who are not in its stream of majors but take its courses as requirements, electives, or prerequisites for other work.

In ways ranging from the general and qualitative to the precisely quantitative, the number of students enrolled in a department's courses and graduate programs serve as a major determinant of the operating budget it receives—particularly of the quantity of operating support, the number of graduate assistant positions, and the additional positions for faculty appointment in the following year. The stronger these budgetary factors are, the greater is the departmental incentive to register large and increasing enrollment. Once again, there is a calculus of mutuality, in that the members of the department have strong incentives to value, in particular, the additional faculty positions that will make it possible to add more members. The kinds of teaching responsibilities that require heavy work are duties to be shared in a more or less proportionate fashion.

The faculty member can hope to gain professional satisfactions (and many indeed do) from these teaching responsibilities. But the more distant they are from his research interests of the moment, and from work with advanced graduate students who may become part of the coin of his and the department's academic visibility, the greater is the competition for his energy.

The role of the department chairman—the administrative officer representing the department to the several levels of the administration and responsible for assignment of course duties and budgetary resources and for personnel administration—contains the classic "linking-pin" stresses of which Rensis Likert has written. The higher levels of university administration regard the chairman as a first-line supervisor, responsible for interpreting and enforcing university policies and regulations and for making sensible allocations of the department's budgeted resources. Department members regard the chairman as a colleague and as their agent in bringing to the department what it needs from the university administration. In situations of conflict and scarcity, the chairman cannot be totally satisfying to both forces all of the time.

Universities differ in the extent of discretionary power accorded the department chairman and in the expected length of service in that position. In occasional instances, the chairman of a department persists in very long service—decades, rather than years. If this is known to be likely, he can use his powers of budget allocation, teaching assignment, and personnel recommendations as sanctions over rank-and-file members of the department. But most professors have lifetime tenure, and there are limits to purely authoritarian control. The chairman must secure mostly voluntary cooperation from his colleagues, and they have avenues of redress if they feel abused.

Much more usual is frequent rotation of the chairmanship among senior members of a department, one of them taking the duty for two or three years, with reduced responsibilities in course teaching and at some penalty to his own research and his work with graduate students because of the time required for administration. Then, the incumbent secures honorable relief from the chairmanship, which passes to another senior member of the department.

This procedure has three consequences. It emphasizes collegiality and consensus methods of operation. The incumbent is aware that next year, or the year after, the colleague with whom he must disagree, or on whom he seeks to foist an unwelcome duty or decision, may be the chairman instead of himself. It produces a quite variable skill of administration over time, because capacity for administration is unevenly distributed in a typical group of university faculty members. This amateur and uneven capacity results in the devolution of large, effective power on skilled, long-service (and usually, female) administrative assistants who are noncompetitive in role with the academics of the department. And rotation results in greater emphasis on the internal needs of the department than on the wider concerns and administrative pressures brought to bear by the higher levels of the university administration.

Program and Process Relationships: Departmental View

When a campus is organized according to academic specializations or scholarly disciplines, with a distinct budgetary unit for each, the faculty and chairman of each department face both complementary and competitive relationships with other departments: academic process and operating interactions; relationships in the design of curriculum; competition within departments for priorities; and budgetary relationships between departments.

Faculty in two fields are sometimes strongly dependent on one another. Historian and linguist, chemist and physicist, lawyer and political scientist may trade mutually helpful backgrounds and techniques and may share in the training of students who are, in effect, hybrid products of the respective specialties. Academic departments may also rely on each other in a milder form of complementarity, any given department sending students to the department which has the expertise and the jurisdictional mandate to provide essential background. Service courses offer institutional efficiencies through economies of scale. But the students arrive from a variety of majors, and the design of a service course is often, necessarily, a compromise that does not quite fit any one of the components of student flow into it.

Thus, we find at many universities, that the mandate of exclusive jurisdiction partly breaks down. An example is the proliferation of introductory statistics courses on many campuses. The mathematical statisticians may offer to majors in the mathematics and statistics department an introductory statistics course that presumes mathematical background and ability. They may also offer an introductory service course for nonmajors with less mathematics training. At a large university, we are likely also to find educational statistics, engineering statistics, psychological statistics, business statistics, biostatistics—all offered in the respective departments and each tailored to the most important applications in a particular field and to the needs for learning and the passing standard that the department feels it is desirable to impose on a particular stream of students. A single, large-scale introductory statistics offering might be considerably cheaper than this menu of specially tailored courses (and it might be better statistics), but it would entail compromises of course design and administration. These compromises have to be evaluated as a loss in seeking the large-scale solution. Students taking the large-scale service course may be dissatisfied with it. Too many of them may do badly in it, from the point of view of the sending departments. And the course may not contain enough of the special topics and applications desired by each sending department.

A department is a coalition of faculty with mutuality of scholarly interest in the shared discipline and a collective interest in the welfare and prestige of its members and of the field on the campus. The department has a strong interest in offering and manning service courses, and defending its jurisdictional mandate, if it has a strong philosophical commitment concerning instruction in its field and if the rules of budgetary allocation on the campus reinforce the departmental interest. This reinforcement occurs if departmental justifications for additional teaching positions and other components of budget are keyed to student enrollment, for the department can then use the additional appointments to satisfy ever-present needs for rounding out its roster of complementary specialties or adding an occasional star or exceptionally promising junior faculty member.

If the campus budgetary mechanism is an internal budgetary market driven by the volume of instructional activity, the department can maximize its resources by: (1) maximizing its capture of student enrollments by making its major fields attractive, and by retaining the course elections or requirements of its major students as nearly as possible within the rules of what it can decide about curriculum and how it can influence its students; (2) having other departments specify its offerings as required courses or as preferred electives, and making its courses attractive to students over the whole campus as free electives; and (3) developing curricula and emphases that will attract more majors.

The budgetary standards written into the resource allocation mechanism also exert profound influence. For example, the laboratory sciences typically claim that they cannot conduct instruction properly unless they have a large amount of building space, equipment, and operating support per faculty member and per student. As we shall see in Chapter Nine, these standards are necessary for the budgetary mechanism; once adopted, they are not easy to reopen as an explicit issue of resource allocation (although the allocation may fail to approximate the standard, exceeding it temporarily if the department's enrollment falls after a large allocation of space or equipment was previously made, or falling below it if enrollment rises too quickly to allow the allocation to catch up). A significant change in the preferred style of work in an academic field, leading to a demand for an increase in budgetary standard, is likely to arouse acute controversy between the department and the campus administration.

An academic department is responsible for the design and offering of graduate and undergraduate degree programs, and sometimes for specialties within the field. Each subgroup of the departmental faculty is most interested in the courses, students, and research activities in its specialty. Elements of competition and complementarity appear in the struggle to define programs, evaluate their worth to the department and the campus, set priorities, and allocate budget. There is a contradiction here between the Law of Indefinite Augmentation and the Law of Competition at the Margin. The forces of complementarity and independence give rise to the first of these laws: a plausible tendency to add new sources of funding, new units of organization and program commitments, and even new elements of purpose to the institution because they do not appear to conflict with what is already being done and may indeed add complementary strengths to it. But the Law of Competition at the Margin warns that if more is done in one direction it may redirect energies and the volume of activity away from another, and that resources drawn in to support the augmented activities or the added program commitment or element of purpose may at the margin have to be financed by cutting other departments within the institution or by making allocations from the small amounts of discretionary funds and reserves available.

If a department faces a campus-wide requirement of justification for resources according to student work load, the department must, in considering a proposed new program, consider whether that program will attract additional enrollment without decreasing it in existing activities. If so, the new program can be financed by budget augmentation; but if not, the potential losing factions within the department may oppose the improvement of position of the potential gainers.

The department may also assert priorities that run counter to wider interests perceived by the campus administration. For example, during the period when doctoral programs were being expanded, many academic departments saw needs, and their interests, best served by a sharp increase in doctoral-level instruction. If faculty wanted to pursue this more rapidly than additional net resources (faculty positions, support budget, and so forth) could be made available, they often did so by reducing the resources allocated to undergraduate teaching and allowing undergraduate class sizes to increase while assigning faculty to new doctoral-level courses and tutorial instruction. Only an assertion of counterpressure by college deans or campus-level administrators could prevent this shift in emphasis. Also, many departments had been admitting graduate students as master's degree candidates. Some of these students might eventually enter doctoral programs, but many were interested in terminal master's degrees. Many academic departments deemphasized or eliminated these terminal master's degree programs, consolidating their attention on doctoral students. Unless the administrators at a higher level saw some harm to institutional interests, they tended to be complaisant about such departmental actions. Only when the PhD hiring market turned sour, beginning around 1970, did many academic departments begin to wonder whether their cutoff of terminal master's degree candidates had been wise.

When negotiating its budget with the campus-wide administration, a department can expect ready acceptance of any proposal it makes for reduction of budgeted resources. But it must expect an uphill fight to obtain increased resources. A department's proposed reallocation of effort can be separated into two distinct components: reductions of activity in area A, and increases of activity in area B. The latter must be scrutinized carefully. Under significant resource constraint, the campus administration has a negative bias about such expansions, and a positive bias about proposals for budget reductions. In such a climate, the only safe departmental strategy is to avoid showing the possibility of any budgetary reductions, and to press for budgetary expansion to support desired growth.

Funds from foundations and federal research agencies for training grants and research support have provided a seeming escape from resource allocation dilemmas. If a vigorous faculty group could find outside funding for what it wanted to do, and if what it wanted to do was academically respectable or even innovative, then that group was not likely to be opposed, by the department or by the higher administration. Once obtained, such funds resulted in concurrent demands for enrollment and for space to house the expanded program. Some farsighted administrators cautioned about the institutional liabilities if such outside funding was discontinued. But, in the short run, enthusiasm for expansion muffled arguments about future risks.

Organizational Problems

The conventional form of departmentalization presents three typical problems of organization: (1) inconsistencies and gaps in assigning academic program responsibilities to the departmental and school or college units; (2) inadequate internal cohesion and clarity of objectives; and (3) rigidity. Each of these is discussed as an analytical issue.

A curricular example of gaps in program responsibilities is the interdisciplinary degree program. Each student in such a program get parts of the work toward the degree from each of several departments. In some universities, an interdisciplinary faculty committee oversees the program and the progress of students in it. But these faculty members have many other responsibilities. It is not unusual for such interdisciplinary programs to starve, in due course, for lack of attention, because no formal unit of organization sees its welfare as depending on the performance of students in the program or on the survival of the program. Research units have been created at many American universities as responses to another kind of incomplete mapping of program responsibilities—the existence of a significant, multidisciplinary research area. This type of organizational unit is discussed later in this chapter.

The analytical problem, and it becomes a practical issue of academic management, is that an incomplete mapping of academic program responsibilities leaves some significant areas of concern unbudgeted (so that if they are absorbing resources, this is not identified) and unmanaged. There is never a definitive cure for this problem because there are many dimensionally different ways to design curricula and areas of academic study and research. Several of these dimensional approaches to curriculum have already been mentioned: area-studies programs, for which the language, literature, history, and social science topics of an area of the world are grouped together rather than having the student take separate courses on each topic in the disciplinary departments; theme colleges; social-problems curricula, such as social ecology and women's studies; and, most important in size and scope, the various professional school curricula. A university administration cannot foreclose all of those ways that fail to be reflected in the existing pattern of organization. Indeed, in the interest of scholarly flexibility and experiment, it is prudent to leave open some opportunities for departures from conventional programs. Yet it remains a problem to monitor the use of faculty time and other resources and the quality of student and faculty performance.

The second problem of departmentalization is that of cohesion and clarity of objectives. At some universities there is little contact—whether official or informal—among department members. This is especially true in an urban university when faculty members work at home on several days of the week and come to the campus only for course meetings and other specific obligations. In these circumstances, it is difficult to sustain the consensual style of decision-making and administration that is preferred by academic people. Information filters slowly and uncertainly, and low frequency of contact prevents the building and maintenance of any mutual confidence. The department chairman and the administrative hierarchy of the department may, by default, become the only point of reference for students, for faculty members from other fields, and for the campus administration.

An academic department that functions with low internal cohesion but according to a theory of consensual decision is unable to go beyond minimal routines and may function badly even with respect to those. Questions of objectives and priorities—difficult enough to resolve even when people of good will share a high state of information and a strong sense of mutual trust—are left unexamined and unresolved. The social pressure to perform, so important to a voluntaristic scheme of organization, is missing.

The alternative to a consensual style is increased bureaucratization and a larger, managerial role for the chairman. He may be encouraged or compelled to assume a larger role if pressed for decisions and tidy results by higher levels of administration. But when there is a low level of cohesion, department members resist bureaucratic pressures.

Rigidity in academic organization is proverbial. One contributing factor is lifetime tenure, which commits the university for a long period to an academic group. The composition of the group can be changed only slowly, except in the unusual circumstances of rapid growth (with flexibility only during the growth interval, and long-persistent rigidity thereafter) and academic reorganization. The higher levels of administration in a university approach such reorganization with understandable caution. A proposal to consolidate or merge two departments arouses latent questions of philosophical intent and reach. It also arouses questions of power and prerogative, which, in the routines of normal departmental operation, are either dealt with by compromise or left unfaced. In order to be on the soundest possible ground for a reorganization decision, the administrators have to negotiate a solution agreeable to all (which may not be possible, or may have high costs in money and institutional commitments) or they have to obtain expert academic judgments on a reasonable plan of consolidation, because as administrators they are unlikely to have credible judgments. The process is intricate, time consuming, expensive of administrative and academic energy, and risky. What better testimony to the inherent rigidity of academic organization!

Because of this rigidity, the governing board and administration of a university do not permit the casual establishment of an academic department, school, or college. They ordinarily require a showing that there is a sound academic basis for establishing a unit that will have long-term consequences. At the point of initiation, there should be attention to considerations that were all too often scanted during the euphoric expansion in the 1960s: (1) Given a sound academic case for establishing the new unit, what is the specific rationale for it in the particular university? How will it add to the strengths and distinction of the institution? (2) Can the university find a nucleus of exceptionally able and entrepreneurial faculty to start the new unit? The characteristics of this nucleus will set the course of the new department for at least thirty years. (3) Is the new academic unit sustainable over time? The starting nucleus of staff and facilities is usually much smaller than needed for steady-state viability. What is the best judgment of that steady-state size? Can it be reasonably forecast that enrollment will require that large an operation? Are there favorable forecasts of available research resources and extramural funding? Will the university be able to provide resources and commitments, not merely for the start-up nucleus but for the path toward steady-state size?

The school or college is the next level of academic organization beyond the department, and to this we now turn.

Schools and Colleges

The dean of a professional school or college is in a linking-pin position similar to the department chairman, but his role as spokesman to external constituencies is greater. The professional school dean is a member of a council of deans or some similar body with whom the chief campus officer consults. His administrative tasks are usually numerous and burdensome. And he is usually appointed for a longer minimum interval of expected service than a department chairman.

In radical contrast to this is the dean of letters and science.

In many American universities, the college of letters and science consists of all departments in the basic scholarly disciplines. Traditionally, this college served as the administrative frame for approving all curricula leading to the bachelor of arts degree and for monitoring the flows of students through them.

Over time, the academic departments increased in number and size, and many developed master's degree and doctoral programs. Sometimes a dean with a strong personality and exceptional administrative skills has developed ways to cope with larger-scale, increasingly ramified specialization (and the demands for expertise in passing judgments on budgets and personnel actions) and multiple levels of program. More often, because the letters and science portion of the campus accounts for a major part of the total budget, the president and senior administration have developed a campus-wide budgetary mechanism to which the larger departments have direct appeal, and they have assigned functional responsibilities to other positions, weakening the position of the dean of letters and science until it became one of routine.

The graduate dean oversees the content and quality of graduate instructional programs (often with the advisory assistance of a graduate council of senior faculty from the various fields) and the administration of graduate admissions, fellowship support, the status of graduate students, and the mechanisms for examinations and awarding of graduate degrees. With the advent of large-scale, extramurally funded research, the graduate dean has sometimes assumed responsibility for research policy, for monitoring the work of organized research units, and for contract and grant administration. But these last have become complex bureaucratic functions, requiring both accounting and regulatory expertise, and are now often handled by a specialized part of the technical administration.

Some universities, instead of having the college of letters and science as an umbrella over all disciplines, have grouped academic departments into divisions with a dean of each for greater ease and coherence of administration: a division of physical and biological sciences, a social science division, a division of humanities, and possibly other divisions. This design was adopted at the start on the new Irvine campus of the University of California and was achieved, after great internal struggle, at the university's Riverside campus.

The dean of each such division is responsible for most ·important budgetary, personnel, and organizational matters. Thus, he can exert effective leadership and control over department chairmen in his division. This role is most effective if there is not a strong ideological commitment to the notion that all fundamental scholarship is integral, and that the liberal arts curriculum is therefore (in principle) integral, with interdependencies and scholarly standards outweighing the importance of specialization. In some fields, the undergraduate major is now designed as an essential preparation, gateway, and screening device for graduate study in that discipline, not as the in-depth part of a program of liberal education. Both students and faculty then gauge "success" in the undergraduate major in terms of admission to graduate study in the field. At the same time, universities have reduced or abandoned general education requirements in undergraduate letters and science. Both of these developments weaken the case for continuing a single college of letters and science.

There are feasible alternatives to departmental organization according to disciplines and professions. One of these is organization in residential colleges—a tradition made famous by Oxford and Cambridge. At Oxford, the university administers examinations and confers degrees. There are some university lecturers, but most of the academic staff have traditionally been appointed as fellows of colleges. The student receives most of his education, and a great deal of other guidance, through the tutorial system of each college.

In the early 1920s, the Claremont Colleges in California established a blueprint of confederation and intercollege cooperation; now there are five colleges, plus the Claremont University Center. The student is officially enrolled in one college but may take courses and have access to academic and other facilities of other colleges. Each faculty member is appointed to one college, but often with attention to the nature of appointment needs in that field in other colleges as well. The central administration provides some common administrative services to all of the colleges and has developed, on their joint behalf, a computer center and a central library.

The Five Colleges (Amherst, Smith, Mt. Holyoke, and Hampshire, together with the larger state-supported University of Massachusetts) have created an intercollege coordinating office to foster cooperative, academically enriching, and cost-reducing relationships among them. The student is officially enrolled in one college and receives a degree from that college. Faculty appointments are made by the separate colleges, but with consultation beforehand.

The University of California campus at Santa Cruz was established in the early 1960s and was from the beginning organized into largely residential colleges. Each student enrolled at Santa Cruz is a member of a college. With a few exceptions, each faculty member holds appointment as fellow of a college and as a member of a disciplinary board of studies, and his salary and duties are split between the two. Adams and Michaelson (1971) reviewed the tensions created by these dual appointments. It was originally expected that each student would take a significant portion—perhaps one-fourth—of his academic work in courses and seminars offered by his college. The colleges proved to be important in student life and informal learning. But they did not develop strong curriculum offerings. The investment in course development and administration in the boards of studies was much greater. The faculty member faces pressures—reflecting the conventional expectations of research initiative, scholarly competence, and responsibility to teach assigned courses—from the board of studies of which he is a member and from the college of which he is a fellow. The boards of studies perform a vital function, seeing to disciplinary strengths and seeking to assure that additional appointments meet appropriate standards of competence and also add to the menu of specialties available in the discipline. The colleges have had more difficulty than the boards of studies in defining the role of the affiliated faculty member, arriving at criteria for justifying their needs for faculty personnel, and evaluating faculty performance in collegial (as distinct from discipline-oriented) duties. Hence, the colleges have had a lesser role than originally expected in influencing the incentives and the advancement opportunities of the faculty member.

Other Academic Units

Supporting units and activities of a university are exemplified in the academic area by the general library and the computer center, in student services by the residence hall system, and in the administrative structure by the accounting office and the grounds and building department. Of these, only the general library may contribute significantly to the global image of the university's quality and distinctiveness. Even the library justifies its existence mainly by supporting teaching and research. Other such units justify themselves by indirect assistance to the direct contributions that academic programs make to academic goals.

The university library is so central to the academic operation that it receives large subsidy from the general funds of the institution. It supports and defends this subsidy by cultivating complementation with academic departments which, in their turn, put pressure on the university administration.

The quality of a library as a research resource is a function of collection size in each field, the uniqueness of research materials, the timeliness of inclusion and accessibility of new materials in fields where ideas and evidence obsolesce rapidly, and the skill with which cataloguing is done. Scholarly fields and disciplines rely differentially on the library and are differentially concerned with the various aspects of library quality.

Individuals, and particularly undergraduates, often consider convenience and accessibility of library materials more important than uniqueness and collection size. The library administration is caught in budgetary cross-pressures between demands for convenience (which often result in pressures to establish duplicative branch collections and to emphasize budget allocations for circulation service as against acquisitions) and the long-term demands for collection size and uniqueness.

A quite different issue is presented by the demands of advanced students and scholars who are working toward the frontier of a subject. In the sciences, reported knowledge and findings obsolesce rapidly, as Philip Morse (1968) showed in his study of library organization. The ideal library service for scientists has the full range of reported research available quickly, and a capability for bibliographical search and information retrieval. In such fields as chemistry and medicine, abstracting and computerized bibliographical search have become worthwhile. For the conduct of science, as distinct from the investigation of its history or philosophy, most researchers would be content with a library that made its greatest investment in contemporary material and threw away everything more than five or ten years old.

The needs of students in the fields of humane scholarship are very different. They need access to the full range of published works that may bear on a topic, including successive editions of the same book and all other possibly relevant references. They need special collections of materials brought together for unique completeness. The professions, social sciences, applied sciences, and history need these. Serial publications have proliferated in number and have risen sharply in cost. A third collection needed by the humanities is the primary creative or historical record: documents, manuscripts, and uniquely illuminating scraps of the past.

Librarians must be preservationists and collectors in anticipating what may be of future interest to scholars even though there may be little or no current demand. They are also motivated in part by total collection size because library prestige is correlated with size. If librarians must choose—and resources are never sufficient for everything—they are likely to opt for book acquisitions, to meet the condition that the desired source is or will be eventually available in principle, rather than for investments in speed of acquisition and quickness of access.

Librarians administer large, hierarchical organizations and large, institutionally subsidized budgets. Because of the competing and often contradictory demands made by different parts of the university constituency, and demands for relations with insistent outside users, librarians are often experts in political accommodation. Scholars make two different types of demands that have strong cost and administrative implications: demands for special collections, which have long-continuing costs of custody and maintenance; and demands for branch libraries, to service conveniently the immediate needs of teachers and advanced students. If a university is physically dispersed in various parts of a city, it does not operate well as a delivery system without branch libraries; but these create duplication of both collection items and staff services. When they can, chief librarians resist branch libararies and defend the integral character and strengths of the main collection and services.

Interesting questions have arisen concerning the network interaction among libraries. In multicampus university systems, the intercampus sharing of items and services and the systemic management of the entire collection can be questioned by the central university administration or by the funding source. Libraries historically have service attitudes of reciprocity with each other in the United States—interlibrary loan arrangements, and, in the case of some multicampus universities, a shared union catalog. But the head librarian of a campus is often resistant to administrative integration of book acquisition and cataloguing with other libraries, to mandated agreements for collection specialization, and to heavy investments in the speed, reliability, and convenience of interlibrary circulation if such investment would be at the expense of collection size on his own main library site.

The number of new titles published per year has been increasing, at an accelerating rate, and, as will be shown in Chapter Eight, the cost per item has been increasing relative to the general price level, much faster for some types of items than for others.

Leimkuhler and Cooper (1970) put together a number of factors that I have discussed, and they demonstrate interactions among these factors that are important for analytical planning of university libraries. They investigated the characteristics of storage costs and usage costs, explored the implications of alternative rules (age rules and usage rules) for culling active collections, and examined implications of acquisition rate in relation to the size of the existing collection.

Left to itself, the library of a university follows a strong law of growth—in needs for building space, book and serials acquisition and cataloguing funds, personnel budgets for circulation and reference services, and diversification of services to specialized campus groups. New, mostly computerized library technologies are on the way; but in their early stages these have increased budget needs without bringing cost reductions. It has become doubtful whether any one university campus, given its financial limits, will be able to finance a library that meets all the expectations of its academic constituencies. Yet the central administration, in view of these financial limits faces problems of concept, politics, and the traditional (and for many purposes, highly valuable) style of library organization and administration if it tries to bring the library budget under coherent control.

When budgets are tightened, the library's subsidy budget is likely to come under attack for various reasons. First, the library is a supporting activity, not a direct contributor to goal attainment. (It stands in weak complementation to academic goals.) Second, circulation of books is an observable work-load factor, but the penalty to scholarship from a cutback in numbers of new titles is hard to prove (and is tied to the more exotic research outputs, which are not likely to find as much favor with legislative or alumni fundors as does the accommodation of students). Finally, the yardstick of collection quality in each field is a moving target, consisting ideally of the inclusion of everything old and everything new. Because no library can meet this ideal, the issue is how far to compromise. When put in these terms, the subsidy investment in the library collection is very difficult to objectify. Finally, if access to general institutional funds is reduced, library administrators and key faculty find only occasional and partial success in replacing the reduction from external funding markets.

Compared with the library, the university computer center came late. University computing emerged, after World War II, as an increasingly significant handmaiden of research in high-energy physics, chemistry, and engineering. A new industry has emerged, with the United States leading most of the development because of heavy federal commitments to military and aerospace research and development and to nuclear physics and other heavily funded areas of science. The information revolution is much more than idle talk, as a wide range of commercial and governmental data processing applications clearly shows.

University computers were, to begin with, mostly financed by the same governmental sources that provided large-scale extramural research funds in the physical and biological sciences and engineering—the National Science Foundation, the National Institutes of Health, the Department of Defense, and the Atomic Energy Commission. There were some direct grants to institutions for capital equipment and operating funds. But much of the cost of computing came out of project grants to which the services provided by a university computer center could be recharged. The federal agencies wanted to make sure that the price structure adopted did not cost federally-funded research projects an undue proportion of the total costs of computer operation, and so they insisted that the costs of computer service were the same for externally- and internally-funded users. Many would-be computer users, however, had no external funds against which to charge their use of the computer, and the marginal operating cost of keeping the machine running for extra time each day was low. This led to two-price systems, to which the federal agencies reacted negatively, demanding that the projects they funded not be charged more for each unit usage than internal campus users were charged.

The prices of computing, per unit of effective service rendered, have continued to fall. But the rise in use has far outstripped the cost reductions, and computer center budgets have continually increased. Both for research purposes and for a widening span of instructional needs, the whole range of physical and social sciences and most of the professions now use computing services. Demands for different types of service have also proliferated. Traditional batch processing now has a range of needs, including those for very large-scale computational problems and large-scale data handling. And there are now insistent demands for time-sharing service and for numerous types of on-line computing, for controlled experiments, data-monitoring, and process-control.

In the face of these expanding and proliferating demands, the central administration of a university faces several managerial and policy problems. One of these is the need to organize for efficient service to a differentiated user population, part of which has extramural research financing, and much of which accompanies its urgent requests for service with requests for subsidy. Given the economies of scale in batch processing (large configurations are typically much cheaper, per job or unit of computation, than small ones), it has been necessary to assemble components of the total load-factor into a job stream to permit acquisition of one large system rather than a series of small, separate installations. Yet the computer installation and its programming and operations personnel cannot serve ideally all classes of users, and the compromises leave unsatisfied, in varying degrees, the large, extramurally-funded users and the large population of small-scale faculty and student users.

The policy of preventing proliferation of small installations has to have exceptions when the main computer installation cannot be modified to accept some tasks. This argument prevails particularly for machines acquired specifically for on-line data monitoring, process control, or controlled experiments. Universities in the United States have generally permitted research groups to invest in these if they secure external funds to do so, but have not used institutional funds.

Time-sharing, or interactive computing, did not become technically feasible until the 1960s, but both universities and commercial sellers of computer services now offer extensive time-sharing facilities. The university must decide how far to go in providing what is an exciting and convenient enrichment of capability both for teaching and for research, in the face of nearly unlimited budget implications. Some universities—Dartmouth, UCLA, MIT, Carnegie-Mellon, and Princeton, in particular—have gone far in this direction. Others allow funded but not subsidized users to make outside purchases of time-sharing service.

Because of the complexities and risks of multiple-source financing, and because it is necessary to forecast carefully the future load factor when making major equipment acquisitions, universities are moving toward careful forward planning of computing needs. The most recent significant issue to emerge is the planning of networks and interconnections among computer installations, for load balancing and, hopefully, net savings. The Advanced Research Projects Agency of the Department of Defense (ARPA) financed an experimental networking scheme among selected universities, and its technical feasibility is not any longer in doubt. Whether networking will be a cost-effective strategy, as compared with stand-alone systems of individual universities, is not yet clear. The Florida state university system has moved aggressively toward adoption of a network approach and is an interesting test case.

Computer center financing and operation exemplifies the contemporary mixture (and confusion) of the problems of funding, academic policy, service effectiveness, and uncertainties. University administrations have had to strengthen their planning and operational capability in computer technology, which is a curious amalgam of hopes, technical issues, frustrations, and accelerating expenditure.

Meanwhile, major universities have also accelerated their applications of computer methods to accounting, payroll, record-keeping, and other administrative services. The demands for integrity of files and systems in these areas and for adherence to tightly defined processing cycles have resulted in the separation of administrative data processing from computing for academic users in many universities. Administrative computing is financed almost entirely from general institutional funds. The policy and managerial issues in this field are commented on in the discussion of information systems for university management in Chapter Ten.

Libraries and computer centers are but two of many academic support facilities. Also important are some types of multidisciplinary research stations, and also museums, botanical gardens, and other major installations. These often get their start with a major act of academic entrepreneurship, combined with the interest of a donor or a granting agency, when the university administration and key faculty negotiate program and facilities financing. The university administration then finds, after a time, that the ongoing costs of maintenance of the installation become general liabilities and that the installation, like the library and the computer center, has become important to substantial academic clienteles. These long-term liabilities must be faced when the installation is first proposed; once built, it becomes a respectable and insistent client for subsidy support from university general funds.

Organized Research Units

Every faculty member is appointed to an academic department and does some research. Why, then, have organized research units instead of using the units of academic organization to administer research as well as instruction? The answer to this question comes in several parts.

First, an area of research interest may exceed the boundaries of one academic department, causing the faculty members concerned to propose an administrative entity compatible with the multidisciplinary or problem-centered (as distinct from discipline-centered) definition of their joint interest. An institute of international studies may attract not only political scientists but economists, sociologists, historians, and anthropologists.

Second, when entrepreneurial efforts for extramural funding and intricate research administration become necessary, specialized administrative expertise must either be grafted onto the administrative apparatus of a department or school or college, which is generally not organized for it, or be developed in its own right. The administration of substantial research activities also entails decisions on research personnel—some of them highly paid and professionally equivalent to the faculty ranks of a department, but not members of the department. If these personnel matters are dealt with through the largely consensual mode of department decision-making, conflicts of focus and personnel policy may become significant.

Third, the research area may be one in which the sponsor—a federal agency, the state government, or a major foundation—has an interest such that, if the university as an institution accepts the obligation to organize and administer a research program, it is really operating as a long-term partner of the sponsoring agency or foundation. The early development of land-grant universities as the sites of applied agricultural research and extension service is a classic case. Activities quite different in some respects from standard academic interests were incorporated in the university framework. The partnership between various areas of fundamental science and the tasks of problem-solving application was often desirable for both. But there have been many stresses and conflicts. These were mitigated by creation of the agricultural experiment stations and of field extension service offices to care for functions not easily combined with instruction and basic research.

More recent and bigger than the agricultural experiment stations are some of the large establishments of big science, such as the Lawrence Radiation Laboratories of the University of California at Berkeley and Livermore, the Stanford Linear Accelerator Center, and the Draper Electronics Laboratory of MIT. Some of these were established in wartime or during the cold war period, when high priority was attached to rapid progress in applied science and technology for national security reasons. These facilities often operated as closed installations, to which even faculty members of the administering institutions were permitted access only with security clearance. Their relations with the funding sources were close, and their size, relative to the normal scale of academic activity in those fields, was enormous. The conditions of security surrounding such research and the security classification of research results are inimical to ordinary academic principles. In addition, because of the nature and scope of these activities, they could not have been undertaken by the existing apparatus of academic administration.

Cornell University has sought to divest itself of the Cornell Aeronautical Laboratory, and MIT has attempted to spinoff Draper Laboratory. Some individual universities or consortia of universities are still active in administering large-scale research facilities. But even a wealthy nation such as the United States can afford only a limited commitment in each highly specialized area of such fields as high-energy physics, radio astronomy, and oceanography.

State universities serve as chosen instruments of state government for other areas of applied research besides agriculture. An Institute of Industrial Relations was established at the University of California, with Clark Kerr as its first director, because then-Governor Earl Warren was convinced of the importance of research in reducing tensions between labor and management in the period following World War II. The institute therefore received substantial budget from state funds. Similarly, institutes of governmental studies and of business and economic research in some state universities perform statistics-gathering and applied research functions and are funded from state sources. The range of possible areas of mandated concern is as wide as the range of public issues that demand systematic problem-solving attention. Drug abuse, air and water pollution, and health-care-delivery research are three examples of state-financed applied research in public universities.

A research institute may also receive institutional funds for its substantive research program—from an earmarked endowment or from money especially raised through current giving—if the university administration is convinced that the activity is especially deserving of institutional backing for reasons of academic prestige or the need to cultivate an important institutional constituency. For the most part, however, organized research units in American universities receive budgets from institutional sources only for core support or administrative housekeeping. The director of the unit and his research colleagues then have a hunting license to secure extramural funding from government agencies and foundations, and they generate proposals that pass through procedural review (to assure that they conform with legal and policy standards of the institution and do not commit it to unanticipated uses of building space or unanticipated liabilities). The amount of research undertaken depends on success in getting proposals approved and funded.

Let us assume that the work done in the research unit contributes to knowledge. Does it also help to strengthen the teaching operations of the institution, or does it weaken them? Does it improve the net resource position of the institution or weaken it? These questions are considered in more detail in the chapter on resource analysis. All that needs to be said here is that the superstructure of extramurally-funded research, largely administered through organized research units, can be very large. In 1971–1972, when the state-funded operating budget of the University of California was approximately $340 million, extramural research funds (excluding Atomic Energy Commission funding of the AEC Laboratories at Berkeley, Livermore, and Los Alamos) was about $170 million. The fiscal and organizational issues are thus of considerable quantitative as well as qualitative importance.

Summary

We have seen how the main constituencies of a university impose conditions on it and give opportunities to it. Constituency influences are exerted through money and through claims on the institution. The legal structure and formal authority of the institution produce an enabling frame. But students and faculty are guided by the norms of the academic process that were discussed in Chapter Two, and authority is inescapably in the hands of individual students and faculty because they can vary the intensity of their commitment to learning.

The units of academic organization are crucial because they deliver the main products of a university: learning and discovery. Academic departments, schools and colleges, supporting academic organizations such as the library and computer center, and organized research units sometimes operate as quasi-independent entities, with their own laws of growth and separate contributions to university purpose. Much more often, they have complementary relationships with some other units of academic organization. These interdependencies make it necessary to consider the parts of the academic organization as mutually supportive, even though they compete for institutional funds, for the attention of students, and for priority.

In the next chapter, I analyze the units of administration that provide supporting services to the student population and those that provide operating services both to the academic organization and to the balance of the institution. Then it is necessary to look at the representational structures of the university and, finally the presidency.

Chapter 4

Administrative Services, Representational Entities, and the Presidency

Analysis of university organizational structure is completed in this chapter with a discussion of nonacademic administrative units, representational entities that provide communication and oversight within the institution, and the office of the president, which is responsible for coordination, policy formulation, and institutional leadership.

Students and faculty are ambivalent about these administrative structures, which they often regard as constraining, harrassing, and bureaucratic. Yet they expect the institution to work smoothly, and they want a great variety of facilitating services that can be provided only by means of elaborate procedures and organization. Participation, communication, and consultation are also essential, yet these functions require another layer of mechanisms and draw off part of the attention and energy of many from their primary duties. Harmonizing and humanizing these administrative and communicative aspects of the university is an important task.

Administrative Services

The administrative services of a university include student services, institutional support services, maintenance and operation of capital plant, auxiliary enterprises, and general administrative and business services. Within each of these there may be a large array of specialized departments. These services and enterprises facilitate the academic business of the university and provide needed services to members of the university community. Some of these activities develop significant constituency support. For example, the intercollegiate athletics program may be as important for alumni relations and institutional publicity as it is for campus morale; the teaching hospital is counted on by the immediately surrounding community for patient care services and as a regional resource for the treatment of difficult and exotic illnesses.

Before a university takes on a service or function because somebody, somewhere in the institution, wants it, some questions must be asked: Should the request for the service be opposed or ignored? If it is to be performed, should it be bought from the outside market or done by a unit of the university? If it is to be performed by a unit of the university, how should the service be organized and funded? Each of these questions deserves an explicit and carefully-examined decision. Unfortunately, administrative services in universities are in great part the result of accretion through time, rather than the result of consideration of the need, the cost, or the policy consequences.

Student Services. The student's academic business includes admission procedures, payment of tuition and fees, maintenance of records, resolution of delinquency and discipline problems, counseling and advising, administration of financial aid and student part-time work where the university is the employer, and, at the end of the line, assistance in job placement. Some of these functions are performed centrally by one administrative unit. Others are performed by academic departments, schools, and colleges. The level of cost, intensity, and skill with which these functions are performed varies among and within universities, affecting not only the ease with which students can get their business done but also their morale and even their academic performance.

Students have many other problems, needs, and interests besides the purely academic: housing, physical and mental health, transportation, recreation, and involvement with political and community life. For many of them, and for the university as an institution, there is no easy and clear point of division between education and the way of life represented by being a student. Partly depending on whether a university is located in isolation or in an urban area with a broad span of community services and depending also on its history and its definition of mission, it may be involved in all dimensions of student living, or it may provide nothing beyond instructional service, relying on local private markets, public services, and parents. The distribution of student needs and the demands for university services are also not uniform for each type of service and in total. Nearly all students at University of California campuses, for example, use the student health service, but only 20 percent to 25 percent on most campuses live in university-provided housing. Only a fraction—it varies considerably—use athletic facilities. Only a small fraction want child-care centers. A university administration may be under pressure to provide many services, even though only a small percentage of the students uses each. One possible solution is to charge for services, at a price that will (ostensibly at least) cover the cost. This approach avoids implicit subsidy to only a portion of the student population. But the university may also face intense pressure to provide some services at a cost that is subsidized. When it does this from general institutional resources, the money cannot be used for other purposes. If it provides subsidized services to some students and these are paid for from fees paid uniformly by all students, some students are subsidizing others. Faced with a variety of such demands and with the consequences of a series of ad hoc responses to them, a university administration needs to establish policies and procedures for determining what student services it will provide, how they will be paid for, how to alter services offered as new needs arise, and how to assess the contribution that student services make to the vitality of the university community and the academic progress of students.

Capital Plant. Typically, two types of administrative units deal with problems of capital plant: one to plan and control the planning, design, construction, and financing of additions to capital plant; and the second to manage the maintenance and upkeep of existing buildings and the land area owned by the institution. If the university has a substantial capital program, it must centralize most of these functions, which require many different kinds of technical and managerial expertise. At the same time, each building project, from its design phases on, needs to be developed in cooperation with the units that will use it.

Some aspects of upkeep could be decentralized and assigned to the organizational units that use the buildings. But usually, because of the needs for management and supervision of staffs of building trades craftsmen and other skilled workers, it is more efficient to maintain central pools of these workers and manage upkeep centrally, on a service and sometimes a recharge basis. Outside contracting of repair and renovation jobs, and even of building and grounds maintenance, is another alternative, and has the advantage of providing a market referent for costs and efficiency.

The allocation of building space among academic and other units is a perennial problem and is almost always a sensitive issue in the internal politics of a university. The central administration of the campus becomes involved and often creates a special administrative unit to cope with pressures for space allocation. Classroom use and scheduling is intimately tied to course scheduling and enrollment. The efficient approach is to pool all available classrooms (assuming a campus that is compact enough to permit any room to be assigned to any course), and to have the same administrative officer who makes up the course schedule and administers course enrollment be responsible for classroom assignments. But individual schools, colleges, and academic departments demand decentralized control of classrooms and instructional laboratories, not only because particular courses may require specialized facilities, but for reasons of convenience and localized autonomy.

State governments are interested in the efficient allocation of of classroom space in state-supported institutions. It is believed that tightened standards would reduce the claims for capital financing. However, in major universities, classrooms and class laboratories occupy only about 5 percent of the total academic and administrative building space. Most space is devoted to faculty offices, service units, laboratories, and other institutional functions. Space standards have been developed to bring some uniformity and policy coherence to the many types of requirements, but the management of building space remains a difficult problem. There is now considerable interest in replacing the traditional bargaining and maneuvering for space by schemes of internal pricing, so that units of the university would be faced with issues of trade-off between their demands for space and their demands for other categories of resources (Breneman, 1972).

Internal prices (sometimes called transfer prices) can be used, in organizations that have several operating divisions, when one division does work for another. The producing division gets revenue credits according to the price set and the numbers of units of work done, and the consuming division is required to recognize what it gets as a cost to it. This approach can be used to govern many types of intraorganizational relationships besides the administration of building space. The technique and its policy implications are discussed in Chapter Nine.

Auxiliary Enterprises. American universities have operated dairy farms, conference centers, electrical generating plants, forests, student dormitories and apartments, staff and faculty residences, automobile and bus fleets, printing plants, glassblowing shops, and large hospitals. Each of these auxiliary enterprises is the result of a presumption that the university should take responsibility for producing a service for a campus constituency or academic organization, and that it would be better not to buy the service on the open market.

Many auxiliary enterprises operate on the break-even principle, charging their individual or organizational clients enough to defray the operating costs and sometimes enough to cover depreciation and capital charges as well. This policy of self-funding through recharges makes the manager of the enterprise responsible for balancing income and expense. But it does not guarantee that the service will be produced and delivered at an (unsubsidized) price that is as low as the open market price, because the university's service unit may not be operating at the most efficient scale. Also, university policy often accords an internal monopoly to the service unit, and this reduces the pressure for cost minimization.

Some auxiliary enterprises have a customer mix that includes purchasers outside the university. If net income from such external customers is appreciable, it may be taxable as unrelated income and complicate the tax-exempt status of a university corporation under state and federal tax laws. This hazard is worth avoiding by tailoring auxiliary enterprises to a dominant customer mix within the university. But most institutions worry more about losing money than making it in auxiliary enterprises. University teaching hospitals, for example, often charge rates that are at or above those of neighboring community hospitals. But they must still be subsidized because they attract patients with especially costly treatment needs and because some costly state-of-the-art tests and procedures are ordered as part of the education of medical students and medical residents or are associated with clinical research efforts. It is sometimes difficult to separate expenses incurred for these reasons from expenses that would be incurred anyway for prudent and normal patient care.

General Administrative Services. As a large-scale organization, the contemporary university has had to develop many specialized cadres of personnel for the various tasks of general administration —accounting, budgeting, personnel administration, procurement, contract and grant administration, law enforcement and safety, public relations, and fund-raising. The ways in which these functions are collected together for effective supervision and interaction can vary. The contemporary university must face the need for administrative modernization and efficiency (for many universities have traditionally under-invested in administration as compared with industrial and financial corporations). And they must face decisions of centralization or decentralization. If administrative functions are heavily centralized, they may operate in a tidy, professional manner, but without sufficient understanding of the administrative problems and needs of individual academic units. If these functions are decentralized, they may not be staffed by sufficiently qualified professionals and may develop inconsistent procedures and techniques. If the institution builds up administrative capability in these areas both at a central point and in the operating academic units, the total cost is enormous. Avoiding the worst of all three evils requires careful managerial design and effective administrative coordination.

For example, extramurally-funded research requires a great deal of accounting work to record transactions, pay personnel and keep personnel records, maintain control of grant budgets so that the principal investigator, the institution, and the granting agency will all be informed in appropriate and timely ways about the status of each grant, and assure conformity with institutional and granting-agency policies and regulations. At the extreme of centralization, all this could be done in the offices of the central administration. In a more decentralized arrangement, basic financial accounting would continue to be taken care of in the central accounting office, but some decentralized grant accounting and the other functions would be arranged through the administrative offices of schools and colleges. And in a still more decentralized pattern, individual departments or specially authorized, organized research units would do a major share of the work. Decentralized budgetary responsibility for academic operations—known as "every tub on its own bottom"—is an interesting example of decentralization and is discussed in Chapter Nine.

Universities, like other large-scale organizations, must judge whether each overhead service is organized to deliver an appropriate amount and quality of service. Universities have often tried, historically, to get by with lower salary ranges for middle- and higher-level administrative jobs than would be paid for comparable responsibilities in industry and finance. They have counted on the dedication and feeling of security of university employees to compensate for unequal pay or have settled for a lower level of qualification and training than considered necessary in industry. The former produces feelings of inequity, and the latter is usually false economy.

The university faces another personnel problem. Faculty and research personnel share a value system and the attitudes about academic status that such a value system induces. Administrative staff members, including those at professional and senior levels, cannot share directly in this status system and are, worse yet, sometimes the victims of academic snobbery and contempt for bureaucracy. Most universities need to increase understanding between the two worlds if they are to avoid the retreat into bureaucratic rigidity that is an all too natural, defensive reaction of administrators.

The line of advancement in the administrative hierarchy ends in such top positions as director of budget, treasurer, controller, or vice-president (or vice-chancellor) for administration. These are positions of large responsibility and, often, of substantial discretionary power, and universities now pay respectable salaries to incumbents of recognized ability. But the crucial positions of president, executive vice-president, and provost are, with rare exceptions, reserved for those who came into academic administration through the faculty ranks. There are positive reasons for this policy: faculty in a university often demand academic spokesmen and understanding, but ineligibility for the top posts inevitably conveys implications of second-class status to even the most gifted of nonacademic administrators and thus blunts career aspirations all the way down the line. The rewards of service and a sense of professionalism are considered some compensation for these disadvantages. It is a tribute to the strength of these values and to the institutional loyalty of career administrators that many able men and women do make the university a career commitment and will not leave it—except possibly for improved pay and position at another university!

The heads of administrative service units and their staffs are primarily concerned with operations—often involving large numbers of personnel, large budgets, and large populations of intractable students and faculty. Senior administrators participate in policy formulation and planning, but in roles secondary to those of the senior academic administrators who speak to the dominant academic content of many institutional policies and plans. Perhaps this is why the enormous range of operating information that is hidden in the accounting system and administrative records is not better shaped and focused toward policy-making and planning. The academic administrators, in turn, may have tastes and styles that prevent them from making systematic demands for accounting and other information needed for policy-making and planning. These considerations are discussed in detail in Chapter Ten.

There is a set of institutional devices, dimensionally different from the academic organization of the university discussed in Chapter Four and from the units of administration, in some of which

managers of auxiliary enterprises and heads of administrative service units are involved together with students, faculty, and academic administrators. We now turn to these.

Units of Communication, Representation, and Oversight

Quite different in design and character from the units of
academic organization or administration are the many units of communication, representation, and oversight in a university. These
include student organizations, faculty organizations, administrative
committees and task forces, multipartite bodies and committees, and
now, unions.

Both the student government and the faculty government in
an American university have official status. They are recognized and
approved by the governing board, specific powers are often delegated to them by the governing board or the top administration, and
they almost always have some official budget. For student government, the funds often come in part from compulsory student fees
collected by the administration and spent by the agencies of the
student government, under conditions set by the administration.
The faculty government usually has modest institutional funds for
office and running expenses. Additional organizations such as faculty clubs usually charge dues and may have institutional subsidy
as well, in recognition of the importance of a common point of
institutional contact. The official status and financial subsidies of
both student and faculty organizations establish a role for them
within the institution and, correspondingly, limit their adversary
capacity when disputes arise.

Traditionally, faculty government—whether a senate composed of all regular faculty from assistant professors up, or a more
limited representational body elected by eligible faculty—has specific
delegated powers to supervise courses and curricula and has strong
advisory influence in matters of academic freedom, academic personnel selection, and educational policy. Generally these powers are
exercised, to some degree, by legislative deliberation and action expressed in faculty regulations and recommendations to the administration and the governing board. But the main work is done through
faculty committees that report either to the faculty government,

for recommended legislative action, or to the administration, with recommendations and findings on particular issues. Faculty members in each college, school, and department generally have delegated power to adopt some academic regulations by faculty vote and also to make personnel and other recommendations to the administration. But much of the on-going work is done by committees. Multicampus university systems must determine the desired extent of university-wide faculty government and the powers and structure this should have, in contradistinction to the role of the campus faculty in the affairs of that campus.

Faculty members and administrators also serve on committees appointed by the campus administration. Such committees may investigate ways of dealing with a pending policy issue, or they may be standing committees for oversight of a particular function or unit of activity—for example, the computer center. Beyond these formalized involvements, in the faculty government and the structure of administrative committees, a faculty possesses great informal influence on the operation of the institution and the conduct of administration. These contributions are made by individual faculty members and working groups, through their academic departments and research organizations, in the normal course of teaching and research. The extent of faculty involvement in matters of institutional policy and administration is an issue.

There are several competing themes. One is tempted to say that, the better the university, the more conclusive and complete is the institutional influence of the faculty. But many of the best universities in the United States—the older, private institutions—customarily operated on a scheme of more or less benign autocracy. A distinguished faculty trusted an unobtrusive and deft administration, and faculty time was reserved for academic duties. However, as these same universities have become more complicated, as some of the state-supported universities have emerged in the front ranks of academia, and as many problems have emerged that call for the combined attention of the academic and the administrative structures, the formal and informal involvement of faculty in institutional policies and managerial questions has increased.

This involvement creates several problems. First, these activities consume valuable time. Studies of the distribution of faculty time and effort show that, out of a quite long work week, faculty members (other than those with specific administrative appointments) spend an average of about 10 percent of their time on administrative and institutional duties. This has an opportunity cost, for time spent this way could instead be devoted to other duties. Yet the faculty government and the administrators who call on faculty members for committee duties often disregard the marginal cost of a faculty member's time.

A second issue is the use of committees for what should be done by one responsible person. Committees are endemic in all governmental agencies and large business firms; often there is no substitute for them, for reasons of communication, coordination, representational bargaining, or the need to pool specialized judgments. But the committee style is carried much too far in some universities, absorbing great energy for small results.

The third problem is amateurism and rapid turnover of committee membership. If a committee has a long-term advisory or coordinating responsibility, each member must usually spend some months acquiring enough background to be effective. But typically, because of research leaves or regular rotation, committee members are replaced soon after they become valuable by new members who have to begin from the beginning.

Despite these drawbacks, faculty involvement in university affairs is vitally necessary, and committee structures are the main vehicle for this, aside from the recruitment from the faculty of full-time academic administrators (who then become somewhat tainted as academics in the eyes of the faculty rank-and-file). The need to obtain judgments from a wide variety of institutional and representative sources, the need for communication, and the need to build consensus (or at least acquiescence)—all are reasons for the use of committees.

Student government has historically been far less strong and politically assertive in American than in European universities, although extracurricular activities—from athletics to cultural organization to student politics—have been important in student life since late in the nineteenth century. Rising student consciousness in the 1960s led to condemnation of "sandbox" student government and to a growing agenda of protest on university and community issues. As the aftermath of those disturbed times, the minimum voting age in federal elections and in many states was lowered from twenty-one to eighteen and long residence requirments for voting were struck down, propelling the most politically active students into local electoral politics in university towns. Many universities responded to student demands by including student representatives on many committees and by giving student spokesmen regular access to the top administration and to the governing board. In addition, the student governments in some state universities began to lobby in state capitols, causing a new level of nervousness in the university administration.

Student participation in committee deliberations provides a new dimension of insight into problems and evidence that student concerns are being taken into account. Student representatives suffer from the same disabilities—time constraints, amateurism, and rapid turnover—as do faculty members of committees, and these, particularly turnover, are likely to be even more seriously inhibiting of important contributions. But the most serious difficulties arise if student representatives are strongly politicized and regard the committee, whatever its stated agenda, as an arena of contest with the institution and with society. A student role in departmental curriculum committees, and especially in questions of academic personnel, may be challenged on matters requiring confidentiality or faculty competence, and the question of how student views can be taken into account is often disputed. Students and faculty often do have deeply opposing views about matters of academic policy, curriculum, passing standards, and academic personnel, and it is not clear how student participation in deliberations on these matters can be arranged without periodic, severe conflict.

A few American and Canadian universities, and numerous continental universities, have recently developed multipartite structures of representation at the highest, or almost the highest, level of government. Each Dutch university, according to the new law of governance passed by the Parliament in 1971, now has a university council composed of eleven elected faculty representatives, eleven elected nonacademic staff representatives, eleven elected student representatives, and seven members appointed by the minister of education. This council has general responsibility for policy-setting in the Dutch university, and a board of administration consisting of five full-time members, including the rector, has executive authority. It is too early to predict the consequences of this democratization of governance; it may turn out to have great constructive influence on the operation of these universities, or it may prove to be unworkable.

The multipartite structure is a parliamentary body, or a large-scale committee, with representation of each of the significant estates of the university. If it is consultative and advisory, it can be valuable as a source of insights and a channel of communication. If it has determinative power over legislated standards, appointments, and budgets, its multipartite character and its parliamentary form can result in a politicized treatment of many issues that, to the believer in underlying academic values of the sort explained in Chapter Two, bodes ill for the university. That this hazard is real, not imaginary, is indicated by the experience of some of the German universities under the political pressures of democratization.

Even though the national parliaments of European countries legislated democratization, there is no assurance that they will provide substantial funding support or restrain themselves from administrative interventions if they are disappointed by the institutional and academic consequences of democratized governance. In American higher education, which has a very different tradition, the moves toward democratization have been much more cautious than in Europe, and one can guess that funding and supportive constituencies in the general community would be impatient with a university that lost the capacity for executive leadership and effective spokesmanship.

It is not the multipartite form of governance but the emergence of faculty and other unionization that represents the most immediate challenge to traditional powers of governance in American higher education.

In American universities to some extent, but much more widespread in largely teaching institutions, faculty unionism is a rising force, frankly asserting that the economic interests of faculty cannot be successfully dealt with except through collective bargaining. Beyond noting that this development would clearly alter the nature and possible range of faculty participation in the many aspects of university operation where they have been strongly involved in the past, and that faculty unionism would trade economic benefits for a reduced professional role in the institution, I cannot pursue this important topic further here. The interested reader should see Garbarino (1974a).

Garbarino summed up the issues neatly in testimony he gave on April 19, 1974 to the California Legislature's Joint Committee on Postsecondary Education (Garbarino, 1974b, pp. 1–2):

> Collective bargaining is a method of faculty participation in governance, but it is a method that can either supplement other methods or substitute for them depending on circumstances. There are many varieties of relationships that can exist between unions and other governance bodies on a campus. The main types are: *cooperation* in which a union and an academic senate or council coexist with an informal division of labor, often made workable by common leadership or overlapping activist memberships; *competition* in which the two organizations exist, but engage in a struggle over the subject matter of governance, over status as the official representative of the faculty on administrative committees, before the governing board, or lobbying in the legislature; *domination* in which the union controls the great bulk of the machinery of governance primarily through the legal monopoly conferred by recognition as the exclusive bargaining agent.
>
> The type of relationship that exists on any campus depends . . . mainly on the degree of conflict that exists between factions in the union and between the faculty and administration. If conflict levels are low, the union's legal monopoly over representation rights need not be exercised and some powers can be delegated to the traditional senate machinery. As important conflicts arise, the union will find that it cannot let decisions that are vital

to important segments of its membership be left to other organizations.

Presidency

These structures of representation interact with each other and with the academic organization and units of administration of the university, and all come together in the conduct of the presidency. When I speak of the *presidency* or the *senior administration,* I mean the president, other institution-wide officers, and their immediate subordinates and staffs. My discussion here is against the background of the multiple purposes, processes, and sources of funding, covered in Chapter One, the constituency problems and norms of behavior discussed in Chapter Two, and the analysis of organization presented in Chapter Three and the preceding sections of this chapter.

Single-Campus University. There was a time when it was almost possible to do without a central administration—when the lay governing board exercised a dominant influence in institutional operation, regarding the president as its agent, the faculty as its hired hands, and the students as its children.

Today the presidency of a university must cope with five areas of interaction: with the governing board, with a configuration of external constituencies, with the academic organization of the institution, with the administrative hierarchy and its many units of operation, and with the faculty, student, and multipartite organizations, committees, and floating constituencies. (These coalesce temporarily over a particular issue, only to fade away when the issue is no longer salient. Among the issues that can create a floating constituency are: the defense of an academic program that is under attack; a faculty appointment or a student discipline case that becomes a *cause celebre;* or a community relations question or internal demand that reaches crisis proportions. Crisis management is discussed in a few examples in Chapters Five and Eleven.) The presidency or senior administration needs an internal division of labor to handle each of these areas, all of which require communication flow, management of decision sequences, policy formulation to cover classes of cases, and spokesmanship. The presidency must also have some means of internal coordination. Problems do not come neatly packaged but often have impacts on several areas or even on the survival of the institution.

In a simpler time, it was possible to consolidate the presidency in one person, the president. But as universities grew, the need evolved for a division between external and internal administrative functions. The president often dealt mainly with the outside world, particularly with raising funds, and a provost administered the internal aspects of the institution. As I noted earlier, this external-internal dichotomy proved inadequate because many problems contain both internal and external elements. The presidency of the contemporary university is therefore evolving toward new and complicated schemes of executive organization that involve specialization and coordination.

The presidency is deeply involved with, takes signals from, and in a discreet manner may seek to manage the governing board and its committee structure, which now often mirrors all of the above-mentioned areas of interaction. The president is most sensitive to the governing board—it hired him, and it will eventually fire or retire him, unless he resigns first. As a practical matter, the president faces many vetoes on his continuation, vetoes by any of the several internal and external constituencies, depending on the nature of the crisis. This is far less true of the others in the presidency. Cohen and March (1974, pp. 153–194) offer systematic evidence concerning the length of presidential tenure, and brilliant insight into its cyclical vulnerability and the reasons for it.

The presidency has to tend, and periodically engineer changes in, the complex structure of organization. In each major area, large numbers of decisions have to be made. Thus, it is necessary to develop adequate general policies and accompanying procedures, so that most of these decisions can be made quickly, near the points where they need to be made. Only those large, exceptional, or ad hoc cases that cannot be settled in a decentralized way should have to be passed to higher levels. As Cohen and March point out, problems may not actually be resolved at all but may instead be held in "garbage cans" (1974, Chaps. 5 and 9).

The officers of the presidency are divided by title, responsibility, and style of work among the classes of issues which accord with the pattern of specialization within the presidency that is adopted for best functional effect, or has grown as a matter of history. Each such officer must monitor the units of operation actually doing the work at the several levels of the organization within his area of responsibility, deal with policy formulation and adjustment to keep the degree of uniformity needed for coherent decentralized decision, and cope with the many representational and communication agencies and committees, external and internal, that impinge on his area of responsibility. Some power of discretionary decision (or power of negotiation) and some discretionary spokesmanship are concomitants of each senior role.

Coordination within the presidency is a live issue. Struggles for power often revolve around the question of whose domain encompasses a particular problem. Coordination inevitably includes tests of the relative strength of one executive role against another. In these contests, administrators aligned with the academic organizations and their interests have the greatest prominence and prestige; but the units of the administrative hierarchy have the greatest staying power and have control over the accounting system, information base, and managerial structure of the university.

It is difficult to generalize about the number of key jobs needed in the presidency, the design of each job and allocations of responsibility to it, and the best mode of internal coordination. The presidency is a group of roles and individuals, and it is always a delicate question whether to adjust the titles and functions of each job to the capacities and tastes of the individual incumbents (particularly the president) or to attempt to recruit individuals into a predetermined plan of top-level organization.

The presidency needs at least one other major position besides the president, if only to have someone available to act during an absence or illness of the president. Its size is limited by the number of people who can sit around a small table and share views freely and confidently—probably five to seven. The larger the university, and the more complex the issues it faces, the greater the demands on the presidency—but the more compelling, also, the need for setting rules for delegation of responsibility to administrators at the next lower level.

At this level of highly judgmental executive responsibility, it is important to find the most able people and allow some adjustment of roles among them in accordance with the needs identified by the president and the arrangements that members of a small group can work out among themselves. Yet the lines of communication and reporting have to be known throughout the university, and the main elements of the official roles and assignments must be stable enough so that decisions can be brought to the right office and evaluative control of operating units can be maintained.

I have mentioned the early historical division of the presidency into two roles, "outside" and "inside." More elaboration of tasks has now become necessary in the larger universities. One approach is to arrange the tasks according to relational functions of a somewhat specialized nature—academic affairs, research, business and finance, budget development (money-raising), and student affairs—with a vice-president or vice-chancellor for each. This arrangement has some benefits of functional specialization. But problems overlap areas, and a given issue may thus require detailed and coordinated attention from several key people. Also, each operating organization, on the academic side and on the administrative, needs a definitive point of contact with the presidency for monitoring, evaluation, and the treatment of exceptional problems. Thus, an alternative that avoids proliferation is to parcel out the executive roles of the presidency mainly according to a division of coordinating and control responsibilities over the significant areas of university operations: medical sciences, the other professional schools, the arts and sciences, and the whole span of administrative support operations and units. Functional specialties then become defined, and are filled by appropriate recruitment of subordinates within each of these areas. If this approach is used, the president and his chief deputy still need, reporting to them, a specialized planning and budgeting administrator for staff support and for administration of the budgetary process.

Each design has advantages and possible defects. Whichever one is chosen, it weaknesses have to be overcome by communication and coordination among the key members of the presidency. Regular and frequent meetings of all those concerned, and easy communication on an ad hoc basis when issues have to be settled, are essential. It is also essential to work out good procedural controls for routing matters that require attention and decision. Each key member of the presidency also has staff subordinates, and staff-to-staff relationships can be developed to improve coordination.

Besides its control over the numerous sequences of operating decisions, the presidency has available several ways to exercise power. As the university spokesman to both external and internal constituencies, it has the opportunity to convey a sense of the direction. The presidency also formulates policy standards through the mechanisms of proposal, review, and adoption. The presidency selects personnel to fill significant jobs in the academic administration and the administrative hierarchy and exerts some control over appointments to the faculty. And, most important of all, the mechanisms of planning, budget-making, and budget adjustment are controlled by the presidency. The budget, and the decisions it embodies concerning priorities, is the single most revealing administrative signal of what is happening in a university. The budgetary process is discussed in Chapter Nine.

The presidency of a university is subject to environmental constraints and complex internal mechanisms, and thus probably has a narrower range of discretionary choice than does the top management of a large business corporation. Indeed, as important conflicts with external political authorities and with rebellious students and junior staff welled up in the 1960s, the vulnerability of institutional control in universities was revealed. Numerous presidents found that their tenure lasted only until the big crisis that overwhelmed them personally, even though it did not destroy the institution or, in most cases, thin out the executive ranks.

The person and role of the president, in the major American university today, probably reflects the impossible expectations that American society builds into the position of the titular head of a major organization. The presidency is an executive arm; the person of the president is supposed to convey symbolic qualities to numerous distinct and often conflicting constituencies. The contradictions of these symbolic requirements can impose risks on the president as great as those that he faces from substantive decisions that go wrong. The issues and needs of a particular period may call for one type of presidential presence and ability. But as needs and issues change, last year's ideally-suited president may be no match, or he may not be able to adapt in time. But with all its risks, the job of president of a major university—because it is so demanding—is one of the most interesting in American organizational life.

Multicampus University. The complicated form of multi-campus public institution that has now emerged in many states has been described by Lee and Bowen (1973). In a multicampus university system it is not obvious whether: each campus should be free to prosper as a separate institution, subject only to formula budget allocations derived from general budgetary standards for each main function across all campuses, and driven by workload measures (such as student enrollment); or the goal attainments, program commitments, and operating characteristics of the system should be determined in a unified fashion, so that it is a single university that happens to operate at several physically separated locations.

Most student, faculty, and administrative perceptions, and most perceptions of external publics, make the individual campus the natural unit of identification. If this is the context, the observations previously made on behalf of the university administrator concerning complementarity, independence, and substitution of goals and programs now hold for each campus administration and in particular for its chief executive officer. There are good reasons, in the complex setting of university operation, to accord substantial, decentralized responsibility to each chief campus officer and his staff.

For a considerable time, in the University of California, strong campus identities and decentralized administration were joined with the general campus concept. According to this concept, each campus might have its own distinctive style but was expected, as time went on, to develop the full range of undergraduate and doctoral programs in all disciplines and also to establish some professional schools. The timing of the initiation of each new program or school would depend on the readiness of the campus and the availability of funds and would require approval by the president and, in some cases, the governing board.

The chief campus officer, in these circumstances, must jockey for the largest possible allocation of the aggregate multicampus budget, and then he must demand the right to make discretionary allocations. If the central administration is willing to play the game this way, it has two main allocative tasks: (1) to maximize the size of the total multicampus state budget; and (2) to set forth plausible rules for each general function and category of expenditure in order to permit equitable allocation among campuses and minimize disputes. In a regime of expansive state funding, all goes reasonably well. But suppose that justification of the aggregate budget from the state becomes more difficult, and resources are in short supply. Then, suddenly, awkward questions materialize, because the external authorities may require examination of the goals and major resource commitments of the system as a whole. The state authorities, in order to reduce the budgetary claim on them, may demand a look at the entire span of commitments of the multicampus system.

In many areas of academic program, what appear to the chief officer of one campus to be complementary or independent programs are bound to be duplicated elsewhere in the multicampus institution. Many superboards and state coordinating and budgeting agencies, looking at the whole of state-supported higher education, are inevitably asking such questions as—At how many campuses must we have doctoral programs in physics? law schools? teacher training programs?

If a university has one campus, its law school is complementary to, or independent of, other programs. But if both campuses of a two-campus university system had law schools, these two schools would appear as potential substitutes for each other. Rather than having two law schools, why not double the enrollment size of one of them? If policy requires a cutback in law training, why not close up one of the schools rather than continuing to operate both at reduced enrollment and (for a transitional period) inefficient costs? (Of course, along with these efficiency issues there are others to be carefully considered—such as the dislocations and inequities that would attend actions as drastic as the ones indicated.) But the point is that once a higher level of intercampus review is adopted, complementary features of a university are converted into possible substitutes for each other. Indeed, the hypothetical questions mentioned above for law schools are actually being raised, and raised urgently, about program areas that now do face retrenchment.

When the system is viewed as a whole, substitutive program alternatives reappear, which cannot help colliding with the desirable principle of institutional integrity and mutuality on each campus. Campus identity then suffers unless it is built on a specialized and limited mission.

University in Superstructure

Superstructures of organization and control, beyond the individual institution, are growing rapidly. In the United States they are emerging mainly at the state level. Paradoxically, as the national importance of the major universities is becoming better understood, the federal government's focus, funding, and policy initiative are not so much directed toward support of the major universities as to the social questions of student access and enrollment opportunity. In Europe, national ministries have traditionally supplied the money and set government policies toward the universities, and superstructure is being promoted by the ministries or by agencies very close to them.

Superstructure power and its exercise take many forms. In New York state, the state authorities (via that curious paper organization, the University of the State of New York) promulgated a temporary moratorium on all new PhD programs. The moratorium held not only in the directly state-supported State University of New York, where the state funding responsibility makes such action understandable if not very welcome, but also in private universities located in New York and thus licensed by the state, according to special New York statutes, to give degrees. It is not the purpose here to discuss the merits of that moratorium, but only to illustrate the new significance of superstructure as a force to be recognized.

Most American states are making strong efforts to bring all of public higher education under planning and coordination control. A few states—for example, Florida, Rhode Island, and Wisconsin— have encompassed all of public higher education, from university to community colleges, into a single system with one governing board and one central administration. Other states—for example, Illinois —have gone the superboard route, with a new layer of planning, policy determination, and budgetary control. Still other states are developing agency schemes for exerting a rationalized, budget-conserving influence on higher education. They are superimposing on the various sectors—each of which often has its own multicampus administration and governing board—new pressures for coherent division of labor among sectors and among campuses. Using these superstructure agencies, governors and legislatures are trimming duplications of activity and cutting budgetary standards, to hold down the bite that public higher education takes from state treasuries.

The power to decide many things is passing farther than ever from the places where education actually takes place, and from the people—faculty members and students—directly concerned with it. Some presidents may well have the eerie sense that they are administering an institutional shell that will soon be emptied of educational significance, with most of the major decisions passed to the universities from remote, bureaucratic, politically-wired, and academically unaccountable locations.

The technical apparatus for the superstructure is growing: quantitative forecasts, cost analysis and measurement techniques, program identification and control, and in the end, a much more sophisticated range of controls and pressures by means of conditions and restrictions attached to state appropriations. In one sense justification of program decisions and budgets is a good exercise of accountability for publicly-supported universities and other public institutions; after all, they do live on subsidy, and they can quite reasonably be asked to demonstrate what they are doing with the money.

But there are two serious problems. The more important in the short run is that those who man the superstructure are mostly new at their jobs; they vary in quality of training and scope of thinking, and they are vulnerable to immediate political pressures. The more important problem for the longer run is that the schemes of planning that are coming forward in these superstructure agencies may fail to take account of the most significant academic and organizational characteristics of the educational institutions that are brought into the framework of planning and control. To the extent that this failure of concept occurs, the superstructure may be unable to make valid predictions, may make unwise policy decisions—even from the standpoint of state governments (as distinct from institutions), and may damage the quality and scope of higher education.

The long-range remedy for this long-run problem would be for the universities to work vigorously to educate the superstructure planners about the academic and institutional facts of life, providing them with a far more accurate and complete picture of the academic enterprise than they now have. Unfortunately, the present developments are taking place in an adversary climate. Information is a weapon. It is not clear to the universities that they should suffer the short-term penalties of providing more informational ammunition to their superstructure adversaries, in return for the (uncertain) future benefits of greater understanding. Whatever the tactical maneuvering, it is clear that tending the relationships with state superstructure is an increasingly important, onerous, and time-consuming task of the public university presidency.

Federal agency superstructure is also important, particularly as it affects the rules of the game and the prospects for funding of research and student financial aid. At issue in the area of research are: the total amount of federal funding; federal policies toward basic research and toward those parts of applied research in which universities may be strongly involved; the funding mechanisms utilized, including not only the schemes of review and approval but also overhead costing, or indirect cost recovery. Federal funds are used more and more to help the student who faces financial barriers to an education. At the same time, federal training grants and fellowships for the most highly qualified graduate students have actually been substantially reduced through recent actions.

In 1969, the Association of American Universities (AAU) established a Council on Federal Relations with an office in Washington, in an effort to bring more forcefully to the attention of the federal government the interests and needs of the major research and graduate-training centers. However, decisions of the Nixon administration in 1972 and 1973 cut back the very sources of funding that are most important to the major universities. The future of the relationships between major universities and the federal government is at this writing cloudy, to say the least. The National Board on Graduate Education, formed in 1971 to develop information about graduate education and research, has issued a report containing several recommendations on federal policies concerning graduate fellowships and financial aid, support of research, and institutional support (National Board on Graduate Education, 1974).

Chapter 5

Policy
Analysis

Just as decision-making is the core function of management, informed and rational decision-making is the core of effective management. Changes in university policy may, of course, take place not through conscious deliberation but through drift and happenstance. Some of these informal and unnoticed changes may, in fact, be useful adaptations to new conditions, but formal policies and procedures then need to be modified from time to time to catch up with them. Others may be slippages from needed policies and performance standards, and only after they are identified and examined can corrective action be taken. In both cases, a primary responsibility of university management is policy analysis.

Two brief examples of the need for policy analysis may suffice to demonstrate its critical importance. First, many universities have documented an upward drift in average course grades of undergraduates during the late 1960s and early 1970s. Some universities have a generally understood standard of academic performance, and most have definite rules about minimum undergraduate course loads and the circumstances in which a student may drop a course or receive a grade of "incomplete." Each student's grade in each course, subject to these regulations, is decided and awarded by the individual instructor. Thus, an upward trend in the distribution of course grades is the result of thousands of individual faculty decisions. It may go unnoticed for some time unless a statistical compilation is made of academic grades.

Once someone has discovered the facts about this upward drift by monitoring trends, the second step—more interesting and yet more difficult—is to assess the reasons. The trend may imply a slow weakening of academic standards throughout the institution, for example, or it may be localized in particular fields and curricula. It may be associated with reductions in the number of required courses that many students used to take unwillingly and in which they did less well than in their other work. It may be associated with the introduction of pass/fail grading. It may be due to intentional tightening of admission standards or other changes in the academic-ability distribution of incoming students. Finally, it may mean that increasing numbers of students are performing better according to some implicit but unchanging academic standard. Different data and different analytical approaches are needed to explore these possible explanations and to make informed and rational decisions about grading policies and practices, student performance, and academic standards.

A second example of a seeming nondecision in university performance over the past few decades is the sex distribution of faculty. For many years, universities did not gather statistics on the percentages of women faculty hired or promoted, although a casual tour through the catalog listings of department faculties would have been revealing about the proportions. Some enlightened institutions may have prided themselves on applying hiring standards in which sex was not relevant. Other institutions were not troubled at the policy level if some form of discrimination was taking place in the numerous decentralized departmental arenas where most of the hiring and promotion decisions were made. Either way, the result was an overwhelmingly male faculty. The causes are many, some general to society and others specific to academic life and to the ways in which individual institutions operate. Only with the passage of federal antidiscrimination laws and the rise of women's consciousness did universities discover that thousands of nondecisions over a long period of time had made them vulnerable to charges of sex discrimination and that affirmative action to redress salary inequities and the relative absence of women from faculty ranks was expected of them.

These two examples illustrate the desirability of analyses of institutional policy and practice in light of demands for institutional accountability and change; and this chapter is devoted to ways the university can respond to this need for explicit analysis and decision.

Place of Policy Analysis

Many administrators have hoped that the mechanics of the planning, programming, budgeting system would meet this analytic need; but the equivocal experience of the state of California and its university with this approach to a new rationalism, as described elsewhere in this volume, has not been encouraging. PPBS systems, as so far realized for higher education, start with the definition of activity-defined programs and a classification of these programs and then align resources for these activities and specify multiyear horizons for them on the basis of activity indicators. Because the operational definition of objectives and the measurement of achievement toward these objectives are still difficult and incompletely resolved, the dream of planning toward long-range goals and budgeting for results remains (some would say, blessedly) incomplete.

Meanwhile, the spirit of an informed inquiry leading to wiser choices, which PPBS has promised, can be realized in policy analysis without the formal baggage of PPBS. As Weathersby and I have written (1972, p. 55):

> Policy analysis . . . uses decisions as the major organizing principle instead of activities. In higher education, these decisions might be student admissions, tuition, faculty staffing, library acquisitions, new construction, or new academic program development, among others. The approach of policy analysis is to bring careful analysis to bear incrementally in specific decision problems and build a planning and management "system" on a case law or precedent basis.

A policy analyst begins with the necessity for decision, identifies the variables relevant to the decision, seeks the relationships between the variables he can control and the remaining relevant variables, examines the values associated with the outputs of consequences of the decision, evaluates alternative strategies characterized by different specifications of the control variables, . . . and designs decisions, implementation, and evaluation processes . . . [for] . . . the decisions of an administrator.

Policy analysis should be used whenever a decision is important enough to justify an investment in analytical assistance—that is, whenever such assistance may make a difference in the quality of the decision. Some decisions, of course, are intractable, in that the institutional response must be made in terms of politics, personalities or tradition. Some others must be made without enough lead time for analytical assistance, even though analysis might otherwise be helpful. (Here, one can ask whether the institution needs better early warning, so that major decisions are resonably well anticipated.) Thus to demonstrate the possibility of policy analysis it is necessary to identify decisions of some importance with a degree of tractability and with enough lead time to permit analysis.

It must be emphasized that policy analysis is important at every level of institutional decision. I choose to classify institutional decisions as procedural, substantive, and constitutional for purposes of examining organizational processes. These three types of decisions are not necessarily in ascending order of importance—from procedural to substantive to constitutional—but they do tend to occur in descending order of frequency; and each of them is well suited to policy analysis, as the remaining pages of this chapter illustrate.

Procedural decisions involve a search for a mechanism or a system for dealing with a class of problems or events. Substantive decisions involve a commitment of resources or power, or a change in a policy standard for a significant class of events. Constitutional decisions entail major adjustments or overhaul of the charter and mission of the institution or major changes in the distribution of its power to act. In order to see how policy analyses can be used in making important decisions of each type, it may be helpful to examine illustrations of all three.

Procedure: Search for Mechanism and System

As will be evident from the discussion in Chapter Ten, data systems evolve in the natural settings of operating responsibility. There are opportunities and even demands for conscious design of these systems, both to support operations in particularized but often interrelated areas and to serve as data sources for planning, policy formulation, and evaluation.

These data systems are one example of the investment in mechanism. They support the administrative framework for institutional allocations and defense. They support the learning process and the numerous activities incident to that. But they are not the main business of the institution. A university can be great with primitive data systems, or it can have marvelous data systems and yet be undistinguished academically or fiscally inefficient. So it is, or so one might think it is, with other aspects of the procedural side of the university. Even so, the modernizers (myself among them) argue that universities will do well to install the best data systems they can afford and tolerate.

In several other areas of major concern, however, procedural mechanisms are the crux of the institutional process. They gain moral and political content because the mechanism is the binding force. Let us look at two such procedural mechanisms.

The first is the elaborate consultative mechanisms that develop in most universities to deal with academic matters—courses, curricula, academic plans. (If an academic unit is separated from the rest of the institution for all jurisdictional, academic, and administrative purposes, consultative mechanisms are needed for its budgetary and administrative relations with the president and the senior administration, and for dealing with internal problems.) As was shown in Chapters Three and Four, the traditional parties in decision-making are the administration, in its hierarchy of units and responsibilities, and the faculty, both as members of academic departments and as members of the faculty senate. Now students are often participating, too, in the affairs of departments, schools, and colleges, and through student government organizations and spokesmanship.

Appropriate consultative mechanisms often exist, by formal regulation or by custom, for approval of academic appointments, courses and curricula, changes of major policies or regulations, and organization or reorganization of academic departments. The proponents of an action cannot simply secure the approval of the final authority—dean, provost, president, or board of trustees. Advice and opinions must be gathered from the sources that are entitled to be consulted. Actions often occur slowly because of these consultative steps, which are not necessarily pro forma. In matters of faculty appointment, for example, administrators are usually cautious about acting without the advisory approval of departmental faculties and faculty senate committees.

Several kinds of policy work relate to these traditional consultative mechanisms. One is the task of extracting conclusions of some sort from the process—hopefully, the right conclusion, but sometimes almost any determination rather than an indefinitely prolonged delay. A second is the task of determining, in borderline cases, which of several available consultative mechanisms is the appropriate and credible one to use. A third is the development of a new consultative mechanism for a new problem area.

Pressures for retrenchment in programs and budget allocations, for example, have compelled reexamination of existing commitments. This unwelcome necessity is generally perceived first by the senior administration, which sees all too clearly the reduction of resources. Academic departments and program groups that might be candidates for consolidation or closure (and, often, the students in these programs) want the opportunity to defend themselves, not only by direct appeal to the administration but through review by objective, representative, and (hopefully) sympathetic faculty. Faculty senates are often invited to the party without being sure that they want to be there. When faculty groups contribute discerning and hard-headed judgments about priority and institutional economy, the administration is pleased to share with them the burdens and pain of cutback decisions. Hence, many universities are developing new review and selective priority committees that cut across departments and colleges to make recommendations about where least-loss reductions can be made. When this kind of consultation works, the administration avoids the onus of unilateral and allegedly arbitrary actions.

Faculty collective bargaining—a spreading trend that may be accelerated by current fears of retrenchment, dismissal, and loss of real income—is dimensionally different from consultative mechanisms that assume the presence of interdependent and semiautonomous but not deeply conflicting interests within the institution. Almost inevitably the rise of collective bargaining means a concurrent decline in the extent of faculty involvement in policy-making and management. At the least, the character of existing consultative mechanisms has to be transformed in various ways. Partly for this reason, faculty groups in major universities are more resistant to unionization than they are in institutions where the sharing of power is less assured. Policy analysis should be used to examine strategies for preserving the positive involvement of university faculties in the institutional process, to avoid the trauma that would attend conversion to collective-bargaining.

A second class of procedural mechanisms has been developed to assure due process to individuals and sometimes to groups that are not in the standard rubric of the institution (for example, political groups of students and staff that want to hold meetings). Procedural fairness and equity for individuals have long been part of the university tradition. The scope of these concepts has widened in recent years. Decisions concerning an individual and previously considered within the scope of administrative discretion may now be regarded as cause for individual appeal. The widening of due process is particularly evident with regard to students and student organizations. Disciplinary cases and cases involving the denial of privileges to politically oriented student organizations must now receive exacting treatment because of the increased sensitivity in the campus community and also because of the increasing rigor of due process standards promulgated by the courts in cases of arbitrary dismissal or disciplinary action.

For university staff, also, formalized grievance procedures and other due process machinery have become necessary over a widening class of issues. Personnel management of the administrative side of the institution—even where formal collective-bargaining agreements providing for grievance mechanisms are not in effect—has become complex. For faculty, tenure provides due process protections rather than contractual rights of job security. Here too, the scope has widened. One example is the increasing enforcement of rights of long advance notice for nontenure faculty and the pressure on some universities to show cause for refusal to grant tenure.

One function of policy analysis is to design due process procedures that get the business of the institution done in an effective way and yet meet court-imposed standards and institutional perceptions of fairness. There are often heavy costs: administrative costs of case preparation and costs of educating decision-makers about assuring a defensible basis for the actions they take; costs of the time spent by members of hearing panels or the costs of hiring outside professionals as hearing officers; and costs of administrative energy. Impatient critics of the university—legislators, donors, influential alumni—are often baffled when told that the administrators who are in charge of a university cannot simply take summary actions against a faculty member considered obnoxious to the public or against an obstreperous student or against an organization that is alleged to have abused the university or the general community. There is a cost to the seeming lack of power for institutional defense, although part of the rejoinder is in terms of libertarian values as well as requirements of due process.

Many universities also discovered, during the agonies of the 1960s, that they had no explicit regulations to cover many matters but had counted on generally understood customs to convey the boundaries of appropriate conduct. When these understandings broke down, and at the same time due process became an inflamed procedural issue, universities had to promulgate extensive regulations under crisis conditions. Thus, policy analysis can be used to determine how to establish standards of conduct and to evolve mechanisms for writing acceptable rules. The more due process, the longer the rule book.

Substance: Search for Problem, Resources, Commitment

Substantive decisions are those that entail resource commitments to organizational units, programs, personnel, and activities.

Because the pattern of resource allocation (see Chapter Nine) is adjusted at least annually in the operating budget cycle, and because most matters of consequence do have resource implications, there are numerous decisions for which systematic analysis could be used to determine final choice. However, many decisions are made without this systematic preparation. In some, time dominates, and an issue that could otherwise be dealt with systematically has to be disposed of through ad hoc and informed judgment. In others, institutional politics dominates, and what might otherwise be a sensible study prior to a decision is opposed by a faction strong enough to compel treatment of the problem as a power issue. In perhaps the great majority of cases, history dominates, because the pattern of resource allocation is too deeply ingrained to permit many of its facets to be reexamined at one time. Work-load adjustments based on past experience are more the rule than the exception in the highly stable environment of a university. Finally, in some instances, external action (by a funding agency, donor, or jurisdictional organization) dominates, so that little is left to the university decision process except to pick up the pieces after a unilateral determination has been made elsewhere. The use of policy analysis for substantive decisions is illustrated with summaries of three cases.

Year-Round Operation. Anticipations of heavy enrollment expansion at the University of California in the 1960s and beyond prompted those making planning studies to suggest extending the calendar beyond the standard nine-month academic year. In 1960, the Coordinating Council for Higher Education (CCHE) was organized under state law and directed to study alternative plans for year-round operation (YRO). In 1962, before the CCHE endorsed YRO (its recommendation came in 1964), the university decided to adopt the principle on the general (non-health science) campuses. In 1966, these campuses shifted from a semester to a quarter calendar for the regular academic year, and the Berkeley campus established a ten-week summer quarter. A year later a summer quarter was initiated at the Los Angeles campus.

Although academic reasons were cited for YRO, the fiscal advantages dominated much of the discussion. The idea was to expand the regular enrollment by enlarging the state-provided operating budget to pay for a summer quarter (replacing the largely fee-supported summer sessions that most of the university campuses had long offered). By accommodating more students, the university expected to avoid part of the huge capital outlay that would otherwise be required to meet expanding enrollment. The 1964 CCHE report estimated that, from 1967 to 1975, the increases of operating budget for university and state college summer quarters would be $109.7 million, but the capital outlay savings would be $177.2 million. A consulting firm, hired by CCHE to reevaluate YRO, also concluded that net savings would occur in both the universities and the state colleges. The legislative analyst repeatedly reported to the California legislature that YRO would enable the state to meet its educational commitments at a saving. In 1970, however, the state Department of Finance, Budget Division, did an analysis showing that the consequences of continued YRO would be "to *increase* substantially the total tax-supported costs per FTE student . . . without appreciably increasing the utilization of the facilities of FTE production on a yearly basis" (Weathersby and Balderston, 1972, p. 75).

How could YRO be claimed to increase costs? Most of the answer is contained in a shift of concept. For many years, appreciable numbers of regular university students had attended the fee-supported summer sessions, at little or no cost in state-budgeted taxpayer dollars. The shift to YRO increased summer enrollment and utilization somewhat. But it also increased the state budgetary obligation—by substituting state funds for student fee support, and by providing an expanded curricular offering to attract students and meet educational policy goals. In addition, another prop under the YRO policy was removed because the state was not providing the amounts of capital funding for enrollment expansion that were previously postulated in the plans on which the analysis of YRO savings depended.

Subsequent careful restudy of the problem was undertaken by an analytical team headed by George Weathersby. This study developed three simulation models to estimate the consequences of alternative proportions of summer-quarter to academic-year enrollment, alternative average class sizes, and trade-offs between operating costs and capital outlay costs through time. As Weathersby puts the wry conclusion of this exercise: "Where did all of this analysis lead? In 1970 the university abandoned YRO because it cost too much. Conceptually, YRO appears cost-effective, on the average YRO is analytically cost-effective, . . . but at the margin *for the University of California* YRO was not cost-effective. Because of UC's high summer session productivity, because of the state's decision not to appropriate requested capital outlay funds, and because of the slackening growth in enrollments, the university decided that there were no real cost savings in YRO. In fact, YRO for the university required major cost increases for which no funds were available" (Weathersby and Balderston, 1972, p. 93).

The planned enrollment growth of the university for the remainder of the 1970s has now been estimated to be much smaller than was originally contemplated. And during the 1980s, in higher education generally, it is likely that there will be some years of static or declining enrollment.

Academic Demand for New PhDs. Fewer than one hundred major universities produce the great bulk of new PhDs in the United States. Propelled both by the high national priority given to scientific research in the 1950s and 1960s and by forecasts of heavy demand for college teachers, these universities expanded their graduate programs substantially, and many additional institutions initiated doctoral-level instruction. As early as 1965, Cartter took a skeptical view of the predictions, and in December of 1970 he presented a highly influential paper to the AAAS (Cartter, 1971). Wolfle and Kidd (1971) followed with a summary and interpretation of numerous current studies of both supply projections and demand analysis.

How many PhDs will be needed is of interest to federal agencies in their plans for funding university-based training grants, graduate fellowships, and centers of research activity. At the state level, the major public universities must justify their institutional support budgets partly on manpower grounds. No individual institution is the "dominant firm" in the national market for producing doctorates, but the University of California, for example, does account for about 6 percent of new PhDs awarded, and it perforce has a concern about the employment prospects of these graduates and the academic and other career destinations available to them.

Radner and I, with the assistance of Sharon Bush, undertook

an analysis of the academic demand for new PhDs during the 1970s and 1980s (Balderston and Radner, 1971). We concentrated on academic demand for new doctorates, making no analysis of the number of doctorate holders who might be employed in governmental and industrial research or in other professional activities. Also, we did not project the supply of new doctorates. To estimate academic demand, Cartter had first constructed an estimate of each year's total FTE enrollment in colleges and universities, then applied to this figure an incremental student-faculty ratio, then estimated the total increment of new faculty to be hired each year by adding to the increase of faculty numbers the replacement rate of existing faculty (for those who die, retire, or migrate out of academe), and, finally, applied to the total new faculty to be hired a percentage figure for those hired with the doctoral degree. According to a crude disaggregation, higher education in the United States is composed of three types of institutions (two-year colleges, four-year and comprehensive colleges, and universities), with two basic modes of organization and financing (private and public). These six sectors have had different rates of enrollment growth and different policies regarding student-faculty ratios and hiring with or without the doctorate. We produced disaggregated estimates of total new faculty and new faculty with the doctorate in each of these sectors. First we used no-change assumptions (the same as Cartter's) and simply showed the composition of academic demand for each sector. Then we explored the consequences of: a different and higher enrollment projection that had been developed for the Carnegie Commission; several incremental student-faculty ratios, reflecting different degrees of willingness to enrich or thin out teaching resources in each sector; and several percentages of doctorates hired, to show the different effects of possible future changes in hiring policies. We then performed a sensitivity analysis showing how much variation from Catter's single path for the future might be caused by different (multiplicative) combinations of assumptions. The long-range enrollment projections show an enrollment dip for part of the 1980s. We therefore explored implications of *smoothing* policies in faculty hiring, as against riding the projected enrollment curve up and then riding it down again. Finally, we discussed some implications of the analysis for public decision-makers, state and federal; for doctorate-granting institutions; for institutions not now offering the doctorate but contemplating initiation of doctoral programs; and for the student contemplating doctoral training for an academic career.

We could not examine the composition of demand according to individual fields or disciplines, although that is important both for public decisions and for institutional planning. A report subsequently issued by the National Board on Graduate Education (1973) extends previous analysis, includes some observations about trends in individual fields, and makes national policy recommendations. We were able to draw some inferences for consideration by doctorate-granting institutions. We found that "future academic demand for doctorates, without reference to fields of specialization, could vary over a wide range as a function of future policies of higher education finance and future staffing standards. If stringent financing conditions prevail in the 1970s, academic demand will be below the level projected in Cartter's study; whereas the demand could, under the revised assumptions we have explored, exceed his estimates by a factor of two of three." Our analysis also shows quite clearly two other important demand factors: "(1) the 1980s, by reason of an expected downturn in higher education enrollments, will be far worse than the 1970s; and (2) the enrollment expansion of the 1970s implies a considerable expansion of total faculty positions in higher education, but the composition of this expansion— weighted toward public four-year colleges and with an even more substantial growth of two-year colleges—compels reexamination of present patterns of doctoral training for academic careers" (Balderston and Radner, 1971).

We went on to discuss the desirability of changing the emphasis in doctoral training for academic careers toward preparation for teaching or of redesigning some programs specifically for career preparation.

We also observed that, in view of the long lead-time entailed in establishing new doctoral programs and getting them to a reasonable level of vitality, it will normally be unwise for a university to launch new programs because "the sequence of efforts and decisions . . . would produce . . . a catastrophe for it and its students in the mid-1980s."

Retrenchment Decision.[1] The mechanism that was developed for retrenchment decisions at Princeton included several key features: (1) formulation of income and expenditure estimates according to major components on a multiyear basis; (2) establishment of a representative, institutionwide priorities committee whose task would be to advise the president about important actions and through whose reports the Princeton community would be made aware of the issues facing the institution and of the basis for recommended steps to face these issues; and (3) support of the functioning of the priorities committee both by intensive work of subcommittees and by staff analysis guided by these subcommittees.

All three ingredients of the process were important. The multiyear income and expenditure forecasts were necessary to guide the senior administration and the trustees in assessing the scope of the fiscal problem, determining the predicted size of the gap if no new actions were taken, and thus making it possible to determine how aggressively to investigate income-increasing measures (for example, raising tuition or room and board charges) and expenditure-reducing measures.

Of the series of policy analyses referred to in the study, perhaps the most interesting—because it dealt with a highly sensitive issue—was the analysis and discussion leading to the decision to close out a graduate program in Slavic languages and literatures. The priorities committee established eight general criteria to guide such analyses (Bowen and others, 1972):

> (1) The quality of the faculty and of the program of graduate instruction, as they can be inferred from the opinion of other scholars in the field, the views of faculty members in related disciplines at Princeton, and any available evidence based on the opinions and experiences of graduate students.
>
> (2) The number and quality of students who have applied for graduate study at Princeton in the field, who

[1] I draw here on the report of the demonstration project at Princeton University sponsored by the Ford Foundation (Bowen and others, 1972). The study group was headed by William G. Bowen.

have accepted admission, and who have completed the program.

(3) The future of the whole field of study in terms of scientific and scholarly trends and in terms of national needs.

(4) The national contribution of the Princeton graduate program, viewed in the context of the number of other strong programs, whether or not they are operating below their desirable size, and, in general, whether suspension of a program at Princeton would have a seriously adverse effect on opportunities for graduate study.

(5) The comparative advantage of Princeton in the field—that is, the ability of Princeton to make a particular contribution to the field in question because of special factors such as a long tradition of good work in the subject, unusually strong library resources, and so on.

(6) The interactions between graduate study in the field in question and graduate work and scholarship in other fields at Princeton, and the likely effects of suspending work in the field on other programs and faculty members.

(7) The interaction between graduate study in the field and the quality and variety of undergraduate offerings in the same field.

(8) The costliness of work in the field, measured in terms of instructional costs, student support, library costs, space costs, and so on.

The department in question was less strong in rating and reputation than most other graduate programs at Princeton. Careful attention was given to the viability of continued undergraduate offerings in the field if the graduate program was terminated and to the problems caused for students in related fields. The extent of savings in library budgets was carefully estimated and the net expenditure reduction per year was calculated.

There is no way to provide balm to those whose direct stake in the institution is reduced or eliminated by this sort of action, but the report indicates great care in assessing the necessities of the situa-

tion and arriving at mechanisms which dealt fairly with the merits
of difficult choices and conveyed the decisions credibly to the university community.

Constitution: Adjustment of the Charter

Extensive changes in the mission and boundaries of a university or major alterations of its structure of organization change
its terms and conditions of operation and its distribution of power.
In effect, these are changes of the charter, even though they may
not entail changes in the legal language of incorporation.

The spectrum of interinstitutional cooperation goes all the
way from informal sharing arrangements in one or a few non-
sensitive areas to outright merger of two or more institutions into one.
The features of a number of patterns of voluntary cooperation were
explored in a research conference that included both doers and
analysts. The resulting report (Kreplin and Bolce, 1973) identifies
incentives toward these forms of change, discusses the obstacles that
often thwart it, and gives examples of mechanisms and strategies
for fostering various forms of cooperation between institutions.

Given that institutional identities and demands for independence are ordinarily strong in academic life, the first question is
whether anything can be gained by interinstitutional cooperation.
The idea may be to save a bit of money on the business-manage-
ment side or, on the academic side, to arrange some expansion of
opportunities for students or faculty or both.

In the absence of significant external requirements for various forms of sharing, success often depends critically on leadership
skills and on the particulars of the situation within and between
the institutions concerned. Even where there is a good case for
mutual advantage (as demonstrated by analysis), the many parties
have many ways to frustrate interinstitutional cooperative efforts.

The path toward a scheme of cooperation and the means of
administering it varies according to the kind of cooperative effort
envisioned, the situation in each of the institutions concerned, and
the incentives and sanctions available. As the Kreplin-Bolce analysis
shows, both the process of moving toward agreement and the mechanisms of administering it can be informal and unpublicized or

highly formal, public, and contractual. Among formal consortia, perhaps the most interesting patterns are illustrated by the Washington, D.C., Consortium, which is evolving interinstitutional agreements, administered with energetic initiatives but not with program-operating responsibilities, and by the more deeply intertwined arrangements of the Claremont Colleges and University Center, where each of the colleges has its own board and faculty, but the Claremont University Center seeks to facilitate cooperative interchanges between the colleges as operating entities and is specifically responsible for such jointly used facilities as the research library and the computer network.

Merger of two previously autonomous institutions into a single entity is illustrated by the formation of Case Western Reserve from Case Institute of Technology and Western Reserve University. This cooperative effort entailed an essential commitment to transform two institutional structures into one and the intricate work of consolidating academic departments and arranging new divisions of labor. No doubt some residuum of previous identities will last for a long time, especially in alumni organizations and relationships. And perhaps background nostalgia will also survive for a time in the patterns of thinking of individuals and groups within the combined institution, just as it often does after merger of business corporations. To capitalize on the positive opportunities for combining academic strengths takes not only the formal commitment and leadership of the governing board and presidency but also a great deal of sensitivity and skill throughout the faculty leadership of the newly formed institution.

Public systems for higher education sometimes face integrating and consolidating pressure from the legislative and executive branches of state government, the state instrumentalities created by statute, and the pressures brought to bear through policy enactments and the budget. Multicampus university or college systems, organized as segments of a state pattern of higher education, already offer some consortium attributes. Each system typically has a single governing board, a central administration, and one budget, and operates according to systemwide policy standards. The extent of campus-by-campus differentiation of role, function, and autonomy is determined by internal institutional and administrative choice.

Policy analysis is often directed to significant issues within these multicampus entities, but it can also be directed toward the proposed alteration of segmental boundaries and structure and of the role of coordinating bodies. At this stage the most basic commitments of the charter may be rewritten. For example, the State of Wisconsin has now put into a single structure the multicampus University of Wisconsin and the other publicly organized institutions of higher education. Such a new structure may make it easier to settle the allocation of students to campuses and to deal with problems of articulation—the conditions under which a student may move from one campus to another in his or her chosen program of study. But it also raises important new questions of similarity and differentiation of academic personnel standards and pay scales, budgeting standards of other kinds, and allocation of functions and roles.

At the stage of policy argument over the desirability and the design of a proposed change of structure, analyses are often contributed by institutional representatives, study commissions and outside experts, staffs of executive and legislative agencies, and factions in the wider community. Because a significant redistribution of political and institutional jurisdiction and power is involved, the quality of policy analysis needs to be high, but, the analysis from each of these sources is inevitably shaped for advocacy. At one stage in the rethinking of the California structure, for example, the legislature's Joint Committee on Higher Education received a staff report recommending consolidation of the university and the state colleges into a unified system, including statewide coordination for the (largely locally financed) community colleges, and development of increased regional coordination (California Legislature, 1969). The CCHE later formed a Select Committee on the Master Plan. In testimony before that committee, the heads of all three public segments (the University of California, the California state colleges, and the community colleges) advocated that no changes be made in the segmental structure (Coordinating Council for Higher Education, 1972). Meanwhile, the legislature organized a new Joint Committee on the Master Plan, which issued a draft report in early 1973. Its proposal to reorganize the Coordinating Council into a California Commission for Postsecondary Education, with a new composition and new powers, was enacted into statute in 1973. As of early 1974, the Joint Committee was active on a number of fronts. It proposed a constitutional amendment to change the terms of university regents and establish a method to screen qualifications of nominees for appointment by the governor; it made resolutions calling for planning studies by the new Postsecondary Education Commission; and it made resolutions proposing various policy directions and standards for public higher education in California.

Most of the assembling of views and positions about what should be done in these sensitive areas comes about through submission of published reports and public testimony. Good ideas and evidence may influence the formulation of statutory enactments and policy directives, although the final form depends on the intricate workings of the political process. I provided testimony, for example, on the sensitive issue of tuition and financing (as did a number of other people), but the eventual outcome in terms of state policies will, of course, be determined by future governors and legislators (Balderston, 1972).

Summary

The modification of a master plan involves philosophical values, elements of legal and administrative structure, issues of resource allocation and allocational mechanisms, and questions of the organization and performance of educational activities. Only the naive would doubt that these major changes would leave unaffected what happens between teachers and students, but inability to assess the educational impacts of master plan alternatives is the biggest missing link in much of the thinking that goes into these changes. It is here that more searching policy analyses could have great effect.

Chapter 6

Market
Indicators

The accomplishments of a university—in the large, and in the long run—are the distinctive contributions of its graduates and its faculty to the worlds of ideas, expression, and action. A university that is doing what it should in new scholarship is a stimulus, shelter, and testing ground for innumerable individual and collective creative efforts in science, intellectual invention, critical insight, and the arts. Such an institution will be well represented in the networks throughout the world for sharing new findings and new approaches in the scholarly disciplines and the professions.

A university can point proudly to former students whose leadership in their professions and whose energy in their community make them outstanding members of society. Those students who reach the point of original contribution while they are students— for example, in their dissertation research—can often be counted on to become future leaders of scholarship.[1] The university can congratulate itself mainly for having made shrewd bets on the

[1] That students are significant contributors to new knowledge as students is illustrated by the estimate that in chemistry, 60 percent of all research findings are contributed by dissertation candidates. See National Board on Graduate Education (1974, Chapter 2).

future success of some of these students when it enrolled them; for others, the student experience generates a real transformation of life possibilities and permanently alters the trajectory of life expectations.

The life transformation of its students and the propagation of knowledge are the fundamental, long-range functions of a university. Yet the assessment of how well a university is doing in these obligations is complicated by philosophical difficulties and by the problems of evaluating the significance of lives and ideas over very long horizons—working lives of thirty to fifty years, and idea-lifetimes that are sometimes as long or longer. Neither the data to trace what happens over these long periods nor the techniques of disentangling the specific impact of one university from the numerous other forces at work in intellectual life and in society are well developed (Balderston, 1970). Alexander Astin, an expert on the measurement of educational outcomes, makes a strong plea for better longitudinal data and for the design of measures that will help universities to assess their effect on students (Bowen, 1974, pp. 23–46).

Although administrators need to keep these long-term issues very much in mind, they must concentrate immediate attention on institutional and scholarly processes, resources, and short-term indicators of a university's position and prospects. These operational indicators are the focus of this chapter. Because ultimate results are so long-range and so difficult to assess, an operational approach examines the views currently held about the university and its academic quality by those whose decisions affect it: prospective students; employers and others who deal with graduating students; evaluators of research proposals for funding; donors and appropriators of money; and decision-makers in the academic marketplace. In each of these markets—those for entering students, for outgoing students, and for high reputation among its constituencies —a university can and must know where it stands with respect to market indicators of academic quality as well as quantity.

Markets for Entering Students

Undergraduate Market. Entering freshmen come mainly directly from secondary schools. Any university, facing this market, seeks to enroll a target number of first-year students that satisfies several fiscal, academic, and policy criteria. It must do so against the pressures of competing destinations for high school graduates and in the context of its mission and of the policy standards that, especially for state-organized and supported universities, impinge on it from the state-level superstructure. In this market, the reputation of the university within the youth community is of peculiar significance because decisions about going to college and what college to attend are influenced by peer views. The visibility and attractiveness of a university to prospective students have a direct influence on their choices. Prospective students consider the quality and character of student life, the availability of particularly interesting academic programs, and the positive views of their friends about a university.

Other influences on institutional visibility include the generally available handbooks of colleges and universities (such as Barron's *Profiles of American Colleges* and various underground guides that report on the living styles in colleges), the impressions that students and their parents get from the mass media, and the advice of high school counselors about the educational attributes of colleges and universities. Prospective students also attempt to assess colleges and universities by reading their catalogs and other sales literature.

Among the predominantly or solely undergraduate institutions, several shorthand quality indicators are the extent of academic selectivity in admission; the extent of nonlocal attendance, regionally or nationally; and the proportion of those completing the degree who go on to post-baccalaureate study. These factors do not indicate what a college might do to provide an education that would be meaningful to a particular student, but they do show where a college stands in the conventional pecking order of academic quality. Structural features that may or may not imply quality but that often affect attracting power are enrollment size (there are several versions of a preferred minimum and a preferred maximum size for different kinds of undergraduate experience); size of library collection; location (urban, suburban, small town, rural); faculty quality, of which two generally available indicators are the AAUP-rated faculty pay scale and the percentage of PhDs on the faculty; and educational style (coeducational, denominational). In addition, some institutions such as Bryn Mawr, Oberlin, Swarthmore, and Williams have gained national visibility by unusual academic strength, and some have distinctively appealing programs and calendars, such as Antioch, Beloit, and Colorado College. Some institutions have also achieved social cachet more securely than others. If such cachet is combined with academic reputation, an institution has elite status within the undergraduate market.

Universities compete with undergraduate colleges in attracting undergraduates. They usually have the advantage of greater public visibility. But some institutional features of a university may exert a negative influence on the perceptions of some prospective students while positively attracting others. These attributes include institutional scale, location, and reputation for undergraduate education (as distinct from fame for graduate education and research). For example, even though large size confers benefits in terms of the range and depth of academic resources available, it also implies a climate of impersonality and lack of coherence in undergraduate life that can deter some students and dissuade their parents. Similarly, some universities located in or near the central city of a large metropolitan area may be able to attract faculty, research staff, and graduate students more easily than undergraduates because many students hope for a congenial, collegiate environment for living. Universities in small communities far from any metropolitan area, however, do not appeal to students who put high value on the urban scene and cultural opportunities. Finally, some large universities that are highly attractive to graduate students have an equivocal reputation among potential undergraduates. This is especially true of those public universities such as the Big Ten, Berkeley, and UCLA that have large enrollments and utilize mass-instruction methods for elementary and some intermediate undergraduate courses. Although high-quality undergraduate education is available at such universities, only those students who can quickly develop the knack of searching out opportunities and kindred spirits and can discipline their own learning effectively are able to take full advantage of the wide range of academic resources available.

The preceding discussion concentrated on attributes of visibility, reputation, and institutional character that contribute to the position of a college or university in the undergraduate market. The cost factor—tuition, living costs, less financial aid—is also of prime importance both to the institution and to the student and the student's parents. To compete in the undergraduate market, a university must be interested both in the academic abilities of potential students and in their willingness to attend. Typical indicators of ability are high school grades and, because high schools vary so much, the scores of high school seniors on CEEB Achievement Tests and Scholastic Aptitude Tests. Willingness to attend an institution is influenced by whether a student has heard of it, is attracted by it, and can afford to attend it.

Although universities should consider in an integrated manner the academic abilities, tuition-paying capacity, and financial aid requirements of prospective students, they have not had good techniques for doing so. Jewett (1971) has estimated, however, the essential cross-distribution between academic ability (as measured by SAT verbal scores) and parental income, and he has used this distribution for an integrated admissions-tuition-aid model and applied the model to Ohio Wesleyan University for the remaining years of the 1970s. His method of analysis can now be employed by other institutions.

In order to forecast the number of Ohio Wesleyan's prospective students at various dollar intervals of financial aid need, Jewett utilized information concerning the nationwide family income distribution and its change over time, information from the College Scholarship Service on ability to pay, and a forecast of future tuition and other attendance costs at Ohio Wesleyan. (He excluded student transportation costs and other geographical market gradients mainly because income-distribution data by state or region was not available.)

Jewett forecasts declining numbers of prospective male and female students for Ohio Wesleyan in the preferred segments of the cross-distribution between SAT verbal scores and amounts of needed financial aid. He demonstrates that the entire cross-distribution, and not merely the average of either the academic ability measure or the indication of ability to pay, must be considered in a thorough analysis. His model also has implications for the fiscal planning of enrollment-related net revenue (tuition and fees minus financial aid) and also for such issues as recruitment strategies, the adjustment of financial aid offers to different categories of students, and policy preference regarding ratios between male and female entering students.

As Jewett points out, there is need for additional research into other significant dimensions of student academic abilities and into the issue of willingness to pay (as distinct from ability to pay) as indicated by parental income. Nevertheless, he has made a significant contribution by showing major parameters of the future market for incoming freshmen students, relating these to both academic and fiscal considerations, and realizing a readily usable admissions planning model for a particular institution. This approach could be adapted to the circumstances of other colleges or universities to determine the size of the national market-segment of potential students within which they must find new entrants.

One additional factor, still to be explored, is the geographical distribution of potential students according to each academic ability/financial-need segment definition. Most colleges and universities draw entering students much more heavily from an immediate geographic market than from more distant locations of parental residence and high school attendance. Private colleges and universities of the highest general reputation can and do emphasize geographical balance in assembling an inflow of entering students, especially if they are able to offer financial assistance to offset the greater travel as well as psychic costs of attendance by students from distant areas. Studies by Hans Jenny (1970, 1972) and Jewett (1971) demonstrate that private colleges face real problems—because of the financial aid costs—in recruiting disadvantaged and minority students.

Another significant compositional consideration is the distribution of students according to academic fields and interests. A university has not only a target of new enrollment-taking capacity but a distribution of this capacity among academic areas that have, in the short run, largely fixed professorial staff, budgets, and special facilities. Student enthusiasm for particular areas of study shifts much more rapidly than the capacity of these specialized program areas can be adjusted, upward or downward, to absorb enrollment. Also, the university usually seeks some balance. Thus, if a university can do so, it very actively recruits new students in areas of surplus capacity and discourages students who are likely to go to programs that are already overenrolled. One trouble with this practice is that many entering freshmen are uncertain about their plans and need time to explore several fields of study as well as to gain some general education. Another problem is that American universities, unlike those in Europe, do not enroll undergraduate students in specialized faculties. If engineering has a four-year curriculum that accepts entering freshmen, it does separate them from other undergraduate streams. But most entering students are enrolled in letters and science colleges that allow students to choose and change major fields with little penalty, especially in the early stages. Thus, it is both administratively and educationally difficult to achieve balanced enrollments of undergraduate majors.

Although the public university faces some of these needs for fiscal and academic balance of undergraduate admissions, much of its undergraduate admission policy is determined by other considerations. The prime one, shared with other public institutions, is the set of state policy standards for access of state residents to higher education. These standards must be met within the state's demographic profile: the numbers of young people of college-going age in each future year from the state's households, plus predicted inmigration of students, minus those students who go to private institutions within the state and to out-of-state institutions of all types.

Total student flow to public higher education within a state is then allocated among the types of public institutions in accordance with state policies. This is usually not done by a centralized application-and-admission system for all segments of public higher education, but rather by setting eligibility standards and fee structures and relying on the natural choices of individual applicants to achieve adequate balance. The role of the public university, in a configuration of public institutions that includes community colleges and four-year colleges, is usually to accept both entering freshmen students and transfer students for advanced undergraduate study. The policy issues thus include negotiated rules for curriculum organization, articulation, and transfer rights, and often place the university's administrators—who deal with the state authorities—in a position of some antagonism with the academic policy interests of departments and colleges.

The private university may worry about having enough students who meet the combination of fiscal and academic constraints it seeks to enforce, and it may therefore recruit on a regional or even a national basis. The public university, on the other hand, faced in the 1960s the problems of sharply expanding numbers and the need to balance its obligations to take undergraduate enrollment against its aspirations for growth and eminence in the professions and in doctoral programs. Over time, with the growth of other types of public institutions, public universities had lost their politically safe base as the locus of mass higher education. Their internal logic of academic growth and considerations of university mission in a wider system pushed them toward increased relative emphasis on graduate study. They then faced increasing criticism as inadequate contributors to the meeting of state commitments to educational access, and criticism of their high-cost status as graduate and research institutions.

Both the private and the public university will soon face decreasing undergraduate enrollments because of the impending decline in the numbers of persons of conventional college-going age. The number of eighteen-year-olds will reach its peak in 1978 and then will decline well into the 1980s. The most selective private institutions, and those that draw from a truly national market, will be very little affected. But private institutions that have a much more localized demand, and state universities that draw undergraduate students who are a significant proportion of the total number of collegegoers from a state's population, will either have to drop minimum eligibility standards or settle for stagnating or declining undergraduate enrollments.

Graduate Market. A university that has many graduate professional schools, doctoral programs, and research establishments gains institutional visibility from them that attracts graduate students. Enrollment size and selectivity of admission influence the quality perceived by undergraduate and graduate students, though the markets, and the market indicators, for incoming graduate students are quite different from those for undergraduates. Separate, segmented markets exist for each of the doctoral fields and for each graduate profession. Thus, the major private and public universities draw from nationwide pools of BA degree-winners, and applicants are carefully screened by the separate academic departments, as well as by the office of the graduate dean. Departments recruit actively for these outstanding students, and they offer their own fellowships, assistantships, and grants-in-aid to strong candidates. Some outstanding students receive nationwide competitive fellowships for doctoral study and are then able to choose what program to enter without regard to local financing. One important market indicator of the eminence of a program in a given field is the proportion of these competitive fellowship winners who choose it.

Graduate training, whether for the doctorate or in the professions (medicine, dentistry, law, architecture, business administration, and others) is more specifically pointed to career than are undergraduate programs. Thus, for the graduate student, who is older and more focused, both career prospects in a specific field and the academic quality of a specific program offered in a particular department are significant aspects of choice. University administrators, faculty members, and disciplinary associations, all sensitive both to placement prospects and to reputations for quality, seek to reinforce the highest possible standard of academic and career potential in their graduate admission decisions. These standards, and also the systematic ratings of the quality of graduate programs that are discussed below, influence the choices that prospective graduate students make among programs.

The market for graduate students has until recently been heavily affected by differences among programs in their level of federal support. In the 1950s and 1960s, solidly established doctoral programs in the sciences provided full support for graduate students once admitted. With the advent of job placement difficulties, beginning in the late 1960s, and the precipitate decline in federal fellowship funds, many of these programs have had to reduce the numbers of entering students they would accept—at the same time that newer universities were attemping to expand their struggling doctoral enrollments.

Variable Entry. From two quite different sources, pressures have arisen for more varied treatment of entering students. First, the students—particularly undergraduates—are demanding freer circulation between study and other activities and freer transfer, for a variety of academic and other experiences, between institutions. The Carnegie Commission's report, *Less Time, More Options* (1971), argues the merits of greater flexibility of response by educational institutions to the student urge for stopout, stretchout, or intervals of work experience, travel, or just plain dabbling. Although this flexibility has educational merit, it does create new problems. Stopout lengthens the elapsed time, though not the full-time equivalency of students, in work for the degree. The intricate pattern of attendance also increases the variability of attendance—semester by semester or quarter by quarter—of students already enrolled, increases the likelihood of errors in short-term enrollment planning and course scheduling, and thus may increase institutional costs.

The second pressure for variable entry is the increased sensitivity that universities now display toward the special needs of new groups of students. One of these groups is made up of students from cultural and minority circumstances. Their admissibility needs to be evaluated with regard to other indicators of academic potential than the conventional ones, and their initial needs as university students for guidance and tutorial assistance may be greater than average. A second group is made up of students of mature years, including midcareer people who need academic training to make career changes and women who need new academic backgrounds to reenter professional work or career employment after raising their children. The market opportunity of a university to attract these two groups depends on the size of the pools of potential students, on recruitment, and sometimes on the willingness of the university to design new programs or special arrangements for flexible reentry into academic work.

Markets for Graduating Students

Undergraduate Output Market. Some undergraduates leave the university when they earn their degrees. Some transfer to other universities and colleges. And some withdraw, without a degree and without immediate plans to return to the same institution or go to another. These three streams of existing students give different signals of what the university is doing to or for students.

Undergraduate education, particularly for the highly motivated student who does well, is often pregraduate. Thus, one series of market indicators for a university is the rate at which its students go on to postbaccalaureate study, the kinds of programs and institutions that accept its students, and the inducements, such as nationwide fellowships, offered these students to undertake graduate study. Some highly selective liberal arts colleges and the major universities find that their pregraduate function is important. As many as 80 percent of Swarthmore graduates undertake graduate work; the percentage of those who go on from the Ivy League universities is nearly as high; and about half the BAs of major public universities go to graduate study. Another indicator is the rate at which BAs eventually complete the doctorate or other advanced degrees. The University of California, Berkeley, can point with pride to National Academy of Sciences data showing that of all those earning the doctorate in the United States from 1966 to 1972, 2,229 (more than from any other single institution) had been Berkeley BAs.

The recent decline in demand for PhDs has been accompanied by increased pressures for admission into many professional degree programs. The numbers and rates of BA students who enter graduate professions, and the quality of the graduate schools to which they gain admission, are indicators of the value of a university's undergraduate education.

Employment markets, especially for entry-level jobs, are subject to rapid shifts and display local and regional differences. Thus, a university cannot assess conclusively how well its recent graduates are faring by comparing their placement distribution in a given year with that of its own students in prior years or with that of other universities located in other regions. Nevertheless, most universities could do more than they have to obtain systematic data about graduating seniors and follow-up data on graduates. Such data would provide market indicators. They would also be useful in considering both the philosophical issue of whether career and career success on society's current terms are important indicators of the university's educational contribution to its students and the interpretive question, as regards the liberal arts, of how to evaluate the widely dispersed distribution of these graduates over occupational destinations.

Exiting undergraduates who leave without a degree give a different series of indicator signals. One group, disaffected with all further education (and sometimes with conventional society on any terms), drops out and stays out permanently. Some students take stopouts and then transfer to other institutions; some enroll elsewhere immediately. No institution is ideal for everybody at all phases of maturation. Nevertheless, careful study of the academic, financial, and personal status of each of these exiting students, and of the reasons why some elect to transfer, may reveal defects in the university's treatment of its undergraduate students.

Grading standards in both colleges and universities are subject to many vagaries, and thus grades cannot be employed as an indicator of achievement among institutions. The recent upward creep in grade-point averages, together with wider use of pass/fail or pass/pass grades, further muddies the use of grading as a basis for evaluation. A firmer indication comes from other measures of the quality of student achievement at the time of completion of the baccalaureate degree, such as the absolute performance of seniors on the Graduate Record Examination, the Law School Aptitude Test, the Aptitude Test for Graduate Schools of Business, or the Medical School Admission Test, or by their academic achievement relative to their initial status, as evidenced by such generalized measures as the ratio of GRE scores on completion to CEEB achievement scores at entry, by the rate of persistence to the degree of a cohort of students relative to their initial ability distribution and the given passing standard, or by student maturation and capacity for responsibility in career and in society.

These latter indicators assess *value-added* by the institution, and in the long run are fairer measures of institutional performance than are measures of absolute quality. By the criterion of maximum value-added through educational exposure of each student, both in the intellective and in the affective aspects of development, a highly visible and elite institution that insists on a very selective admission policy will often be of lower quality than an institution that admits students of lower educational ability and attainment (as conventionally defined) and then assists them materially to improve their educational performance. Unfortunately, this is not, of course, what is generally accented in discussions of quality in higher education, where the connotations of high absolute performance are read into the term. According to this more conventional usage, there are a few general indicators of high quality (not concerned with quality assessment of individual students or particular specialized programs). One major indicator is the ability distribution (conventionally defined) of students at the time of admission: the minimum cut-off point, the median or average, and the proportion or absolute number of incoming students of exceptional or superior academic ability. The first implies what the institution is doing to protect itself and the bulk of students from the absorption of resources in purely remedial work and the drag of poorly motivated or failing performance by a significant fraction of the student body. The second implies something about the expected level of average performance around which the academic programs of the institution can be designed. The third is a signal of the appreciation of the merit of the institution by students who are outstanding at the time of admission and have the widest range choice of where to go to college (market competition for National Merit Scholarship winners and runners-up is thus quite intense). If they maintain their performance through the dangerous years of maturation, these high-achieving students also then convey both to other students and to the faculty what is possible by way of maximum attainment.

Similarly, at the time of completion of the undergraduate degree, different implications can be drawn about marginal students (those who pass a minimum standard), students who are grouped around the average academic outcome for the institution, and students in the small upper tail of the achievement distribution. One model of quality is to take in only those students who exceed a high minimum ability standard and then, as nearly as possible, guarantee academic and maturation success to those students (and their parents). This has been the implicit role of the high-quality liberal arts colleges in the past.

Another model, much more nearly approached by the large public universities that have high-quality faculty for graduate programs and research and use them also for undergraduate instruction, is to enforce a fairly high minimum passing standard for graduation but also to accept a high variance in intellectual performance between the minimum passing standard and the best work that undergraduates do. The best of these undergraduates, according to this model, are able competitors of first-year graduate students (who are immediately available to the faculty for purposes of comparison) and with high probability, these ablest undergraduates go on to graduate study in their major field or into the graduate professions. The standards of minimum acceptability and of respectable mediocrity are lower for undergraduates in the major public universities than in the elite liberal arts colleges, but the standard of excellent performance for undergraduates is as high or higher than in these colleges.

From this standpoint, also, the elite private universities (the Ivy League plus Chicago and Northwestern) can enforce on their undergraduates a higher minimum performance standard than can the large public universities. They also, probably, enforce a generally higher standard of median performance, although this is not so clear. They probably cannot find a different accent on excellence for the upper tail of the achievement distribution than is available in the large, strong public universities.

Graduate Output Market. Among the mechanisms that could be used for judging the quality of graduate programs are the use of visiting committees of prominent scholars and professionals to evaluate departments and the promise of their graduates, the aid of outside readers to review a year's production of accepted dissertations in a department as evidence of the level of graduate work, and even the reading of a national sample of doctoral dissertations in the field to see whether outstanding ones come from the institution in question. Such questions as these can be asked about student work: What are the major frontier issues in the discipline, and to what extent is research effort and achievement focused on them? How close are dissertation projects to these frontier issues, and how close are graduate courses and seminars to them? And to the extent that instrumentation and methodology enable faculty and advanced students to work on frontier issues, is there evidence of their successful use?

Other market indicators include the number of recruiters who visit the campus to interview pending graduates, the placement and salaries of students on graduation, and their career success and trajectories after five, ten, or more years. For example, a university can monitor the hiring market for each doctoral and graduate professional degree, by keeping records on where its graduates are placed and how well they do in their careers. The market for new PhDs has received a great deal of attention, as illustrated in the chapter on policy analysis. The booming PhD market of the 1960s has soured in the 1970s (Cartter, 1971, 1974; National Board on Graduate Education, 1973a, 1973b). Traditionally, a university's strongest PhD programs could place many of their new PhDs in research universities and in postdoctoral science fellowships at the great scientific laboratories. Those PhDs who showed less scholarly and research promise went to college teaching posts or industrial research. The reputation of a PhD program was strengthened by the first group of placements, but, as Breneman (1970) argues, the second group had either a neutral or a negative effect on the national reputation and rating of a program. In the much more difficult market now facing new PhDs, a university can still use the placement pattern of its graduates as an indicator of its reputation and success in each field, although as Wolfle and Kidd (1971) point out, new PhDs—exceptionally talented and energetic as they are—are very unlikely to be unemployed, and thus the proportion of reputation-increasing placements is almost bound to be lower in the 1970s than it was in the 1960s.

The placement of professional school graduates can similarly be used to assess how well each professional school is doing. For example, after their required year of internship, medical school graduates go into clinical residency, research preparation, or practice; their choices and placement as residents in the best-known teaching hospitals or as faculty members and medical researchers with well-known medical schools is one mark of their success.[2]

Law schools send their best students to be clerks for prominent judges in the state and federal judiciary, and their placement as well as the starting salaries of all graduates and the numbers who

[2] See Held (1973) for an analysis of the relationships between the geographic origins of medical school graduates from 1955 to 1965, their choices of internship and residency, and their eventual location in medical practice.

are well placed elsewhere serve as market indicators for the law faculty. But because of the proportion of law graduates who take up financially unrewarding but socially challenging work in such fields as poverty law and environmental law, a law school should not necessarily regard the salaries of these graduates as indicative of failure simply because their early earnings are low. This example illustrates the problems of using overly conventional market indicators.

In other fields, such as engineering and business administration, the rates of placement with major corporations and the starting salaries can serve as indicator. Again, however, an appreciable fraction of these professional school graduates elect to go into small firms or even to strike out on their own, and these choices should not be regarded as having negative implications.

Follow-up at successive points in time to determine the career lines of professional school graduates provides significant indications of the strength of a program. Among the measures that can be employed are the proportion of graduates showing professional leadership, the extent of their memberships in professional organizations, their involvement in community and professional action, and their pattern of advancement. Are they working in the same field in which they studied? Are they independently established? What proportion have disappeared or dropped out of the field? Although many professional schools have fragments of information about this, few are systematic about follow-up or use the evidence they get to adjust curricular and admission strategies. Private universities, to cultivate alumni interest and annual giving, have sought energetically to follow the careers of past graduates. Public universities do some of this, for the same reasons, but they need more follow-up information than they have had.

Markets for Academic Reputation

What are the significant reference groups whose views about the academic reputation of a university are important? As indicated earlier, peer attitudes of present and prospective college students are important, partly because they determine what kinds of students select toward, or away from, a particular university. But the youth style in a university may be more important to potential students than to other constituencies. Universities that gain a reputation for good teaching and a good atmosphere for undergraduate learning can attract more motivated students than can those known as party schools or as centers of the counterculture or, at the other extreme, as eminent graduate institutions where the undergraduates are, so to speak, second-class citizens; and yet this reputation may not affect the institution's standing in other markets.

Parents, alumni, taxpayers, and the general public also hold views about a university. Locally, these are attained via the local news media and also through contact with students, employees, and the institution's campus. Regional or national visibility is often attained through news media treatment of intercollegiate athletics and of newsworthy events involving the institution—events which may, of course, convey negative connotations, such as Santa Barbara's experience with the Isla Vista riots and bank burning or the Kent State episode. Universities gain some man-in-the-street visibility through news reportage of exotic scientific events or happenings, as illustrated by Stanford's early heart transplants and Berkeley's discovery of new transuranium elements. But while the views of laymen are significant to the university for a variety of reasons, such views may have only a frail relation to its academic quality and reputation as judged by academic standards.

Interinstitutional Comparisons. Informed opinions about their own and competing academic programs are held by academic scholars and administrators. One way to calibrate this opinion is simply to ask the right people about the quality rating of various departments in a field and then assemble their opinions in some systematic way. This procedure was used by Alan Cartter at the American Council on Education for the Cartter ratings (1966) and for the succeeding Roose-Andersen ratings (1969). Assuming that there is at least a modicum of agreement about the standards of good research and good training among the scholars who are peers in a discipline, such judgments of specialized experts in a given field are worth a good deal. Academic scholars have and use judgments of this sort when deciding where to send their most promising students for graduate study, what departments to use as sources for new PhDs for academic appointments, what examples of curriculum change to emulate, and, if it comes to that, where to move if a move would be desirable.

The Cartter and Roose-Andersen ratings have developed something of a life of their own, tending to reinforce the positions of strongly-rated departments and giving an all-too-convenient negative signal about those that are rated poorly. The ratings do offer the general university administrator access to collective judgements of academic reputation in each discipline. Departments rated as inadequate can be identified readily, and then the president, provost, or graduate dean can explore in detail what to do about them. Important as the academic opinions about reputation are, however, they are often based on fragmentary evidence. Other market indicators based on more objective information are needed.

Getting Research Funds. One such indicator is the absolute and relative success of the faculty in a given field in competition for resarch funds from the federal agencies and foundations that award funds on a merit basis. Evaluation by academic peers is not always made only on the basis of the quality of the researcher and of the research proposed. But the reputations of the evaluators as well as the evaluated are on the line, and the signals forthcoming from this process are important. Besides, the receipt of research funds makes a great deal of work possible and provides support for graduate students. No major university can afford, financially or otherwise, to ignore the grant-getting performance of its faculty in the areas for which substantial basic research funds are available.

Success in obtaining funds for applied and mission-oriented research is often important for the financial base of a university and is indicative of the entrepreneurial energy of faculty and research administrators. But it is not as clear a signal of academic eminence as is the receipt of peer-evaluated funds for basic research.

Indicators of Faculty Distinction. Research funding reflects the reputation and the aggressiveness of faculty (and getting it may be facilitated by helpful support on the mechanics of proposal writing). There are other measures of faculty distinction, both for the scientific fields for which research funding is a signal and for those fields where there is little or no outside funding. One indicator is honors received and evidence of prominence in the scholarly societies of a field. Another is service on editorial boards of the scholarly journals. Still another is the receipt of honorific fellowships and appointments—Nobel Prizes, Guggenheims, appointments to the Institute for Advanced Study in Princeton or to the Center for Advanced Study in the Behavorial Sciences in Stanford, and memberships in such organizations as the National Academy of Sciences and the National Academy of Engineering. These kinds of recognition are frosting on the cake of scholarship that is primarily based on research productivity. Sheer quantity of writing is not, in principle, the main thing.

On some scientific fields, attempts have been made, through the development of citation indexes, to identify the most important articles and authors. Opinions may differ about what ideas and contributions are important and about whose reputation is deservedly outstanding. But scholars do judge the work that comes forward, and they are serious in these judgments. The individual scholar is dependent for his or her academic reputation on having produced something and on having it recognized as significant. A departmental group of strong reputation generally contains a number of prominent senior scholars, and it should also have some highly promising junior contributors who are struggling to establish reputations. The collective reputation of their department, as well as their own reputations, is important to a group of scholars because important positive or negative consequences flow from that reputation.

Faculty relations with professionals outside their own discipline can also serve as a market indicator, especially in the professional schools that have active practitioner constituencies but also, to some extent, in the sciences. These indicators of prominence include, for example, the use of faculty members as advisors to practitioners, professional groups, and federal and other agencies; faculty involvement in practitioner and broadly based professional societies; and evidence of progressiveness and reformist impact on scholarly and practitioner outlook and standards, such as by coupling instruction and research in a prominent area of concern, collaboration with other disciplines, and the approbation of scholars in other fields of the work done in the school.

Competition for Academic Staff. Tenured faculty are tied to one institution in the laboratory sciences more than in other fields, because of the complex arrangements for laboratory space and equipment and the problems of obtaining grants and research funding. In all fields, however, there is some movement of tenured faculty, who resign from one university to take appointments at another. Unless a senior professor is recruited by another institution specifically to take up a prominent administrative post, the resignation of a valued senior faculty member is a signal for both the gaining and the losing institutions.

There are of course, numerous individual motivations for such a decision: personality conflict with others in the same field, dissatisfaction or a conflict of principle with some important issue of university policy, or disagreement over terms and conditions of work, including salary. But the losing institution does get a negative signal, with respect to the last set of motivations. And if the gaining institution can actually attract a well-known senior professor at a small increase in salary, or none, this is a clear signal of perceived upward movement by that professor. Universities that have high rates of resignations by tenured faculty, whatever the reasons, are receiving adverse signals about the health of the body academic.

In contrast to the tenured faculty, new PhDs come on the market with a maximum expectation of mobility. They have to expect to sort out choices over a wide geographical and institutional set. Each year, the major universities' doctoral programs in a given field produce a relative handful of new PhDs with truly outstanding prospects of academic success. The success of a given institution in attracting its high choices among these outstanding candidates for junior appointment is an indicator of the quality of its new blood and of its competitive standing as perceived by young men and women who have the most intense motivation—prospects for doing good work in their early years—for making acute and careful judgments. If a university or a department is in trouble, one of the surest signals is failure to get acceptances of appointment offers made to outstanding young candidates. Such a failure does not necessarily show up in unfilled positions, because a university that needs staff can always find somebody. But knowledgeable academics can usually tell, at this stage of recruitment, how a university is doing.

Resource Base

Finally, it is necessary to discuss a few general aspects of the resource base of a university. Without adequate resources, it is difficult to achieve significant results. The size and quality of a university's capital plant and the total annual operating budget are two aggregate measures. The university's capital endowment is a third. The wealth of an institution can be better judged, however, by the amounts of space, operating budget, and other resources per faculty member and per student. A university's library— its total collection size, quality rating, and distinction in special collections—is another very significant resource. The achieved position and the rate of change of all of these resources are market indicators. The annual capital outlay budget for academic buildings and equipment signals the rate of change of capital plant. The annual increase of the operating budget may signal either expansion or a deepening of quality or both. The acquisition rate of the library is important for both the currency of the collection and the ability to repair gaps in the existing collection.

All of these are indicators of the ability of a university's trustees and senior administration to marshall support. Faculty members see these indicators as measures of the buoyancy of the environment in which they work and as measures of the effective energy of the stewards of the institution; and competing institutions watch them carefully in hoping to better themselves. Few university presidents have earned accolades for clever retrenchment; the great presidents have almost always been great expansionsts. As we shall see in the chapters that follow, there are other ways to get signals of the skill with which a university is led and managed; but increases in the market indicators for a university are the most commonly used gauges of managerial success.

Summary

The first step in getting beyond opinions about institutional success and systematic measurement of academic quality and excellence can be made by obtaining objective information on various market indicators. For most indicators this is a straightforward task of institutional research and can be done with a modest investment of effort. A sample box score would include the following:

Market Indicators	*Data Sources*
Quality of student input	Test scores (for example GRE) and changes in test scores
Student achievement and output	Percent going on to post-baccalaureate study and achievement there
	Placement and career information
	Outside review of student work (for example, dissertations)
	Test scores (for example, SAT)
	High school class rank
	Number of state or national scholarship and fellowship holders who choose the institution
Departmental reputation in the field	Total size of faculty cadre in the field
	Number of specializations represented
	Effective borrowing of strengths from related groups
	Access to or availability of laboratory space or other critical resources
	Amount of extramural research funding
	Generalized opinion rankings (for example, Cartter and Roose-Andersen ratings)
	Library size and accessibility
	Number of faculty publications in scholarly journals
	Special awards, citations, and so forth to faculty

Institutional image	What it is famous for, what its distinguishing characterization is with other institutions, with practitioners, and with the general public

A more detailed list of quality indicators can be found in Appendix A.

A cursory examination of these listed data shows that a surprising number can be used on a regular basis without new primary research. Some, of course, would require a large data collection effort—for example, the mandating of GRES for all graduating seniors in an undergraduate program or the assembling of expert judgments and detailed institutional knowledge about developments in the scholarly fields and about what is going on in each department or professional school. In those fields suffering from some disagreement or ambiguity about their boundaries or about what is most important, this is a task in which prominent people will find some areas of agreement and some important areas of disagreement.

A troublesome feature of this whole array of market indicators is that academic quality is shown to be multidimensional. An institution or program is of high quality because it shows up well on several indices. One is tempted to suppose that a system of weights could somehow be agreed upon among these indices so that institutions or programs would be capable of comparison over time and of comparison with each other at any time, but as yet, no systematic analysis of this type is possible. For the interim, university managers must rely on their own best judgments and a diversity of data to assess institutional performance within multiple markets.

Chapter 7

Cost
Analysis

Traditionally, academic leadership has been concerned about ideals, missions, and values, to the exclusion of concern about costs except as an unfortunate inhibition. It fell to the business management of academic institutions to account for the funds used and to keep the operation going. Now there is a joining of these two domains of responsibility, and we must talk about cost analysis in the context of what is to be decided and what it is that our universities are trying to accomplish.

Cost analysis is useful for: (1) operating and management; (2) providing critical inputs for planning major changes in capacity, program structure, or institution policies; (3) obtaining comparisons between institutions, to help us share insights about what targets to set; (4) justifying to funding sources (public and private) what prices we charge for educational and institutional services and what resources are needed.

Operating and Management Uses

We all have to make, and live by, budgets for the institution as a whole (or for a multicampus or multiinstitutional system with a single budget), and for numerous types and levels of programs and operating units within the institution. Cost analysis is essential for constructing and controlling these budgets. It is needed to monitor what is happening to each budgeted activity as changes occur in the work-load level of the activity and in the environment (increases—or only too rarely, decreases—in the prices of things purchased, and shifts in the demands for educational and institutional services).

Costs are often a factor in day-to-day decisions. Most institutions are sufficiently complex to require written operating policies in many areas. When a change in one of these policies is contemplated, cost analysis is usually employed to determine various aspects of the proposed change and to predict various of its consequences.

David Humphrey (1972), of the office of Educational Development at SUNY, wrote: "We have not explored the possibilities for reallocation of our resources in more cost-effective ways . . . Improvements are possible in program management to determine the efficiency of activities in relation to their cost. Instead of automatically decreasing services in response to 'budget cuts,' we should be capable of rearranging and reallocating our resources to allow for continuation of the services in the face of decreasing budgets." Whether Humphrey's prognosis will turn out to be correct we do not yet know, but it is clear that both political and institutional forces will constrain budgeted expenditures while maintaining the pressures for increased student enrollment. Powerful incentives will exist for justifying activities and making them more efficient as well as for pruning away costly operations that cannot easily be defended.

The structure of incentives within an institution presents problems. We know that budgetary rules intended to recapture unused resources can actually operate perversely, causing managers to be sure they spend all they have so that money is not taken back at the end of the fiscal period, and to avoid reduction of the previous level of budget. We also know that there are sharp differences between the style of operation of organizational units that can be regarded as self-supporting performance centers and those, such as the library and many student services offices, that face an open-ended service obligation. Cost analysis, coupled with attention to the design of the structure of authority and organization, may facilitate increasingly efficient management of particular activities.

Planning Uses

Costs and cost predictions are important in developing plans and designing planning models. Cost-effectiveness and trade-off studies are very helpful in the review and reworking of institutional commitments and priorities. There are numerous examples of planning and decision issues for which cost concepts and measures that are appropriate to each situation are important.

When new buildings and other facilities are planned, it is as important to analyze the initial costs and the stream of future operating, debt service, and maintenance costs as it is to obtain good architectural and engineering design. Some institutions that did not look ahead when they went through substantial building programs later found themselves strapped for operating funds to met the ongoing requirements of maintenance and operation of their expanded plants.

Facilities planning over long future horizons may compel the study of patterns of future growth in enrollment and programs and the examination of usage rates and standards for accommodating such growth. A recent model developed for this purpose—including review of facilities utilization and the interactions between capital costs and operating costs—is the CCHE-FAM model, which was developed for the California Coordinating Council for Higher Education by Mathematica Corporation, with the involvement of staff groups from the council and member institutions.

A proposal for a new academic program is often accompanied by the assertion that the new program will be mounted within existing resources—"it will not cost anything." University presidents and their planning staffs have learned to be skeptical of such assertions. A new doctoral program or professional school or experimental undergraduate college almost always needs a nucleus investment for the initial phases, just to open its doors. Then it will induce further costs to be borne by related departments, the library and computer center, and the administration. And finally, the program will reach a size of enrollment and faculty and a depth of resources that will enable it to be academically and fiscally viable for the long pull. If they can be secured, or even guessed at with some shrewdness, the estimates of nucleus costs, transition costs, and steady-state annual program costs need to be in hand when the decision is pending—in other words, when the information can have some effective influence.

Many colleges and universities are considering part-time degree and extended university programs. A new educational clientele must be identified and the institution's mission must be adjusted to meet the new need. Such new possibilities require not only close study of the size and character of the educational program that may be needed but also of costs, sources of funding, and mode of organization.

There is much talk of new educational technologies and new patterns of organization of instruction, and some new approaches have been initiated. Sometimes these proposals are put forward with the stated intention of saving money. It takes careful and costly design effort, involving cooperation between academic people and those who know the new technologies, to put coherent proposals together. Analysis of initial costs and future patterns of operating costs is hazardous, because the realization of the technological and educational design is a developmental problem in itself. And the cost per student or per unit of service can be estimated only if there are reliable forecasts of the future volume of activity.

Systems of higher education must plan whether and when to add whole new campuses. During the decade of euphoric expansion—roughly from 1955 to 1965—many state systems laid out large designs for future growth. Robert Sanderson (1969) developed a new approach for long-horizon planning problems. Starting with total projected enrollments for a university system and with estimates of the cost of adding enrollment-taking capacity at existing and potential new campus locations, the model is formulated as a network in which non-zero flows on certain arcs incur fixed charges. The model computes a minimum total cost expansion program for accommodating gross enrollments, showing the stages at which to expand existing campuses and build new ones. It does not take into consideration such factors as graduate-undergraduate mix or disciplinary mix. The presumption of continued growth no longer holds for most state systems, but this analytical technique can be applied to other kinds of problems.

Many universities have begun to overhaul and modernize their business and administrative systems. Cost analysis is important in this context when an opportunity for cost reduction or efficiency improvement can be identified. This was my experience as vice-president for Business and Finance at the University of California, when a planned purchasing system was installed to capitalize on the university's purchasing power in procurement. The new system made campus-level purchasing agents responsible for negotiating master contracts in various areas; individual orders are placed within the terms of those contracts. The savings have been very substantial, and there have been very minimal administrative costs or dislocations because existing offices are utilized.

Some new administrative systems require cost analysis to demonstrate their feasibility and desirability. Nearly every campus now has computerized accounting. Many are on the way toward increasingly complex information systems, which may or may not reduce the cost of administrative routines but which are quite definitely intended to increase the amount, quality, and timeliness of information available for academic and administrative management.

Comparisons Between Institutions

If any figures are available, it is inevitable that they will be cited and used for good arguments or bad ones, for good purposes or bad, and regardless of whether the numbers are trustworthy. Institutions gather and share information on costs per student year and on unit costs of various programs and activities. Such figures are frequently reported to or generated by the state and federal agencies concerned with higher education. Institutions like to get cost information, first of all, to have some basis for knowing whether they ought to be proud or worried—some sort of comparative standard. Such comparisons may be especially important because typical efficiency signals of the market type are not directly available, as they are to industrial corporations. Second, an institution may be able to direct attention to areas of operation that show significantly higher costs than are being reported by comparable institutions. Higher education institutions, like other social enterprises, find they can learn from one another.

The National Center for Higher Education Management Systems of WICHE developed a Resource Requirements Prediction Model (RRPM). (See NCHEMS, 1973a, 1973b.) This model emerged from earlier efforts to design cost-tracing simulation models at various universities. One of the purposes of the RRPM development is to have common classification schemes and data definitions that enable institutions to generate cost figures and to share them in meaningful ways.

Cost Justification

Cost justification always sounds self-serving, and sometimes indeed it is—but where would the world be without advocacy! As a practical matter, a college president or dean or administrative vice-president may need to show that there is a good cost basis for a decision, as compared with the alternative courses of action that were rejected. And, indeed, there is often good discipline in assembling the cost justifications for decisions—unless the concepts are jumbled or the figures are trumped up. Only the unwary administrator who underestimates his critics will do that today.

External constituencies—state or federal funding agencies, foundations, alumni and other donor groups—have increasing appetites for cost and efficiency information, and so do institutional boards of governance and various groups within the university. Many institutions must now, in addition to all the other cost analyses, go through the rite of overhead costing to establish the case for indirect cost recovery in annual negotiations with federal research-funding agencies. NCHEMS has produced a study and task force report on *Cost-Finding Principles and Procedures* (1972), but controversy continues about concepts and measures for cost determination.

Within institutions, some activities are set up as self-funding cost centers and obtain their incomes by making either accounting or cash charges for their services. These centers have to establish their recharge prices, and cost is usually the basis they use. There are problems of setting these prices properly and holding managers responsible for efficient service and cost control. Certainly it is essential to have careful review of both the cost basis of such prices and the institutional impact of the recharge, self-funding concept in each such case.

Finally, cost analysis—particularly a demonstration of a rising trend—provides the most plausible justification for raising tuition and student fees. Inflationary trends in educational costs and the evidence about them are discussed below.

Measurement Problems

When it comes to measurement, we can borrow some approaches from the extensive background of empirical, practically-informed cost studies in the business world and from the analytical contributions in econometrics and management science. In fact, one might almost turn the issue upside down and ask why cost analysis has been such a baffling problem in our colleges and universities!

There are four important cost measurement issues: (1) What resources are being absorbed? (2) How does resource use vary with changes in the volume of activity? (3) Is the pattern of resource use efficient? (4) What is the trend over time? As I discuss each of these, I shall give a few examples of cost measures and also comment on the problems that have plagued attempts at cost measurement.

Resources Absorbed. The accounting systems of higher education institutions are rooted in the tradition of fund accounting for financial stewardship. To this are joined classifications of the departmental or organizational units and of expenditure categories.

The first step in measuring resources absorbed is to determine the appropriate boundary for the resource absorption process and find out whether the data available from the system of accounts are in a form consistent with that boundary. These difficulties are minimal when the measurement is confined to the costs directly incurred to operate conventional units—for example, the English department or the general library.

Measurement of the costs of a complex flow of activities is more difficult. For example, how do we determine the cost to an institution of having all of its upper-division English majors in attendance during a given academic year? An analysis must be made of the absorption of direct instructional resources by English majors, both in the English department and in other departments of instruction (via such devices as an Induced Course-Load Matrix of the kind used in RRPM). And the use by English majors of other pooled resources, such as the library, the administrative and student services offices, and the financial aid office, must be examined.

There are startling variations in the average annual allocated cost per student by type of major or program, as well as differences by level of student. Until some cost tracing is done, the enormous magnitude of these differences may be unrecognized. We have generally been aware that the institutional cost per lower division student is lower than the cost per student at the graduate level. But it has not been clear until recently that the graduate cost per student year in some fields of engineering and the laboratory sciences is as much as ten times the per student year cost in some social science and humanities fields. Furthermore, the yearly average cost of engineering undergraduates is higher than the cost of graduate students in many areas of the humanities. Some of these differences in unit cost are due to the much greater volume of students in some fields and to the need for a base investment in a given field if it is to be of reasonable strength. But other differences are due to the budgetary standards that have been built into college and university operations. These standards can be traced, in good part, to the large facilities and equipment overheads that have been justified in some fields on the ground that the work of the field cannot be effectively pursued without them. In any case, it is sobering to look at such large differentials in cost per student year, when the work-load basis of budgeting does not take into account the disciplinary distribution of enrollment. In private universities, the tuition and fees per student are not significantly different from one field to another.

Even for the tracing of current levels of resource absorption in an activity that is easily identified via the accounting structure, recorded expenditures are an incomplete measure. Accounting systems record outlays. Those accounting systems that are on an accrual basis permit the recording of liens and the spreading of an outlay over the relevant future periods. But recorded current expenditure rates do not give adequate measures of true cost for many purposes, and here are some of the reasons:

(1) Many institutional operations have both joint costs and joint outputs, so that identification of the cost level of a given activity may require a (partially arbitrary) allocation of joint cost pools over several activities and allocation of a unit's total imputed costs over the functions it performs or the outputs it delivers.

(2) Institutions are accustomed to absorbing volunteered resources that do not enter the accounting system and do not get recorded as costs. An example is the teaching time volunteered by clinical faculty members of medical schools.

(3) Our tradition in the area of capital accounting is not to do depreciation accounting for buildings, equipment, and major maintenance and renovation. As a result, we are often surprised by mysteriously rising costs of current building and equipment maintenance, and many institutions face periodic emergency pressures for replacement of capital items for which replacement reserves have not been planned.

(4) Many implicit costs and opportunity costs go unnoticed because decision-makers are preoccupied with a narrower boundary of their responsibility than is really sensible.

Student time is not generally recognized to be scarce and valuable in institutional planning and operation. Thus, we underestimate our ineffectiveness (and the frustration we impose on students) when we do not take account of the time spent in waiting lines for simple bureaucratic services, the delay costs of waiting for library books that are misplaced or not recalled or not in the collection or not present in sufficient numbers. And, focusing as we normally do on what it costs the institution to operate, we do not usually think of the student's foregone opportunities and earnings as a significant cost factor in higher education. Yet estimates indicate that these foregone earnings are a major contribution of the student to his education and are a very real part of the social cost of higher education (Schultz 1971, p. 20).

Even within the pure business side of institutional management, we have been slow to control cash requirements and recover maximum interest earnings and investment yield on financial assets.

We typically do not charge ourselves for working capital employed or account for the differential usage of working capital by operating units that are slow to settle accounts.

The above examples of implicit and opportunity costs convey the impression that the true costs of many institutional activities are very much understated by our traditional practices of cost analysis. On the other side, we should also look for implicit revenues and benefits that we deliver up to society as a whole, to the surrounding community, or—within the institution—the delivery of unrecorded value from one part of the institution to another. We have reason to be interested in this wherever a change is contemplated or a significant opportunity arises for spelling out what is really accomplished. For example, in most universities, faculty members spend significant amounts of time on administrative duties —for internal administration of departmental affairs and, often, in assisting with myriad tasks of keeping the institution going. A man-hour of faculty time, from this standpoint, tends to be regarded as having a zero cost to the institution. Committees are appointed with gleeful abandon by deans, presidents, and athletic directors (not to mention the committees brought into life by other faculty committees!).

There is good reason for caution toward proposals to tighten up and eliminate the essential types of institutional involvement by both faculty and students—involvements that absorb energy but that also help to bind the institution together. At the same time we should take thought to the uncontrolled proliferation of demands on faculty time, and we must be wary of proposals that assume—as do some current proposals for increasing classroom teaching assignments—that the reallocations would occur at no cost to the institution.

Variations in Volume of Activity. It is something of an achievement simply to put cost (figures) into the proper buckets and thereby to estimate the relative sizes of cost components. But there are wide classes of managerial decisions for which the relevant question is: How much will costs vary with volume? Some examples are: (1) How much will a summer session add to the total annual cost of building maintenance and utilities? (2) If ten additional students, beyond the expected norm of twenty-five, enroll in English 103, will this add to teaching costs in the English department, and will it reduce teaching costs anywhere else? (3) If the target size of the entering freshmen class in the school of engineering is increased permanently by one hundred students, how much will this increase expected institutional costs in the first year, the second year, the third year, and so forth? (4) If a new program is initiated for part-time adult students, how much will this increase the work load in the registrar's office?

In these simple examples, the pertinent measures of volume or usage vary from case to case. The summer session will require, say, sixty days of regular in-term maintenance attention for the buildings that are used, as against the shut-down summer level. The ten extra students in English 103 may add no costs at all, or may add some work for an instructor's assistant, depending on the staffing policy; but where will the enrollees come from, and will any costs be eliminated because one or more other courses have to be canceled, or will all other courses still be offered and staffed without any cost changes?

The permanent increase in engineering's freshman class size will increase costs everywhere in the institution, but its full effects on teaching costs, year by year, depend on: how many entering engineering students stay as engineers, transfer to other programs within the institution, or flunk out or withdraw entirely, year by year; and the distribution of the first-year, second-year, and so forth, students over courses in engineering, in physical science, in humanities, and elsewhere.

We can measure different aspects of the instructional volume of an institution or a program by using the following quantity indicators: (1) head-count students, or those who have educational exposure and are present in the institution at some time during a year; (2) student credit hours, derived by multiplying the enrollment in each course by the number of semester or quarter credits each enrolled student earns in the course; (3) FTE student enrollment per year, obtained by adjusting total head-count enrollment for the extent of part-timeness; (4) number of degrees granted, a measure of net certification output; and (5) value-added, which means taking, for each student, a measure of his or her learning state at the start of a program, a measure at the end of it, and estimating the amount of improvement.

Each of these quantity indicators may need to be measured separately, according to type of program or discipline and by the level of degree. In some institutions and state systems, an effort has been made to construct a consolidated quantity measure by weighting the number of FTE students at each degree level by some factor to give approximate reflection of the differing instructional burdens of the various levels of student. For example, lower division students might have a weight of unity, upper division undergraduates a weight of 1.5, first-stage graduate students a weight of 2.5, and second-stage graduate students a weight of 3.5. The weighted FTE enrollment approach has been used to justify work-load budget requests. But there is a degree of circular reasoning in using it for cost analysis, because the weights are intended to reflect approximate cost differentials.

For some analyses of cost variations, one measure may be inherently better than another. The use of many student services, for example, varies according to the number of head-count students and not according to full-time equivalency, whereas direct teaching resources are geared to FTE enrollment. But the choices between volume measures sometimes depend on the policy attitude of the decision-maker. Some believe that resource allocation should be evaluated according to the amount of institutional exposure it delivers, and for this purpose, cost per head-count student is a good measure. Others want a measure corrected for full-time equivalency, because they are interested in the volume of instructional exposure. Still others, believing that net certification output is all important and that uncompleted academic programs are worthless to the student or to society, want to see cost per degree granted, which means eliminating from the volume count all students who do not persist to the degree. Value-added is the most sophisticated of these measures and has been the least used.

It is also desirable to keep track of the number of visitors to the college information center, the number of books checked out of the library, and the number of general ledger transactions per month in the accounting system. These are typical measures of the level of activity for various intermediate services or functions, and the costs of these services vary with changes in these volume indicators, not with changes of more general institutional volume rates such as enrollment.

Now let us look at the evidence about the way costs vary with volume changes. Here are some activities whose costs rise less than proprotionately with increase of volume and whose cost per unit therefore falls: (1) The unit cost of instruction falls as enrollment in a particular course rises, subject only to the availability of classroom facilities (the mode of course organization does have to shift with the addition of instructional assistants and other aids to instruction at high levels of enrollment). (2) The unit cost of a kilowatt hour or a computer computation is reduced at high average levels of volume, because the basic equipment investment is characterized by economies of scale. (3) The general administration budget on a campus can be held to a declining percentage of the total campus budget for the larger, as against smaller, campuses of a multicampus system.

Unit costs may increase with increases in the volume of activity. Familiar causes, in industrial plants, are the saturation of available plant capacity and the necessity to pay premium overtime to the work force at high levels of output. Similarly, this can happen when excessive enrollment is piled into an academic institution or various subunits. But the first evidence of saturation is likely to be a higher level of delay, frustration, and compromise in filling the program needs of students, while the dollar expenditures per student may actually continue to fall.

Less obvious, but more interesting analytically, are the kinds of activities whose unit costs increase for reasons of technology or organization when volume increases. In very large library collections, book acquisition and processing require extensive search of the existing collection and its records, and the staff also searches for unusual and rare items to add to the already large, specialized collections. The unit cost of acquisition and processing (apart from the actual purchase price of each new book) therefore may be higher in large libraries than in small ones.

Administrative costs for security also may increase more than proportionately with increases in campus size, partly because police duties must be handled in a more impersonal and professional way at the largest campuses, and partly because the big campus is like a big city—it has low social cohesion and, as a result of size alone, special problems of controlling mass behavior.

Efficient Cost. The cost estimates generally made in universities are much cruder than the cost curves we remember from the economics textbook. The economist's short-run average cost curve for one product is drawn by assuming that it is known how to find the least-cost way of producing each possible level of output, and then connecting the points. This, of course, assumes much more than we usually know about cost behavior in higher education. When we trace a cost magnitude, we get a unit-cost figure at one particular level of output, which is all that can be observed for a recent time period. To get another point, we have to go to the historical record for some other time period when the output rate was different, or we have to get a cost estimate from some other institution that is comparable in other respects but operates at a different output level. And then, if we connect the two points, we do not necessarily have a segment of the economist's short-run average cost curve. Why not? Because the economist assumes that, with a fixed and known technology and a complete menu of input prices, it has already been decided how to get the best input combination for each level of output. But our cost observations are simply snapshots of the ongoing situation, and we cannot assume that anything has been optimized in the management of each activity. In fact, our cost investigations are often made with a view to discovering how to do better.

Suppose, for instance, that we had data from three similar four-year colleges as shown in Table 1. Plotting these as shown in Figure 2, we find that, for this narrow range of enrollment, some of the costs are higher than others *at the same enrollment level.* The best approximation we can make to *efficient cost* for this set of data is to find the lowest cost per student at each of these enrollments and connect the points, as is done in Figure 2.

We have two kinds of evidence that recorded cost experience is often far above minimum costs. First, plots of cost per student year, for each general type and quality of institution, show that some institutions have much higher unit costs than others at the

Table 1

	Year One	Year Two	Year Three	Year Four
College A				
Enrollment	800	850	850	750
Cost/student	$2400	$2300	$2400	$2500
College B				
Enrollment	600	650	750	800
Cost/student	$3000	$2700	$2400	$2500
College C				
Enrollment	850	900	950	850
Cost/student	$2300	$2200	$2100	$2600

same level of enrollment. A second kind of evidence comes from Radner and Miller (1970), who studied the variations in student/faculty ratios (faculty being one major cost component). Strictly speaking, this is an input ratio rather than a cost measure, because the salaries of faculty are not included. But here, too, the student/faculty ratios varied widely for each type of institution, even after corrections were made for the percentage of graduate enrollment.

Part of the observed range of variations can be explained by institutional policy commitments to comfortable size or to quality, and part can be explained by differences in disciplinary composition of programs and by the presence of programs that are high in resource cost because they are in transition. Radner has sought to derive indications of the efficient frontier of student/faculty ratios. Carlson (1972) utilized a nationwide sample of institutions of each type. Data included enrollment, program mix, faculty, and cost characteristics. Carlson estimated the lowest combination of resource-inputs required for each average amount of enrollment and other characteristics—in other words, the efficient frontier of average resource usage. He also estimated the incremental change in resource-inputs for a change in enrollment and other characteristics and computed the distance between the actual observations and the points on the frontier.

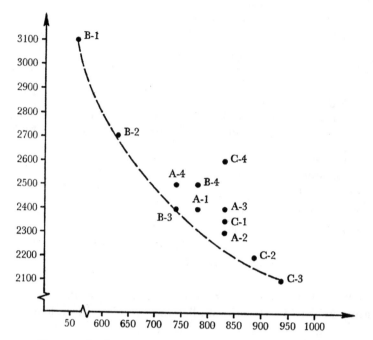

FIGURE 2. Cost observations and "efficient cost."

    In performing this analysis, Carlson assumed that production
and cost relationships were dependent on other measurable characteristics of the institutions. He included such variables as student
mix and program mix in the analysis, and he also performed separate analyses for each type of institution: public and private universities, public and private comprehensive colleges, and public
and private liberal arts colleges. For each type of institution, Carlson used a linear programming procedure to calculate both average
production behavior and the "best possible" resource utilization.
    Two other approaches to the measurement of efficient cost
deserve mention. Large-scale simulation models of the WICHE–RRPM
type can be used to estimate what the consequences of growth and
program shifts might be, provided that the estimated structure (the
set of estimated coefficients) remains stable over the range of possible changes (NCHEMS, 1973a, 1973b). Richard Judy of the University of Toronto and his colleagues at the Systems Research
Group (1972) have developed the CAMPUS model in various forms.

Its purpose is to throw light on possible efficiency improvements in an institution.

Finally, Howard Bowen and Gordon Douglass (1973) have made interesting use of the idea of putting together constructed cost functions from simple building blocks, to explore the effects of course proliferation, class size, and mode of instruction.

Cost trends. In *The Turning Point,* Jenny and Wynn (1972) find that, for forty-eight private liberal arts colleges, the annual compound rate of growth in total expense per FTE student year was 6.8 percent from 1960 to 1970 (see their Table E, p. 11). The compound rate for the period from 1960 to 1968 was 6.4 percent, implying considerable cost acceleration toward the end of the decade. Total income per student grew at the rate of 6.4 percent for the decade and 6.3 percent for the period from 1960 to 1968, showing a widening gap or cost-income squeeze. The number of institutions covered in this study is large enough so that these findings convey a clear message about the cost problems of one major type of institution.

Earl Cheit (1971) covered a few private four-year colleges and examined trends in the other types of institutions, public and private. Forty-one institutions were interviewed in detail, and their data on broad categories of cost and income were assembled and analyzed. From this, Cheit made the judgment that twelve of the forty-one institutions were "not in financial trouble," eighteen were "headed for financial trouble," and eleven were "in financial difficulty." Cheit examined components of the income and expenditure patterns of the institutions surveyed to find likely causes of financial pressure. For the institutions in financial difficulty, these cost factors were general inflation, faculty salary increases, student aid increases, rising expenses of dealing with campus disturbances, and some cost rises associated with growing institutional responsibilities and aspirations. Cheit also found that the squeeze was accounted for by lags in the growth of income needed to offset these rising costs. Cheit (1973b) performed a follow-up of his earlier study and found that a number of colleges had achieved better control of their costs. (But in late 1973 and into 1974, inflationary factors were causing severe new cost problems in all types of institutions.)

Costs can increase either because unit prices go up or because of increases in the amount used of particular resources. Recent evidence concerning both of these factors is reviewed in Chapter Eight.

Longer-term cost and productivity trends in higher education are also important as background for current concerns. June O'Neill's valuable study (1971) gives estimates of the long-term changes in cost per student credit hour, both in current dollars for each year and with correction for trends in input prices. Not adjusting for changes in the mix of student credit hours produced by level (graduate, upper division, lower division), she found that the current-dollar cost per credit hour rose by 3.4 percent per year, compounded, from 1930 to 1967. When input price trends were removed, this fell to 0.3 percent per year. Further adjustments, to deal with the change in mix by using cost-based weights for the different levels of instruction, cut the compound rate of increase still further to 0.1 percent per year.

The O'Neill study is required reading for all of us. She observes that the quality content of instructional output may well have changed over this long interval, but that, aside from the adjustments for student credit hours by level, it is not possible to make specific corrections for quality changes. Still, we are left with the impression that the real productivity of instruction in higher education may have been constant or slightly declining over a long period. In the face of general increases in output per man-hour in other sectors of the American economy, this implies that higher education has to make increasing relative claims for society's resources for what it produces.

O'Neill was able to make only rough adjustments in her study for the use of higher education resources to produce outputs other than instruction. This entanglement of input usage is a characteristic problem in cost analysis, and it means that there must remain some doubt about the interpretation of many of our findings.

Trends in instruction costs will remain difficult to analyze until we have a better understanding of the cost interactions between instructional, research, and other activities. Even within the domain of instruction, the costing of particular programs is a vexing problem because of interdependence between programs in the flow of students and in the reliance of several instructional areas on joint resources. Thomas J. Walsh and the present author contributed a comment to *Minerva* (1971) concerning the pattern of expenditures and budgets for sponsored (or as some say, organized) research. In this, we updated UC Berkeley data reported by Betz and Kruytbosch and commented on the problems of interpreting how much resource use is induced by the presence of sponsored research on a campus.

Cost measurement should be done in all institutions with a weather eye to the problems of joint resources, cost interaction among programs, and joint contributions to the objectives of the institution.

Analysis of Costs of Graduate Education

Graduate education is intertwined with: (1) basic and applied university research, both extramurally funded and institutionally supported; (2) undergraduate education, through sharing of the same faculty and other institutional resources, through the involvement of graduate students in undergraduate instruction, and through the incorporation (after time lags) of research findings and graduate instructional materials in undergraduate courses; (3) public service obligations, because some graduate students are involved in public service functions (for example, medical residents with duties of patient care in hospitals), and because some research activities have significant public service aspects.

Joint processes make for difficulties of cost analysis. Cost analysis for graduate education is thus an inherently complicated problem. Costs analyses differ in design and content depending on the breadth of view taken, the purpose for which cost magnitudes are to be estimated, and the time horizon contemplated for decisions or policy recommendations.

National Costs. What does graduate education (a type of program, or in total) cost a nation in the long run (a generation or two), and what proportion of society's efforts should be devoted to it? A student completing a graduate program has an expected career life of thirty to forty years, in teaching, research, a practicing profession, or (occasionally) a career only indirectly related to graduate preparation. A university constructs new buildings with an expected service life of forty years or more. The United States gains the fruits of new knowledge and perspective from the research activities it supports over a time horizon of a generation or more. Seen in this light, graduate education has imputed costs and consequences that raise significant questions about what the purposes and priorities of the nation are and ought to be.

For this kind of cost analysis, it is important to estimate both operating and (annualized) capital costs of graduate education, and also to estimate these as real social costs, including the social opportunity costs of resources employed, going beyond and behind the estimates of money costs (to obtain estimates of true opportunity costs) and beyond the question of specific financing by individuals, institutions, or agencies, to count up all contributed resources, however these contributions are financed.

Student Costs. At the opposite end of the spectrum is the estimate, by or for an individual, of the cost of attendance in a graduate program. This cost often has a large bearing on the decision whether to start and the subsequent decisions whether to persist in the program. Before committing to graduate study, the prospective entrant can first estimate annual fees paid to the institution where he or she will study, the other cash outlays for living, and cash outlays specific to study (books, supplies, and so forth). If the student knows how long the program will take, he or she can estimate the gross cash outlay to complete it and, against this, offset expected annual cash earnings (during the academic year and the summers), any fellowship or grant income, spouse's earnings, and gifts from parents and others. This gives the student an estimate of net cash outlay to complete the program, to be financed from prior savings or by borrowing. Both outlay and income are subject to variances and contingencies (will an assistantship or a fellowship be renewed? what if we have a baby?). The time required to complete the program is also subject to numerous risks, including academic failure, financial pressure, and variation in degree progress—especially, for doctoral students, the time to complete a dissertation.

Two controversial elements in the calculation of the individual's cost forecast for graduate study are income foregone during the process (the difference between earnings while in graduate study and what would have been earned if not in graduate study) and living standard foregone (penury is an actual delight to few people). Foregone incomes surely figure in broad estimates of costs to society, but whether they also influence the prospective student's decision to enter is debated.

The prospective student's estimate of total cost is, of course, affected by the probability of completion and the estimated number of years of study. Looking ahead, the prospective student faces a decision tree, with various branching points on both the expense and the income aspects of the future interval of study. There are well-known methods of summing up the expected value over all paths of a decision tree, but it is hard to estimate the costs and incomes and probabilities of various events.

The prospective student could also use an interest rate or discount rate for an investment calculation and compare the discounted money outlay for graduate study with (assuming successful completion of the program) the discounted value of the income differential for the subsequent career relative to what his or her stream of annual future incomes would be if he or she went directly to work without going through graduate study. This kind of investment calculation is seldom performed by students as a basis for their decisions to enter graduate programs, and there are other, nonpecuniary factors that may control the decision. In a very rough-cut way, however, students often try to think through their choices with some attention to the economic worth to them of graduate education (or the size of the economic penalty), and economists have performed these kinds of calculations in studies of the "returns to education" (Becker, 1964; Schultz, 1963; Eckhaus, 1973; Schultz, 1972). Besides serving as some guide to personal decisions these estimates of investment returns of education are a partial (and some believe, a dominant) basis for social decisions about the merits of investments in human capital.

Institutional Costs. When a university contemplates establishing a new graduate program, it must estimate, from the present initial base of faculty, library, building space, and other capabilities, the likely, long-range, incremental commitments of costs and the long-range incremental income from outside sources. Only if this is done can the university make a reasoned planning choice, for the difference between long-range incremental costs and long-range support expectations is the amount that the university will have to support from general institutional funds.

The new program will have start-up costs and transitional operating costs each year on the way to steady-state viability. A discipline or professional field, to be offered in a comprehensive way, needs to cover all areas of specialized study, and each of these specialties may need several faculty at different levels of maturity. This faculty cadre, in turn, may need to be supported adequately by a group of postdoctoral researchers and technicians. The estimated size of this faculty and professional staff, together with the number of graduate students needed to justify the program financially and give it academic vitality, is the critical mass of the program. Suppose that there is an estimated *critical mass* of the program (measured in total number of affiliated faculty, FTE faculty allocated to the program, head-count and FTE students, other staff, and associated space and equipment) for steady-state viability. (Unfortunately, there are only primitive notions of what this viability requirement is in most fields.) A comparison of the present base with the steady-state requirement provides an indicator of how much enrollment the new program would have to attract, in relation to current and future enrollment demands in other fields, and how much expansion or redirection of resources, including faculty, the institution would have to finance from its own or external sources.

A second cost issue is the speed of transition from the present to steady-state viability. Very small graduate programs typically have high costs per student year, because the nucleus and start-up costs have to be borne but enrollment is small. A slow and deliberate transition over a period of many years, which is all that many universities can afford, has the predictable consequence that unit costs are high and that drawing power (in competition with other, established programs) for high-quality students and recognition of the program's academic quality are poor. At some risk, an institution can avoid some of these transition costs by a planned, rapid build-up to steady-state size. Perhaps it is a commentary on the state of management in universities that this kind of simple planning exercise is often not done (especially by the proponents of a new program, who at the time of a decision to initiate want to show that, like pregnancy, the decision to begin can be painless and even rather fun), and different paths to viability are not considered.

There are radical differences in the costs of achieving steady-state viability for major graduate programs. Here are a few of the author's guess-timates in 1971 prices:

(1) Medical school (175 FTE faculty, medical undergraduates entering class of 130, plus clinical residents, and basic science PhDs equal in number to the medical undergraduates): capital cost, $100 million; operating expenditures, $30 million per year (excluding hospital subsidies and major extramurally funded research projects).

(2) Law school (100 FTE faculty, 1000 total students): capital cost (building and library), $5 million; operating expenditures, $4 million per year, excluding major research funding.

(3) A physical or biological science field (30 FTE allocated faculty, 240 FTE doctoral students): capital costs (building and equipment), $5 million; operating expenditures, $1.75 million per year, excluding major extramurally funded research projects.

(4) A social science field (20 FTE allocated faculty, 200 FTE doctoral students): capital costs, $2.5 million, including $0.5 million for special library collection; operating expenditures $0.75 million per year, excluding major extramurally-funded research.

Not only are there large differences from field to field in the estimated amounts of capital budget, operating expenditures, and size of faculty and student body; but all of these amounts are much larger than is usually envisioned in the early phases of discussion and planning of major new commitments. Smaller planning targets than these, however, are likely to mean that a university launching a new program will later be in for some unpleasant surprises when the true size of needed funding becomes evident.

Major universities that already have a wide span of graduate programs and undergraduate curricula face a different issue than that of estimating the costs of planned choices of new directions. Here are three interesting problems for program cost analysis in an ongoing situation: (1) Where are the university's resources now going (that is, considering the total operating expenditures of the institution in a given year, what amounts out of that total can be imputed to each existing program, including a segregated cost for each graduate program)? (2) What should the cost be to provide needed improvements in specified graduate programs—especially improvements that money can buy in the near term? (3) What present costs would be avoidable if specified programs were dropped, and over what time horizon would expenditure reductions be realizable?

The first of these questions is the sort that cost-simulation schemes—such as the NCHEMS/WICHE Resource Requirements-Prediction Model—are intended to answer (1973). Cost imputation is intended to classify the range and levels of academic programs; obtain statistical indicators of major interactions among parts of the academic program span of the institution; and assemble estimates of the resources employed and the students enrolled, by standard resource-input and student categories. Then the model is run to obtain total direct costs, total costs, and costs per student for each academic program or major. The computer program contains allocation rules for dividing up various cost pools among their uses.

This sort of cost imputation has its limitations (particularly in the arbitrary treatment of allocations from cost pools in the handling of the problems of jointness).

Nevertheless, it is instructive to discover that costs per student year may vary between academic fields by as much as a factor of ten, that some undergraduate programs apparently cost more per student year than do some graduate programs, and that even direct costs per student year are subject to very large variations between fields in the same university. Such differentials are not necessarily bad, and may be mainly rooted in real differences in the way in which academic work has to be conducted in various fields. However, the disclosure of differentials of large magnitude often triggers useful questions among those responsible for seeing to the effective use of resources.

Other approaches to program costing, essentially based on budget analysis and cost accounting techniques, have also been used to arrive at cost imputations for graduate programs. Powel and Lamson (1972) did an exhaustive review and critique of these methods, and McCarthy and Deener (1972) wrote a useful, brief commentary on the problem, based on Powel and Lamson.

It should be noted parenthetically that the usual methods

of working from a university's data to arrive at a cost imputation for each graduate program provide a point estimate, for a fiscal year or other time period, of what total program costs or unit costs actually were. Such estimates are not necessarily what the economist wants as the elements of a firm's cost function relating total cost to total output of a good, for such a cost function presumes that for each possible output level, the technology is known, the input prices are known, and the inputs are combined to minimize costs for that output rate. Each point on the cost function is an efficient point—costs could be higher if the production process is not optimized for that output rate, but they cannot be lower with the given technology and input prices. Quite apart from such issues as accuracy, data definition, and allocation techniques for estimating graduate costs, it cannot be presumed that a cost estimate, when completed, is an efficient point. I return to this question below.

The second institutional question about costs is: What are the incremental costs of making improvements in a given program? Desired improvement resources typically include: added faculty positions, to round out coverage of specialties in the field or to add intellectual strength; fellowships and assistantships, to attract more and better graduate students; equipment, library, and space allocations; and research support, both for faculty and for advanced graduate students. If the program in question is small, such requests may simply mean that those who want more resources are seeking to expand toward steady-state viability. But because of the competition for resources, decision-makers at higher levels have to ask whether key people in the program would make use of additional resources to bring about improvement of the program. And they also have to decide whether the requests have sufficient priority to be met from resources available for allocation at the margin.

The third institutional question is: What costs could be avoided if a specified graduate program were dropped? This painful question is now arising with some frequency in hard-pressed graduate institutions, and many factors—equity, academic policy, and appropriate mechanisms of decision—outweigh cost considerations. Analysis usually demonstrates that immediate reductions of expenditures are small. Reallocation of clerical and administrative staff is relatively easy. But to reassign or vacate faculty positions—except those of the most junior staff—often takes time measured in years rather than months, unless the university faces a genuine fiscal emergency and so is ready to take the risk of setting aside tenure. When a program is closed, a university has obligations to graduate students who are in the pipeline; if senior faculty leave for other positions and can shift their graduate candidates with them, the transition is easier and faster.

Funding Agency Costs. Many graduate programs and their research activities are supported by funds from various sources outside of the university. Foundations, federal agencies, and private donors may supply fellowships. Funds for research projects may come from any of numerous extramural sources, and are used in part for the salaries of faculty and graduate students associated with these projects. Funding agencies often stipulate that funds are to be used for specific purposes. Adequate financial stewardship and grant administration by the university can cope with these agreements, up to a point. But when several components of funding are used to support intertwined activities, funding agencies can never be quite certain that they are getting what they think they are paying for.

Costs of Jointness of Research and Undergraduate Instruction. In most American universities, some faculty members perform only one function and all of their salary costs can be assigned to that. But most faculty members do some undergraduate and some graduate teaching, supervise some dissertation research, and perform some research—with or without extramural funding. Methods of measuring the pattern of faculty effort include: time-reporting by every faculty member each term by means of a simple accounting form;[1] in-depth interviews of a sample of faculty members to determine the time spent on numerous distinct activities and the mapping of these activities onto single or joint outputs;[2] and work-

---

[1] Such public universities as the University of Texas and Ohio State University have done this in order to report in prescribed ways to the state budgetary authorities.

[2] University of California (1970). This method has been amplified and refined in the recommended scheme of measurement published by the NCHEMS task force on Faculty Activity Analysis.

sampling or diary-keeping for specified periods (Williams, Blackstone, and Metcalf, in press).

All of these approaches involve self-reporting by faculty members. Their typical disclosure of a very long work week and of a large amount of teaching time is regarded with skepticism by public budget authorities partly for that reason. But the problem is deeper. If a faculty member does less of one thing, what is he likely to do more of? One indication of complementarity is that graduate students usually seek out, for graduate courses and as supervisors of dissertation research, those well-known members of the department who are active in published research and who are most likely to have extramurally-supported projects. The teaching of these faculty members is likely to be at the frontier of the subject; when the time comes for placement in academic employment, they have wide contacts and their recommendations carry weight; and they have funds to support dissertation candidates. It may seem odd that many of these key faculty members also share vigorously in undergraduate course teaching, an activity that almost surely competes at the time margin with the more closely-coupled activities of research and graduate teaching.

Salary costs of faculty may be funded partly from extramural grants: for full-time research in the summer months; sometimes for research leave during part of the academic year with concomitant release from other departmental duties; and occasionally a regular expectation (that some major private universities have recently found is risky) that extramural grants will take care of a part of the faculty member's academic-year basic salary.

Can more of both graduate education and research be accomplished because they are performed in the same setting? More specifically, is the amount of graduate education likely to be increased if research funding is augmented while departmental funding for graduate instruction is held constant? The answers differ from field to field, but in those areas of scholarship where dissertation research requires supported outlays and where there is a close research relationship between faculty supervisor and dissertation candidate, the answer is probably yes (Breneman, 1970).

In scientific departments with research establishments that

involve faculty, graduate students, other research and technical personnel, and significant amounts of space and equipment, Breneman found that graduate student places have to be rationed because of requirements of laboratory space, equipment access, and time for detailed faculty supervision. He found that this produces incentives to screen entering graduate students carefully, start them early on research that will lead to a dissertation, monitor progress carefully, and keep the elapsed time to the degree as low as possible.

In such research establishments, one possible indicator that the size of research activity exceeds a minimum for academic viability might be the presence of an exceptionally high ratio of postdoctoral and professional researchers (not holding faculty appointment) to the number of graduate students in that field. Disciplines vary in the extent to which a year or two of postdoctoral research experience is a *de facto* necessity for the young academic and in the extent to which postdoctoral research costs are built into the resource base. Thus, comparisons of different fields in the same university would not be as indicative as would interuniversity comparisons in the same field. After some point, the presence of these nonfaculty, non-graduate-student researchers is likely to increase the flow of research results while having small marginal effects on the quantity or quality of graduate education.

If we examine the implications of reducing the amount of funded research in laboratory fields while seeking to hold graduate enrollment and quality of work constant, several effects can be foreseen. One is the selection of dissertation research topics that will not cost much in terms of equipment and supplies. In some fields, this effectively debars the PhD candidate from doing thesis work on mainstream topics. Another probable consequence is that, because money is not forthcoming for part-time employment of graduate students, more of them will seek other employment prior to completion of the dissertation—the elapsed time to the degree will increase for many, the risk of noncompletion will increase, and the reduced amount of cooperative involvement between the faculty supervisor and the graduate student will have adverse affects on the quality of the research apprenticeship.

The above observations also bear on the question of competitive quality or reputation of graduate departments in a given field.

Universities that are fortunate to have strong academic cadres for graduate study in a field can expect that: their key faculty will compete successfully for research grants that are awarded on the basis of peer group judgments of scientific merit; their key faculty will attract exceptionally able graduate students and will face strong demands to provide places for postdoctoral researchers; and the strong department will make intense demands for space and for support budgets from institutional funds to accompany the large-scale, extramural funding and the robust doctoral program for which it is responsible. In this competitive milieu, the basic rule is: The better and richer a program, the greater its ease of attracting additional resources and people. The main variables relating to quality are all positively correlated with each other.

In most of the humanities and some of the social sciences, the main scholarly tradition is much more one of individual work, by both faculty member and dissertation candidate, than in the technology of graduate education presumed above. Major investments in specialized library collections may be required to support the work of specialists. The research performance of an individual scholar in these fields is a function mainly of his quality of mind and his energy—and of the availability to him, at critical intervals in his work, of extended periods of uninterrupted time for reflection and writing. The scholar benefits from an atmosphere of stimulus and striving among his colleagues, and a good department in such a field has that atmosphere. The same general considerations of research productivity hold for dissertation candidates as for established scholars, with the added element that the faculty sponsor of a candidate can help him or her enormously by encouraging wise choice of an important problem for a dissertation, and by finding ways to assist the candidate with the craft of scholarship and with access to needed library materials and primary sources.

The question of jointness, especially as a matter of the size of funding for research relative to the size of the graduate department, has a much less clear answer in these fields than in those employing laboratories, capital equipment, and a style of research that requires group interaction.

Costs of Jointness of Graduate Education and Undergraduate Instruction. Does the presence together of graduate education and undergraduate instruction enchance or inhibit the quality and intensity of undergraduate study? How does the presence of the graduate operation affect the costs of undergraduate instruction? How does the presence of undergraduate instruction affect the institution's costs of offering graduate instruction? In other words, does the multiprocess, multiproduct university display higher academic efficiency than the single-product undergraduate institution (and, one might add on the side of research, than the single-product, free-standing research corporation)?

In Chapters Two and Four I explored conceptual issues of complementarity, independence, and substitution. Stephen Dresch (1973) argues that graduate education is much less subsidized at the margin than is generally supposed. This becomes clear when the cost relations between graduate education and undergraduate instruction are reexamined in the light of complementarities and contributions to undergraduate instruction (partly through the use of graduate students as part-time instructors at low prices).

There is little doubt that, at the margin of faculty time, research and graduate instruction compete with undergraduate instruction. And there is competition between these activities at the budgeting margin for clerical support, library service, and various other inputs. It is also true that those immediately responsible for these activities usually feel that their domains are underfinanced. And, in fact, the institution may be attempting a menu of operations that exceeds available funds. Perceptions of inadequate financing do impose frustrations, but the possible relative starvation of undergraduate instruction in this competitive regime, where the aggregate may be underfinanced, is not really the issue. The issue is whether, in their inherent design as multiprocess, multiproduct organizations, universities can deliver a quality of undergraduate education equivalent to that offered by strong liberal arts colleges and do it more cheaply than the liberal arts colleges can, by sharing undergraduate and graduate resources (faculty, libraries, laboratories, and graduate students as instructional assistants). Judging whether the quality can be the same is difficult, for the university can offer the undergraduate student access to research libraries and laboratory equipment that the small single-function institution usually cannot afford at all, and it can also promise that the student will have some contact with distinguished senior faculty who are prominent in research. But the strong liberal arts colleges can promise that an able faculty will concentrate its full attention on the undergraduate student, a promise that the university cannot make. Nevertheless, the hypothesis of improved efficiency through the exploiting of joint resources by universities is an interesting one, and detailed comparative analyses are much needed.

To summarize, the total cost of a particular program of graduate education is a function of: the *scale* of resource comitment in the field, the size of the graduate program, and the interrelations of that program with research and undergraduate programs in the same field and with other neighboring academic areas; the *methodologies* of scholarship and the modes of graduate instruction and study that are specific to the field, and the standards of scholarship and style of work that are characteristics of it; the *quality* of the program and the intensity of aspirations for quality improvement (the latter receiving heavy transition funds from institutional sources if quality improvement is attempted on a crash basis); and the *efficiency* of use of resources, including (on a multiyear basis) the effectiveness of choice of a path of further development of the program.

Evidence about graduate education costs. The Gradcost Study (Powel and Lamson, 1972) and the McCarthy-Deener essay (1972), which was based on it, contained some empirical evidence of the range of cost per student year from field to field. Powel and Lamson had to hedge their use of such evidence very carefully, because of differences in the practices of institutions in assembling cost data, differences in definition, and so forth.

Table 2 presents comparative costs for master and doctoral programs as reproduced from Figures 3 and 4 of McCarthy-Deener (pp. 37, 38). To produce this table, Powel and Lamson adjusted cost data from a number of different studies by using a standard definition of the full-time equivalent student academic year. The costs estimated are direct instructional costs only. Many of the qualifications and reservations that need to be kept in mind in the examination of this evidence have been discussed earlier. What do the cost figures show? Here are some comments:

Table 2

AVAILABLE ESTIMATES OF RANGES OF UNIT COSTS: 1970 DOLLARS AND NINE-MONTH FTE STUDENT YEAR

Discipline	Number of Programs Offered in U.S.[a]	Number of Program Cost Estimates Available	Ranges[b] of Unit Costs — Direct Instruction	"Full"	Total
			MASTER'S PROGRAMS		
Humanities					
Classics	77	4	2000, 2000— 2500		
English	425	19	600, 800— 2500		
German languages	111	14	700, 800— 3600		
Philosophy	120	13	600, 600— 6200		
Romance languages	165	8	1000, 1100— 1700		
Social Sciences					
Anthropology	72	10	600, 900— 3200		
Business Admin.	262	19	400, 500— 1800		
Economics	194	15	600, 600— 2000		
Geography	101	16	300, 600— 3400		
History	361	16	700, 700— 1700		
Psychology	272	20	400, 500— 7000		
Sociology	191	15	500, 500— 1200		

"Full": For the few available studies presenting data by departments, the ratio of unit "full costs" (total costs exclusive of graduate student fellowships and assistantships and of separately budgeted research costs) to unit direct instructional costs ranged from 1.3 to 1.9.

Total: Total unit costs may be estimated by multiplying direct instruction unit costs by 1.3 to 1.9 and then adding the unit costs of graduate student fellowships and assistantships and of separately budgeted research, as may be appropriate.

Biological Sciences

Botany	84	6	2000,	2300—	3500,	3800
Zoology	98	6	2100,	2100—	2400,	2600

Physical Sciences

Astronomy	30	8	2200,	2400—	6700,	9000
Chemistry	299	22	600,	1500—	4500,	5000
Geology	120	12	1700,	2400—	5400,	7100
Mathematics	372	22	600,	600—	3300,	5500
Physics	256	20	400,	700—	4500,	4800

Engineering

Chemical	118	12	2100,	2500—	5500,	7100
Electrical	150	12	1300,	1500—	4000,	4800
Mechanical	143	12	1400,	1800—	4300,	6900

DOCTORAL PROGRAMS

Humanities

Classics	41	4	3000,	3700—	3700,	4600
English	92	9	1100,	1300—	2600,	3500
German languages	48	9	600,	800—	1600,	2000
Philosophy	65	8	1900,	2100—	3300,	4100
Romance languages	65	9	1400,	1500—	2600,	3400

Social Sciences

Anthropology	42	9	1600,	1800—	3200,	3400
Business Admin.	57	7	500,	1500—	3800,	7700
Economics	91	8	1300,	1900—	3300,	3600

For the few available studies presenting data by departments, the ratio of unit "full costs" (total costs exclusive of graduate student fellowships and assistantships and

Total unit costs may be estimated by multiplying direct instruction unit costs by 1.3 to 2.6 and then adding the unit costs of graduate student fellowships and assistantships and of

Table 2 (cont.)

Discipline	Number of Programs Offered in U.S. [a]	Number of Program Cost Estimates Available	Ranges[b] of Unit Costs — Direct Instruction	"Full"	Total
Geography	34	6	2200, 2900— 5600, 7700	of separately budgeted research costs) to unit direct instructional costs ranged from 1.3 to 2.6.	separately budgeted research, as may be appropriate.
History	91	8	1200, 2200— 3800, 5100		
Psychology	110	10	1100, 1700— 2900, 7600		
Sociology	73	9	1600, 1600— 4100, 4900		
Biological Sciences					
Botany	97	6	3300, 3900— 6900, 7300		
Zoology	95	6	3200, 3500— 4700, 7200		
Physical Sciences					
Astronomy	35	5	4000, 10,100— 15,500, 15,700		
Chemistry	125	13	1900, 2500— 6200, 6400		
Geology	67	8	4200, 4300— 11,100, 13,900		
Mathematics	102	11	1100, 1400— 3600, 6200		
Physics	113	9	1600, 2700— 7600, 11,100		
Engineering					
Chemical	73	7	2500, 4600— 8200, 9100		
Electrical	78	7	1700, 2800— 5600, 5600		
Mechanical	71	6	2500, 3600— 5700, 6900		

Note: Available estimates arose from only four separate studies, in most cases carried out at public colleges and universities.
[a] The basis used by Powel and Lamson (1972) for estimating the number of graduate programs offered in the United States in each discipline is described in detail in their paper.
[b] Cost ranges are presented in terms of the lowest, next to lowest, next to highest, and highest cost estimates. In McCarthy and Deener's opinion some of the figures giving the low ends of the ranges do not represent all the elements even of the direct instructional costs associated with a good quality graduate-degree program.
Source: McCarthy and Deener, 1972.

(1) The range from the two lowest to the two highest unit costs of every field is very wide. The high ones are usually as much as 300 to 400 percent of the low ones.

(2) For both types of degrees, the laboratory sciences and engineering show the highest maximum entries. But their minimum entries are below the maxima of the humanities and social science fields.

(3) Within each field, the range of unit costs for master's degree programs generally overlaps with that for doctoral programs.

(4) The four cost studies that Powel and Lamson used as their source contained estimates for only a small proportion of the total number of programs of each type. Had there been an estimate of unit cost for all programs in each field, the range would have been wider than is reported.

(5) Because research expenditures and organizations are important in association with graduate education, and because the above cost estimates may well understate the resources that have to be locally available to conduct graduate education, the contribution of graduate students to institutional and social product may be substantial, although adjustment is not made for it.

Powel and Lamson (1972) also performed some regression analyses, seeking to test the effects of program size and program quality (as indicated by Roose-Andersen ratings) on unit costs. They found statistically significant higher costs in the laboratory sciences and engineering than in the others. Otherwise, they could not report statistically strong results, although there were apparently some scale economies and some mild indications of a positive association between program quality and unit costs.

Existence of a wide spread in cost experience is confirmed by other types of analysis of college and university resource use. A Carnegie Commission on Higher Education report (1972, Chap. 3 and pp. 82–83) discussed the wide variations that can be found in cost behavior and gave tabular evidence of large variations in student/faculty ratios for each type of institution.

As I pointed out earlier in this chapter, Carlson (1972) used an extensive data file on individual institutions to do an econometric study of costs and of the production relationships at the achievable efficient frontier of resource utilization. He found that variations in cost per student were partly the result of differences in the proportions of undergraduate to graduate students and other defining characteristics of institutions. He also showed that there were significant distances between the average usage of each type of input and the best-practice usage, and that "the ratio of the average cost per student to the frontier cost per student for institutions with comparable characteristics and enrollment mixes ranges from 1.42 to 2.20 across categories of institutions."

Policy-makers can draw two broad inferences from this review of methods and evidence in the realm of cost analysis. First, there is valid reason for concern about the effectiveness with which academic resources are combined and used. Many institutions could do better than they have been doing. And second, valid differences arise from the differing characteristics of academic fields, differing design of programs within categories, and differences in the size, maturity and other characteristics of individual institutions. Thus, a single, uniform, national standard of permissible cost, or even a set of standards with one cost magnitude for each discipline, would do violence to the variety of academic programs in this very heterogeneous industry.

Cost per student year versus cost per degree granted. It is possible to take the estimated cost per student year in each field and, by applying the statistics of persistence and dropout over time (and assuming that the student who dropped out is an unrequited investment), calculate the effective institutional cost per degree granted (Balderston, 1970). Because attrition rates are often much higher in programs that have low costs per student year than in some of the programs with higher costs, the net cost per degree granted is sometimes lower in the latter. There is serious question about the validity of the assumption that the student who drops out of a program before receiving a degree has failed to achieve anything. The focus on effective cost per degree granted could be of interest, however, to institutional administrators who, using this as a criterion of review and even of budgeting, could stimulate graduate departments not merely to amass enrollment but also to pay close attention to final achievement of the degree. Criticisms of the details of curriculum and organization of graduate study imply the usefulness of such a change of focus (Breneman, 1971a and 1971b).

Figures for cost per degree granted are also of potential interest to those who are trying to estimate what subsidy costs the states or the federal government may need to bear to assure that a particular number of fully-trained professionals in a field will be forthcoming. The pertinent issue for this purpose is not the cost per enrolled student year but the cost per degree.

Summary

The appropriate cost concept should be used for each kind of decision about graduate education that is to be faced: long-range, social costs for national policy decisions; one of several forms of investment-cost analysis for a prospective student's decision about entering a graduate program; and, for the graduate institution's several types of decisions about graduate programs, the appropriate cost approach to each.

Costs are important, but are only part of the equation. Institutional cost analysis for graduate education is inherently complicated because of the jointness of processes and outputs. This factor, together with the wide variety of scales and technologies and the lack of standard definitions and measures, gives rise to varying estimates of costs, even according to a given cost definition approach. In addition, estimated costs can differ between institutions for the same activity because of differentials in the efficiency with which resources are combined. In the present state of the art, it is generally not possible to show conclusively the reasons for quantitative divergencies between cost estimates.

If federal agencies seek to establish cost standards for graduate education as a basis for national planning decisions or in conjunction with the establishment of financing and cost-reimbursement formulas, appropriate cost concepts should be used for different purposes. Different cost magnitudes or ranges will need to be developed for different types and technologies of graduate programs, and sound procedures for adjusting costs with trends in input-prices will be needed.

Chapter **8**

Varieties of Financial Stress

Many colleges and universities are facing several crises simultaneously: a crisis of internal governance and control; a crisis of confidence with major external constituencies; a crisis of philosophy and mission; a crisis of market position; and a money crisis. A sufficiently serious state of stress in any one of these areas will be communicated to the others, particularly to the financial area. And the ability to address problems in other areas will often depend on whether money problems can be solved or at least alleviated.

I prefer the term *stress* because *crisis* implies a peak of tension and then its end: death, or transfiguration, or sudden discovery of gold at the end of a money-raising rainbow. Most students of higher education finance agree that only one source is large enough and powerful enough to help all the institutions now facing financial stress—Uncle Sam. To produce a permanent easing of financial stress, the federal government would have to change its policies and allocate several billions of dollars per year of federal money to higher education.

The Higher Education Amendments, passed in 1972, authorized billions of dollars of new financial support to students and institutions of higher education. The amendments were based on substantial congressional inquiry, influenced by the Rivlin report (1969), the Carnegie Commission's recommendations (1971c), and other proposals.

The main appropriation actions of the Congress subsequent to these authorizations, however, have been for student aid. No university president can afford to wait for the full authorization package to materialize. Although federal policy may change, we are not likely to see basic change in the structure of higher education finance, but rather a number of piecemeal ameliorations. Financial stresses will probably persist through the present decade.

Financial Stress Defined and Evaluated

How did financial stresses accumulate? Why did they appear suddenly and almost simultaneously in the late 1960s, especially since the early 1960s had not revealed evidence of financial trouble in most universities? What are the specific varieties of financial crises to which the institutions and their constituencies must seek solutions (Smith, 1972)?

Earl F. Cheit (1971) arrived at a definition of financial stress. Many public institutions are required by law or state financial regulation to keep current expenditures within current income; they are not allowed to run an operating deficit even though their financial resources may be seriously inadequate. Some private institutions do, from time to time, dip into capital or reserves—run an operating deficit—without feeling that they are in long-range financial difficulty. Cheit cites the academic truism that each institution may expect to spend for current operations up to its current income. Neither good financial stewardship nor effective academic management requires an institution to more than break even each year.

Cheit, therefore, felt that the presence or absence of an operating deficit is not a good test of financial difficulty. He believes that the appropriate test is the adequacy of an institution's resources in relation to its mission. He said, "For purposes of this study, an institution is judged *in financial difficulty* if its current financial condition results in a loss of services that are regarded as a part of its program *or* a loss of quality" (Cheit's italics, p. 36). He points out that his definition accepts the institution's perception of its educational mission and academic standards. If its resources are inadequate to sustain that mission and that quality, then the institution is in financial stress. Given the wide variety of institutional types, sizes, and missions in American higher education, it is hard to set forth an external, objectified measure to replace the self-definitions of financial situation given by the individual institutions. Thus, we have no convenient and operational test of financial viability to apply directly to the observable accounting picture of an institution.

Cheit's findings are aptly summarized in the title of his monograph, *The New Depression*. He assembled data on costs, income, and enrollment trends and also gathered detailed interview information on a total of forty-one institutions classified into six groups, ranging from seven national research universities to five two-year colleges. He conducted most of the interviews that comprised his field work, and was assisted by several people who interviewed presidents and other senior officials at some of the institutions. Although Cheit emphasizes that this study (1971) cannot purport to be a strict statistical analysis applicable to all higher education in the United States, it was a serious effort to assess the situation for a group of representative institutions.

Cheit (1971) summarized for Representative Edith Green's Special Subcommitee on Education what he found:

> Almost three-fourths of the schools studied (71 percent) were either in financial difficulty or headed for it. The Carnegie Commission staff estimates (by a national projection of my sample) that two-thirds of the nation's colleges—enrolling three-fourths of the nation's students—are in financial difficulty or headed for it.
>
> My study found that all types of institutions are affected. The major private universities have been hit first, but the others are not far behind. Public and private alike are facing increasing financial trouble. No class of institution is exempt from the problem or free from financial trouble.

He went on to describe the logic of the cost-income squeeze

—a gap of several percentage points between the cost per student per year and the income per student per year—facing different types of institutions, and suggested that "the nation's colleges and universities need between 300 and 700 million dollars in additional operating income. When we recall that this would come from federal, state, local, and private sources in fifty states, it is hardly a frightening sum." Cheit concluded by urging the need for new federal programs to assist the student and to provide institutional support.

Alice Rivlin, in testimony (1971) before the same congressional committee, posed the question of whether there is really an emergency or crisis in higher education finance and then said: "Hard facts are difficult to assemble in this area. My own impression from available studies and conversations with higher educators is that there is no *general* (her emphasis) crisis of higher education finance." She noted:

There are several sets of factors affecting various kinds of institutions in various ways at the same time, some permanent and some temporary.

1. Some major research institutions are suffering from cutbacks in federal research programs or federally funded graduate programs . . .

2. Some, but by no means all, state-supported institutions are suffering from smaller than usual increases in state support . . .

3. Some institutions, especially private ones, are finding themselves overextended as a result of ambitious attempts over the last decade to improve the quality and variety of their programs . . .

4. Some institutions are suffering the combined effect of recent recession and inflation. Private institutions are the hardest hit. Private gifts have dropped sharply, although they seem likely to recover somewhat this year. Students are less likely in a recession to pay the difference between public and private tuition. At the same time, wages, salaries, and other costs have continued to rise steeply.

5. Some institutions no longer offer what students appear to want.

Rivlin concludes the litany of woes with this observation: "It is certainly not obvious that a program of general support for higher education is the appropriate answer to all or even most of these varied financial problems."

These different, or differently shaded, views of the nature and trend of financial position are cited to show the differences in the judgments of experts, and to point the way toward what may be needed for further diagnosis of the varieties of financial crisis.

Five Models of Stress

Five conceptually different models of financial stress are defined and discussed: expanded academic aspiration, time passing, stabilization after growth, conscientious overcommitment, and income tapering. Each is a stress model for an institution of higher education; any one institution may have some combination of these stresses accumulating at the same time.

Expanded Aspiration. To achieve this kind of stress, an institution established a number of new programs in areas of hot competition and recruited key faculty from a limited supply, ahead of enrollment growth. It developed new programs in areas of growing prestige—doctoral programs requiring heavy library or laboratory investment and substantial fellowship funds to enable successful competition for good students. This was done in many areas and moved the institution upward in academic status but also, inevitably, moved it outward toward the fiscal cliff.

Time Passing. This model is closely related to the stress from stabilization after growth, which might also be labeled *rising fixed commitments.* It is almost breathtakingly easy to experience stress from time passing, for two reasons: differentially growing cost factors push up institutional costs relative to income, and the institution ages. Consider the institution having, in base year 1960, three components of operating expenditure: A, amounting to $500,000; B amounting to $250,000; and C, amounting also to $250,000. Let component A grow in cost at the compound annual rate of 4 percent, component B at 6 percent, and component C at 8 percent. By 1970, the $1 million budget of 1960 will have grown to $1.74 million, with no change in actual operations or their productivity.

An annual rate of income growth of 5.75 percent would have been just sufficient to offset the cost rise. But if, in a second institutional example, the three components had been equal in 1960 at $0.33 million each, and if the growth in costs had been the same as in the first example, the budget would have grown to $1.83 million, or 5 percent more than in the first case. These differences in cost structure are not chosen accidentally, nor are the different rates of cost growth. Component A could be faculty wages, component C could be maintenance of fixed plant plus library, and component B could be all other overhead. The first example above could be an undergraduate college and the second a university.

Inflation in the prices of nearly all things universities buy accelerated strongly in 1973 and 1974 and underscored the cost-increasing effects of the passage of time. Fuel costs rose 30 percent or more in a few months during the "energy crisis" in the winter of 1973–1974. Construction wages and prices of building materials advanced rapidly, raising the cost of building maintenance even more rapidly than in previous years. Inflation seriously eroded the attempts of universities to control their costs in this period.

Simple aging—the increase of age and rank distributions of faculty, increase of seniority of administrative staff, increased age and maintenance requirements of buildings—is the other aspect of this model. To avoid upward cost pressure over time in each category, an institution would have to control the age and rank distribution of faculty for a number of years before the need for doing so became clearly evident. To illustrate the aging of faculty, let us assume that the institution has gone through a period of expansion in which mostly junior people were added to faculty. Thus, at the beginning of a given decade, 50 percent of the faculty were non-tenured, 10 percent were associate professors, and 40 percent were (youngish) full professors. Now let ten years pass, with no change in the total number of positions. In each year, let us say that one-fifth of the nontenured faculty comes up for promotion to associate professor and three-fourths make it. One-fourth of the associate professors comes up for promotion to full professor and three-fourths make it. Among the full professors (because the faculty is young), nobody reaches retirement age. By the end of the tenth year, here is the situation: the rank distribution is 10 percent assistant professors, 15 percent associate professors, and 75 percent full professors.

Stabilization after Growth. In this model of financial stress, the potential for trouble is primed by a substantial interval of past growth—significant numbers of new faculty and staff were added, mostly at the junior levels, and capital facilities in copious quantity were added although no old buildings were torn down (pressure of growth forced continued use of old buildings). Underlying the expanded institution is a rising budget for administration, for libraries, and for computer centers. With this priming force, the cost structure of the institution and the age distribution of its faculty and capital facilities cannot fail to produce later rapid increases of costs. The cost increases will not have been foreseen at the time of the expansion because the budget in the early years of expansion could be financed at low entry costs.

There is an interesting corollary to this model of stabilization. If the institution had been able to keep growing, it could have put off the evil day. But to do so, it would have had to grow at more than a linear rate in total faculty, total building space, and so on, and it would have had to keep income growing at least proportionally with enrollment growth. What institution can do all that indefinitely? We can predict that any institution that has been growing will be hit by the stresses of stabilization shortly after its growth tapers off.

Conscientious Overcommitment. In recent years, many universities increased their financial aid to students, not only to offset for needy students the effects of rising tuition, fees, and other costs but also to attract Black, Chicano, and other minority students previously excluded. Once entered into, the commitment to the individual student cannot be cut back, and the institution's first-year program commitment grows rapidly with each new group of students. These financial aid budget obligations, as Cheit points out, are a major source of cost increase for many universities.

Particularly in urban areas, many universities have sought, or had thrust on them, increased community responsibilities. These, too, are sources of budgetary strain. Conscientious commitments of an institution do not have to constitute a large fraction of the budget to produce a financial crisis. If the costs are high enough to produce imbalance when added to ongoing budget, and particularly if they grow at a more rapid percentage rate than other costs, they are enough at the margin to cause severe financial stress.

Income Tapering. The preceding models deal with the dynamics of prices, costs, and expenditures. This model is concerned with trends in income and the possibility that some income components are not sufficiently responsive over time to enable an institution to finance its cost pattern.

Cheit noted in his study (1973) of forty-one institutions that, overall, income trends had failed to keep pace with expenditure trends. Private institutions are hit by two basic income problems: the hazard of pricing the institution out of the market through tuition increases, and the decline of the purchasing power of endowment income. The latter may be offset by increased annual giving and by new capital gifts. But in recent years, increasing tensions between private institutions and their alumni and other donor constituencies have decreased income growth from gifts. Potential market resistance to increases in attendance costs is especially serious for private institutions that encounter increasing competition from publicly supported institutions, which have lower fees as well as enrollment spaces and political commitment to take all qualified applicants.

Universities face an additional problem. In the past few years, extramural research funds from federal agencies and foundations have grown more slowly or have actually declined. Most seriously affected are institutions that have counted on a portion of the direct costs of research to buttress academic salaries (and now must find other funds to meet these basic commitments), and those that have come to depend on the overhead (indirect cost recovery) rate as the budgetary base for other major institutional services such as libraries, computer centers, building space, and general administration.

Cost Trends

What are the various activity and program components in an institution's cost structure? To be considered are: the unit price of each type of resource used, and the trend in that unit price; the trend in the quantity used of each resource; and, because productivity rates of some resources improve over time while others may decline, the effect of productivity changes on the amount of service that the activity or program contributes to the institution.

There are, of course, many serious problems of data, of interpretation of the measures of both quantity and quality of each resource used, and of measures of the quality and quantity of services contributed. Universities differ, from one another and from other types of economic institutions, in their location in labor and other resource markets, in their uses of resources, and in their perceptions of the quality and quantity of the services produced. The best that can be offered here is a series of clues and judgments about the financial stresses caused by cost trends.

Unit Prices. Labor costs, according to the traditional rule of thumb, account for about 80 percent of the operating budget of an academic institution and so will be examined first. The general trend of faculty salaries has been recorded in the annual surveys of the American Association of University Professors. Salary trends for other categories of personnel in higher education have not been studied in the same detail, however, and are difficult to examine on a comparative basis because of wide differences in the definitions of administrative and staff positions and differences in labor market conditions.

Committee Z (Economic Status of the Profession) of the AAUP reported (*AAUP Bulletin,* June 1973) that average faculty salaries for all ranks had risen, after correction for inflation, by only 1.1 percent for the year from 1968–1969 to 1969–1970. (By contrast, in various years from 1955 to 1967, real faculty purchasing power had shown growth rates ranging from 3.2 percent to 4.4 percent per year.) In the late 1960s, institutions were having trouble keeping up with cost-of-living increases, and most professorial ranks—in both public and private institutions—were affected. Preliminary information concerning the 1970–1971 status of the profession showed that all-ranks average compensation failed to keep pace with the cost-of-living rise from 1969–1970 to 1970–1971 (AAUP, 1971).

One measure of institutional labor cost is the average faculty salary across all ranks and disciplines and the average salary of administrative staff across all ranks and types of jobs. This measure, unfortunately, combines the effect of changes in salary at each rank or position with the effect of a change in the roster of personnel and the percentage composition of the work force.

Data from the University of California on the change in unit price for a given type of labor are presented in Table 3. Faculty salaries have been adjusted, over the years, to keep pace with a peer group of major universities. Nonacademic salaries have been adjusted in accordance with findings of the California State Personnel Board studies of wage rates in comparable classifications in business and industry throughout the state.

Table 3 shows that weighted average administrative salaries over the twenty-year period from 1950 to 1970 rose at about the same compound rate as average faculty salaries, but during the decade from 1960 to 1970 faculty salaries rose at a lower rate than did nonacademic salaries. The averages are an amalgam of the respective job classification wage rates and the (possibly changing) mix of people in the various job classifications. Therefore, Table 3 also shows the compound rates of increase for three administrative classifications. These rates are significantly higher than the rates for academic salaries.

Also shown are the salaries of teaching assistants for the same years. Finally, three classifications in the library staff are shown. All three librarian positions showed higher rates of salary increase from 1950 to 1970 than did any of the faculty positions.

Two inferences can be drawn from these data. First, an institution that had a greater than average proportion of its employees in the administrative and subfaculty categories in 1950, and maintained these proportions from 1950 to 1970, has experienced a greater than average upward pressure on its costs. In addition, there has been a tendency to upgrade jobs and create supergrades in order to provide opportunities for salary advancement beyond the cost-of-living adjustments. Thus, the average salary of individuals has risen by more than the rates of increase shown in Table 3.

The second inference is that faculty became cheaper, at given ranks and steps, between 1950 and 1970, relative to teaching assistants and administrative staff of given ranks and steps. Institutions have some choices in determining whether to substitute one

Table 3

University of California Salaries, 1950 to 1970, and Compound Rates of Increase

Labor category[a]	Salary[b]			Compound annual rate of increase (percent)	
	1950	1960	1970	1950–1970[c]	1960–1970
Academic year faculty[d]					
Average faculty salary	$ 6,284	$10,255	$15,505	4.2	3.6
Assistant professor, II	5,040	7,536	10,700	3.8	3.6
Professor, II	8,190	12,900	17,900	4.0	3.3
Teaching assistant, half time	1,200	2,365	3,447	5.4	3.8
Monthly administrative salary					
Average administrative salary	313	432	645	4.1	4.1
Principal clerk, minimum	230	376	530	4.3	3.5
Accountant, minimum	370	676	1,048	5.8	4.5
Principal engineer, minimum	560	950	1,475	5.0	4.5
Librarian, I, minimum	240	415	627	4.9	4.3
Librarian, III, minimum	370	584	820	4.2	3.5
Campus librarian, yearly	10,800	20,325	35,000	6.05	5.6

[a] Roman numerals indicate steps in the salary schedule within the given labor category.

[b] Salary is stated in current dollars for each year, *not* corrected for changes in purchasing power.

[c] No salary range adjustment was made from 1969–1970 to 1970–1971. For the years 1950–1951 to 1969–1970, the compound rates of increase were: average faculty salaries, 4.4 percent; assistant professor, II, 4.0 percent; professor, II, 4.1 percent.

[d] Nine-month, academic year salary.

form of labor for another. Some institutions experienced little increase in the complexity and technology of their operations between 1950 and 1970. If so, and if they had an optimal balance of faculty with other staff in 1950, the sensible policy over the years would have been to hire relatively more faculty than administrators and, where feasible, substitute faculty labor for the kinds of administrative labor whose costs were increasing faster than faculty salaries.

I have pursued this analysis of unit costs and trends because it counters conventional explanations made during the last two decades about cost problems and rational responses to them. According to the conventional argument, faculty salaries are a major cost item, faculty salaries have been rising, and therefore universities should be finding ways to substitute other kinds of labor for faculty labor. Yet in at least one major institution, the cost of other kinds of labor has increased faster than faculty costs.[1]

Commodity Prices. As we turn to other costs of operation, we again look for changes in unit prices. First we observe what has happened to unit prices of the same items. After that, we can look at quality upgrading and increases in volume of various items. The wholesale price index of industrial commodities rose 19.6 percent in total from the base period of 1957–1959 to 1971. Individual components of the index show large differentials, however. Rubber and plastic products rose only 6.1 percent and furniture and duraables rose 10.5 percent; at the other extreme, metals and metal products rose 29.4 percent and general purpose machinery and equipment rose 33.4 percent.

When these price increases for various types of commodities are stated as compound annual rates of increase from 1957–1959 to 1971, as shown in Table 4, the figures provide greater comparability with the rates of increase of wages. Prices of purchased commodities have risen over the decade much less rapidly than wages. Increases in number of commodity units required, relative to other

---

[1] See, however, the trenchant criticisms of this view by Joseph Kershaw, Provost of Williams College, a discussant of the paper presented at the 1971 ACE meeting. Kershaw points out that there is no reason to believe that an optimal combination of faculty and nonfaculty labor was used by most institutions, and he argues also that student/faculty ratios could well be adjusted upward by many. Thus, he attacks the validity of the above argument (Kershaw, 1972).

factors, and increased demand for more complex items may, nevertheless, have caused more cost pressure from these components of expenditure than indicated by Table 4. Further, the impact of increased costs may have been particularly strong during the last three years of the 1960s, influenced—as was the entire United States economy—by the inflation resulting from the Vietnam war. Thus, the relative influence of cost rise in some types of items has been increased.

Table 4

WHOLESALE PRICES, BY MAJOR COMMODITY GROUPS
(1957–1959 = 100)

Commodity	Price index, 1971	Compound annual rate of increase (percent), 1957–1959 to 1971[a]
All commodities	119.6	1.38
Rubber and plastic products	106.1	0.46
Furniture and durables	110.5	0.77
Metals and metal products	129.4	2.0
General purpose machinery and equipment	133.4	2.2

[a] 1958, midpoint of base period, assumed for start of calculation.

Various types of institutions are, of course, affected differently by the differentials in commodity price increases. However, we can reasonably suppose that the institutions that have experienced rapid capacity growth have been most affected by increases in machinery prices.

Library Materials. Price trends in library books and serial publications have exerted an influence on budgets in all higher education institutions. Unit prices of library books, periodicals, and services have risen at different average rates from the base period of 1957–1959 to 1969. Books have gone up a total of 77.1 percent, periodicals rose 89.2 percent, and serial services rose 98.0 percent. These represented, respectively, compound annual rates of 5.3 percent, 6.0 percent, and 6.4 percent.

Recent inflationary pressures hit all three sectors of library acquisition costs. In the year from 1969 to 1970, the United States periodicals index rose from 189.2 to 211.6, or nearly 12 percent over 1969, and a combined index of serials services rose by 8.4 percent (Tuttle, Brown, and Huff, 1970). In the same period, an index of the prices of hardcover books, ranging by field from agriculture to travel, rose overall by 22.7 percent; this same index rose 38.3 percent during 1967–1970, with the greatest increase occurring during 1969. Also during 1969, mass market paperbacks rose only 2.1 percent, whereas the more selective, trade paperback category rose by 29.0 percent (*Publishers' Weekly,* Feb. 8 1971, pp. 53–54).

As striking as the average price increase in each category is the great variation among categories in the amount of increase. From 1957–1959 to 1970, the cost of business and economics periodicals rose 82.1 percent, chemistry and physics periodicals rose 233.3 percent, engineering 123.5 percent, literature 63.1 percent, and history only 56.1 percent. Thus, an institution with a heavy periodicals commitment in the hard sciences and engineering would have found more inflationary pressure on its library costs than one that concentrated on the humanities. Even more striking interfield differences were shown for the serials services. Those in law have risen, since 1957–1959, by 155.7 percent; business by 66.5 percent; science and technology by 554.2 percent; and United States documents by 48.7 percent. Here again, the specific effects of the increases in unit prices of library materials will depend a great deal on an institution's mix of programs.

Educational Resources. Now let us examine, first, the increases in quantity used of each type of resource, and then such fragments of information as we have concerning changes in productivity for each type of resource. In his study, Cheit (1971a) converted each category of expenditure to expenditure per student in each institution, in order to obtain a basis for comparison among institutions. This approach combines the effects of prices, quantity of a resource used per student, and productivity. It is very difficult to go beyond this approach because data are scant.

Use of faculty labor has risen enormously with increases in enrollment. At the same time, student-faculty ratios have apparently increased—that is, fewer faculty are being used per thousand students (Radner and Miller, 1970). Does the increased number of students per faculty member actually represent an increase in the amount of teaching output per faculty member? Some evidence suggests that in many institutions, during the 1960s, the number of faculty teaching contact hours per week in regular classes decreased but was accompanied by increases in the amount of faculty time spent supervising graduate students and by increases in class size.

Cutting the problem another way, we find that the total number of faculty in some institutions increased dramatically. At Stanford, for example, the number of members of the academic council went from 427 in 1955 to 1,031 in 1970, an increase of 141 percent, compared with an increase of enrollment from 7,870 to 11,600, or 47 percent. But there was a sharp change in the composition of the student body: graduate students accounted for 36 percent in 1955 and 45.5 percent in 1970. Staff other than faculty increased by 161 percent, from 2,220 in 1955 to 5,802 in 1970. Stanford was transformed in those fifteen years by plentiful federal research funds, the generosity of its benefactors, and the drive of its leadership. From 1955 to 1970, its total operating budget rose by 572 percent, the instruction budget rose by 632 percent, the research budget by 669 percent, the library budget by 634 percent, and plant operations by 551 percent. Other major research universities had similar growth, and some public institutions grew even more in total budget and enrollment.

Note that staff other than faculty increased by a greater percentage than did faculty, that both grew by much more than enrollment (because of growth in research and increased relative emphasis on graduate instruction), and that all of the dollar budgets grew by percentages far greater than either the enrollment growth or the faculty and staff growth. (An increase of 600 percent in fifteen years represents growth at a compound annual rate of 13.9 percent.)

Educational institutions that have the specified mission of providing the first two years or four years of postsecondary instruction, and that have been constrained by their own policies or by jurisdictional allocations from accumulating research and graduate instructional responsibilities, have experienced growth in enrollment and thus in total faculty (though student/faculty ratios have increased over the past twenty years). They are not, however, likely to have experienced as costly a relative expansion in nonfaculty personnel as universities have because of their simpler organization and smaller involvement in research and public service activities.

As academic institutions have grown over the past decade or two, they have had available to them some economies of scale in administration resulting in increases in the number of administrative staff less than proportional to growth. At the same time, administration of universities has become more complex and, as cited above, some have expanded administrative staff relative to academic staff. Such increases have introduced another independent source of cost increase, for often the increases in proportion are in precisely those types of personnel whose costs rose most rapidly.

Let us now consider the increase in quantity of library resources. The earlier discussion showed that book, periodical, and serial prices rose at a more rapid rate than salaries, and that the major research universities experienced enormous expenditure increases for library materials during the past two decades. But in public two-year and four-year institutions that experienced major enrollment growth, especially in the 1960s, a frequent budgetary device has been to provide funds for a specific number of books per FTE student. Quite natural desires to improve library resources have led to increases in the budgeted factor. From 1965–1966 to 1971–1972 (estimated), the California state college system increased the number of volumes per FTE student from 27 to 35.5. In this same seven-year period, total library holdings more than doubled, from 3.2 million volumes to 7.5 million volumes.

Expansion of the equipment base of academic institutions was also rapid during the enrollment upsurge and particularly during the 1960s. The mechanical core of buildings became more expensive and more elaborate. One simple example is airconditioning. In 1960–1961, only 14 percent of the University of California's total building area was air-conditioned; in 1970–1971, after a huge expansion of total space, 40 percent was air-conditioned, with large cost consequences not only in initial capital outlay but also in maintenance and utilities expense. Many universities, to conserve scarce land, have had to build high-rise buildings. Basic construction methods and more mechanical equipment make these more expensive per square foot. New construction has had a high and rising rate of increase. During the past eight years, depending on the type of construction, the cost index has risen 10 to 12 percent per year. And maintenance costs have also increased.

Scientific equipment has increased in complexity. Electron microscopes cost about $30,000 in 1960, and, with improvements and design conveniences, about $50,000 to $60,000 in 1970. The unit cost of computers has fallen rapidly and continuously with technological advance, but these decreases have been much more than offset by increases of usage. In a ten-university study of rising costs, computers were shown to represent 0.3 percent of operating budget in 1961–1962, 1.0 percent in 1966–1967, and were projected to be 1.7 percent in 1972–1973 (Cornell University, 1967).

In the late 1960s and early 1970s, insurance premiums, fire and other damage losses, and personnel costs for security rose very rapidly. Fire and casualty insurance rates have risen throughout the economy, but, with the spread of student unrest, academic institutions became a new kind of risk. To keep dollar premium rates from rising too high, institutions have been forced to increase the deductible limit for each occurrence—an action that, in turn, forces them to absorb fire and other damage losses from their own resources.

Cheit (1971a, pp. 108–110) cites these increases in expenses as common among the institutions he surveyed. He finds that total costs attributed to campus disturbance—insurance, security, property maintenance and repair increases, and diversions of staff time —amounted to 4.746 percent of educational and general expenditures in 1969–1970 at one institution; and he offers the judgment that one percentage point of the cost increase in each year from 1968 to 1971 came from this source alone.

Increased financial aid to students is an important element of growth in the cost structure of many institutions. Those public institutions that have sought, successfully, to secure added appropriations for student aid, and especially for education opportunity programs, have experienced offsetting increases in expense. Many private institutions that have increased their incomes by raising tuition have felt obliged to devote significant portions of the new revenue to financial aid for needy students. And many have accepted new financial responsibilities toward minority students who were formerly underrepresented in their enrollments. It has been of great importance to American society that our colleges and universities, both public and private, undertake these new responsibilities. But their discretionary resources are clearly not adequate for the job of redressing deep imbalances in the previous distribution of income, assets, and educational opportunity. There is a strong case for new federal finance to meet this need.

Full funding of the Basic Opportunity Grants authorized in the Higher Education amendments of 1972, and adoption of other elements of a comprehensive federal approach to student aid as recommended by the Carnegie Commission on Higher Education (1971), would not only improve student access but would assist institutions that in recent years have found financial aid an increasingly significant institutional cost. Still further help to these institutions would be in order, through adoption of the Carnegie Commission recommendations for educational supplements to institutions from the federal government in proportion to their numbers of federally aided students.

Jenny and Wynn (1971) performed a financial trend analysis for a group of private liberal arts colleges over the period from 1960 to 1968. This and their follow-up study (1972) underscore the importance of financial aid as a growing component of institutional expenditure. For the full decade of the 1960s, Jenny and Wynn report that these colleges had compound annual rates of income growth per student of 6.4 percent, while the like rate of growth in expense per student was 6.8 percent. Thus, for the decade, the gap was 0.4 percent per year. This rate is less than the average shown by Cheit in his study of forty-one institutions of several types. Jenny and Wynn find, however, that their very recent figures, for 1968–1970, show a much larger gap—income growth of 6.8 percent per student per year as against 8.2 percent yearly growth of expense. Student aid expense had the most rapid growth rate of all the expense categories. Jenny and Wynn also calculated the year-to-year marginals—the changes in income and expense—and find that for 1960–1961 about eight cents of each dollar of extra tuition and fee income went to student aid, whereas for 1969–1970, thirty-two cents went to student aid.

Appraisal

We must now step back from details and appraise the overall consequences of the cost push and the failure of institutional income to keep pace with costs. Many of the figures cited go back one or two decades and show that the seeds of financial difficulty for higher education were germinating for a long time. The inflation associated with the Vietnam War and its aftermath has clearly accelerated the cost push of some major elements. The growing competition for the federal and state dollar has worsened the lot of research universities and public institutions. Private institutions, worrying about whether to raise tuition still further, face market resistance to the prices they must charge.

Cheit followed his initial study with another examination of the same institutions two years later (1973). He found that, largely through tight expenditure control, most universities had achieved "a precarious stability." Many colleges also hoped that they were repairing the breach of confidence with legislative and private funding constituencies, with possible beneficent effects on future income. Somewhat counterbalancing these recent improvements, private colleges and universities (like other investors) did not have as good capital gains experience from their endowment portfolios as in earlier years. And both private and public institutions experienced continuing severe cost pressure from the rate of inflation during 1973 and the first half of 1974. But these are continued short-term adjustments—down in some variables, up in others. What of longer-term, underlying forces?

Then-provost, now President William G. Bowen of Princeton University suggested a fundamental relationship that may pertain to all of higher education. Bowen notes that higher education may be a constant-productivity industry surrounded by other sectors of society whose productivity is rising several percent per year (Bowen, 1969). Bowen presents long-term comparisons (1905 to 1966) of direct costs per student in higher education with an economy-wide cost index, as well as detailed cost experiences of a sample group of major universities. The data show a continued relative cost rise for higher education. To get out of this trap, academic institutions can try to gain whatever economies of scale are available and can also use more capital and technology per staff member where this might cut costs per student. But Bowen raises a problem that—in the absence of significant productivity gains in the use of resources for higher education—could be dealt with only by cutting the quality of educational operations as we have known it, by reducing the real wages of those who earn their living in higher education, or by continuing to raise tuition costs and the public subsidy of higher education.

Lack of systematic progress in measuring the output of higher education makes it difficult to do a full analysis of the productivity questions, although trends in cost per student year can be estimated. What is needed, and not now available, is an estimate of trends in the cost of achieving a given amount and quality of educational results. It may be possible, when more is known, to re-organize some aspects of the educational pattern and to use new technologies and, by both of these means, to moderate the cost push. These strategies will take a great deal of time, development money, and—above all—courage. The necessary development efforts are beyond the purse of the individual institution and will require help from foundations and from such special sources as the Fund for Improvement of Postsecondary Education in the U.S. Department of Health, Education, and Welfare.

For the balance of the 1970s, continued cost pressures must be anticipated as enrollments continue to grow. The cost structure of public two-year colleges will probably be least vulnerable to further rapid increases of operating cost per student. The community colleges rely most heavily on academic personnel, and they face fewer urgent needs in other areas of rapid cost increase, such as library expansion. However, to the extent that two-year colleges find that they must expand their higher-cost-per-student technical–vocational programs more rapidly than their academic programs, they too will have new cost pressures. And those community colleges that have a vital role as gateways to new educational opportunity face intense demands for counseling and other educational services. Beyond the 1970s there will be, for many institutions, the problem of living with absolute retrenchment, for total college enrollments will probably fall for several years in the early 1980s.

Summary

This chapter has dealt with cost and income influences on institutions with stable or growing levels of activity. Most universities have been experiencing stability or growth and will continue to do so during the 1970s. As institutions look some years ahead to the problems of adjusting to possible future decreases in their operations (as indeed some of them are already having to do in research areas), they will have to consider, by analysis that is beyond the scope covered here, how to plan the withdrawal of resources from each domain of the institution's activity. In the next chapter, elements of cost analysis and of this chapter's focus on financial trends are used to examine the budgetary process in the university.

Chapter 9

Resources and
Budgets

The budgets of a university are the surest single indication of what it is committed to do or is stuck with as an institution. This is true partly because, underneath the rhetoric of leadership, there is a hard logic in putting funds where institutional necessity points. It is true even though not all funds of an institution are counted as budgeted funds, causing confusion in the analysis of fiscal patterns; and it is true even though some very important resources are not explicitly dealt with in the budgeting process, while money is.

Capital Versus Operating Budgets

In their budgeting schemes, universities traditionally follow a rigid division between capital funds and operating funds; that is one feature of their financial accounting. One reason for this division is that the planning and management of major maintenance, renovations, and expansion of capital plant and major equipment need specialized expertise. Also, many dollars are rigidly earmarked by source, either for an operating or a capital purpose.

199

For long-range planning purposes, the capital and operating aspects of a major program commitment should be considered together—to see that their full magnitude is understood when the commitment is made, and to assure that increments of capital funding and of operating funds will be reasonably in phase. Rigid separation between capital budgeting and operating budgets tends to make disjoint what should be a joint process and may also cause the university's decision-makers to overlook possible trade-offs between capital and operating elements of the decision.

A university's customary treatment of its long-lived (capital) items as against its short-term (operating) commitments would baffle the hard-headed business analyst. Universities ordinarily do not do depreciation accounting on their buildings. The reason usually given is that universities do not have to calculate profit and loss, and so they do not have incentives to look at the rate of depreciation of long-lived assets. But this also means that universities undervalue, in costing various activities, those services that happen to be supplied from the capital plant instead of being accounted for through operating transactions and payroll accounting. There is another problem—universities often fail to set up reserves for major maintenance and for equipment replacement; these then seem to be one-of-a-kind emergencies, rather than normal features of effective managing through time.

Part of the rationale, and probably it was once an enticing one, for the lack of such reserves was that a crisis or potential disaster would rally loyal donors, whereas evidence of prudent accumulation of reserves would tend to discourage them. But this could only work well for institutions that relied on a few wealthy patrons. Nowadays, even the private universities have institutionalized the donor relationship, with organized annual giving and proudly orchestrated capital campaigns. It is now very doubtful whether it is good tactics for any institution—public or private—to fool itself in order to plead emergency.

Universities also observe the convention of capitalizing only commitments for physical plant and equipment, or for long-term debts and financial arrangements. They have not, for example, customarily regarded as a capitalized commitment the contractual obligations to faculty and other long-term personnel. Yet associated with these commitments are important, long-range risks that could be better understood if there were explicit accounting for them.

Budget Horizons

Long-range budget projection is not uniform among universities. Some do not do it at all, in published projections or fiscal plans. And the horizons considered vary among universities that do undertake long-range projections. One state university, for example, has periodically published ten-year fiscal plans or projections and has also developed still longer-range fiscal projections for specialized purposes. These are most useful if there is institutional intent to pursue a fixed path of development and growth and the resource implications of this intent need to be examined. Such long-range projections have to be based on plausible assumptions, but they cannot really be read as forecasts. The assumptions may fail, and the assumed path of the institution, of which the long-range fiscal projection is a price-out, is almost never a completely definite institutional commitment. It may have to be adjusted to new environmental events (for example, a change in the expectations for federal research funding) and also to changes in internal policies and priorities.

Intermediate-range budget projections can be clearly tied to the existing span of institutional commitments and to such indispensable forecasts as enrollment projections. Multiyear budget projections, updated annually, can be built into the process of budget preparation and analysis, and they provide a convenient point of takeoff for the preliminary phases of the following year's budget preparation. Multiyear budget projections are indispensable for showing, on the capital outlay side, the estimated costs—distributed over several years—of completing building projects that are, in the current year, in a planning phase or in an early phase of construction. Unless such multiyear projections are available when the annual capital budget is adopted, rational consideration of it is impossible.

Although long-range and intermediate-range fiscal projections have important uses for planning, the greatest practical preoccupation of administrators is the annual budgeting cycle. The fiscal year just past provides history and the last measured, actual figures; the current fiscal year has a budget to be administered and held in control; and the upcoming year's budget must be prepared, defended, negotiated, and adopted. Every academic and administrative unit of a university is caught up in this iron cycle. The fiscal-year budget, once adopted, contains signals of the most definite of the university's commitments; other projections beyond that adopted budget are subject to change with new information about resources, costs, and priorities. Thus, the budget is to be read not only for what it authorizes and pledges but for what it implies.

Budgeting People

The preceding discussion of budgetary horizons has been cast in terms of dollar budgets, which are indeed the usual mode of resource planning and control. We also need, however, to take note of other important resources—in particular, employed personnel and building space—that are planned for and allocated in a fashion semi-independent of the procedures for dollar budgeting.

Governmental agencies have long practiced *position control* in addition to dollar budgeting. In most governmental activities, the workload of an agency is reflected, through rule of thumb conventions, in *entitlements* for manning the agency—at the first level of activity, in a ratio of so many elements of workload per first-level employee, and then a supervisor for every so many first-level employees, and so on. The table of organization is built this way, with provisions for people to coordinate the interactions between line units, for support staffs in some ratio to the sizes of operating staffs, and finally, for the top executive structure. Each position level is accorded a rating as to salary range. Thus, the total wage bill of the agency can be estimated easily from the manning table and the salary rates, and this wage bill comprises the major part of the dollar operating budget. Nonwage budget items are usually tied by other rules of thumb to the number of authorized employees.

Why not simply budget in terms of dollars and only require the agency head to determine how many employees are needed to meet the workload? Why not do without position control? Classically, there are several reasons. The most important is that, once hired, a civil service employee acquires job and retirement rights that are totally extinguished only on death, voluntary separation, or dismissal for cause after elaborate due process. Also, the assessment of what resources the agency must have proceeds naturally from activity workload to personnel requirements to dollar budgets. Position control provides an additional assurance that an agency director will not step outside the prescribed boundaries of operation. It also enables those who are reviewing an agency's budget request for the forthcoming fiscal period to see how the estimated workload increase translates into manpower requirements, assuming that a standard ratio of units of workload to units of manpower is agreed. Position control also enables budget reviewers to intervene at a critical point if they want to force a productivity increase or a decline in the apparent quality of the service of the agency. This can be done by applying a new and less generous manpower allocation either to the work-load increase or to the total workload of the agency.

Public universities find that position control is most crucially enforced in the student/faculty ratio that is used for determining how many faculty positions the institution will be permitted in the forthcoming fiscal period. Once the budget is agreed to, or once the estimate of what will be agreed to is reasonably firm, the number of new faculty positions allocated (usually on the basis of increased enrollment)—together with the number of positions vacated by resignation, death, or retirement—provides the total of allocable faculty slots that can be assigned to the academic departments. These slots, or faculty FTEs, are precious coin in the resource-allocation process. The budget allocation to each academic department is adjusted to reflect the salary cost of a faculty FTE awarded to it. But mere dollars available do not permit a department to recruit a new faculty member if a slot has not been provided. This procedure prevents a department from engaging in short-term trade-offs between one dollar category and another, when the effect would be to increase not only the department's but also the institution's long-term budgetary obligations.

In addition, many universities have become increasingly sensitive to the need to control longer-term aspects of the personnel resource: its age and rank distributions, and the extent of the institution's ability to hire some new blood each year. Universities share this concern about the priorities of a manpower system over time with all hierarchies that have relatively strong patterns of career-long employment.

Recent studies throw much new light on the long-term characteristics of university faculty flows and provide a means of testing the consequences of different patterns of organizational growth, different promotion policies, and different policies of encouraging or requiring retirement. Among the contributors to this literature are Oliver (1969), Bartholomew (1969), and Grinold and Stanford (1973). Their models, and the empirical application by Grinold and Stanford that involved dynamic programming calculations, are formulated in terms of a rank-structure with specified fractions of those in each rank passing to the next one, staying in the same rank, or passing out of the system each year. Grinold and Stanford show cost-minimizing strategies for achieving assumed long-range targets, and they also show a method for dealing with a current problem that is characteristic of universities going through rapid expansion: the need to determine what promotion policies are required to reach the stated objectives of the expansion in a given number of years. An even more interesting substantive issue facing many universities now is the need to determine the length of time required to stablize the rank-structure after a period of rapid growth. With the onset of steady-state thinking, universities are particularly susceptible to this characterization of faculty manpower planning.

Budgeting Space

Building space is another major resource. Most universities keep comprehensive inventory records of the space they own and control. Records usually exist, also, of the current assignments of space. But the extent to which a particular building or room is capable of accommodating different uses, or must be regarded as a special-purpose type of facility, is often not evident from the records. Rather, it is part of the judgment and lore of the campus administration.

Space for academic and administrative uses is typically not budgeted—there is no regular cycle of review and determination of continued need. Space is initially assigned to a given purpose on the basis of administrative judgments about the amount and type of space that is justified and available and the campus location that is considered appropriate. Once assigned, space is often considered to be all but owned by the unit that occupies it, and reallocation of part of space previously assigned becomes a major administrative issue.

Some types of building space are specifically designed for particular purposes. And buildings that are built through the generosity of donors or with capital grants from foundations or research agencies have strings attached. Thus, both functional characteristics and assigned uses place constraints on the allocation of space.

The mechanism of allocation and occasional reallocation of space is almost always administrative and judgmental. Sometimes general space standards for the amounts needed for particular purposes are used. Only rarely—when the institution must go out and rent offices for a research project and pay the rental with funds provided in an extramural grant—is the pricing of space to a particular activity explicit. Otherwise, administrative assignment and rationing is the rule. Also, once space is assigned, the user has no incentive to economize on its use or to give up space that is not really needed. The unit gains nothing by giving up unneeded space, because no compensation is provided and it loses flexibility for the future. The basic rule, therefore, is: What's mine is mine and what's yours we can negotiate.

Unless regular, periodic justifications are required, management of space allocation is closely checked, and all of the many space allocations are assembled and coordinated with other allocations of resources, it cannot be said that university space is budgeted. Internal pricing of space and other institutional resources, to encourage more rational allocation and more trade-offs, could be an alternative to the customary mechanisms of purely administrative judgment. To my knowledge, no American university is relying substantially on a price mechanism to deal with space administration. The possibility, and some of the drawbacks, are discussed by David Breneman (1971). Internal pricing is discussed in more detail in the concluding section of this chapter.

Techniques for facilities planning and for long-range physical development planning are much more highly developed than are techniques for the administration of space. Enrollment growth in public institutions is one main planning variable, and new programs with special space requirements is another. Public agencies require extensive and detailed justification of facilities expansion and the capital outlay budgets to finance it, and these demands for justification have probably been the main force encouraging the elaboration of techniques for facilities planning. One major, systematic effort is the *Higher Education Facilities Planning and Management Manual.* This is actually a set of six manuals, developed by the Planning and Management Systems Division of WICHE (1971), in cooperation with the American Association of Collegiate Registrars and Admissions Officers.

An ambitious effort to solve the problem of optimal space planning was undertaken by Mathematica Corporation for the California Coordinating Council for Higher Education. This resulted in the design of a facilities analysis model known as CCHE—FAM. Donovan Smith and Gary Wagner started with efforts to modify that model for application to University of California problems of planning for instructional and research facilities. They had to depart from the original model and develop their own cost-simulation model, which was then implemented (Smith and Wagner, 1972). The Smith-Wagner formulation "relates enrollments, class scheduling policies, class size policies and faculty workload policies to physical resource needs and the resulting utilization rates of classrooms and class laboratories. SPACE also computes the faculty needs, the associated current costs, and converts the capital costs to comparable annual costs."

An even longer-term perspective is the planning of new campuses for a multicampus university system. This is now a nonissue in higher education in the United States because of the pending stabilization or decline of enrollments. But as recently as 1968–1969 it was a live topic and received sophisticated analytical attention (Sanderson, 1969). Starting from a long-horizon projection of total university enrollment, Sanderson developed a solution method for least-cost expansion by using network-flow computational techniques.

Budgetary Standards and Indicators

A budgetary standard can be defined as the amount of resources needed per unit of workload in some activity. By far the most ubiquitous example is the student/faculty ratio. It has been necessary to elaborate this ratio much beyond a simple count of the number of bodies in the numerator and the number of bodies in the denominator. Thus, the first level of refinement is to adjust head count downward to full-time equivalents (FTE) and get the ratio of FTE students to FTE faculty. Some institutions accord separate recognition to the more intensive tasks (and the generally smaller-scale character of instruction) in advanced graduate as against undergraduate programs. This led to the development of weighted FTE students/FTE faculty, where higher weights for the graduate components of enrollment would reflect the presumably greater staffing requirement.

Whatever the form, the student/faculty ratio can be used to calculate the number of faculty positions that should be added to the budget to meet the presumed demands of additional students. In its easiest and most plausible initial form, the increment is calculated at the preexisting average ratio.

An enrollment increase of 100 FTE students, at an FTE student/FTE faculty ratio of 20, would mean adding 5 FTE faculty positions. At this point, a second budgetary standard—the average rank-level of new positions—might be invoked, to guide position control and to fix the number of dollars added to the faculty salary budget.

A clever budgeteer might object to this way of calculating incremental faculty positions because the more pertinent issue is: What should the marginal ratio be? Among the considerations that might come into play are: the preexisting size of the faculty; the extent to which the institution's leadership or (for a public institution) the budgeting agency want to thin out the staffing pattern; and close examination of the composition of enrollment increases to determine whether they are mostly in areas where class sizes could be increased with little need for new staffing.

This example may help to illustrate both the uses and the potential weakness of a simply stated budgetary standard. Such a standard makes for administrative convenience and ready calculation of budgetary needs. It can also be used to assess the approximate internal allocation of a resource increment, with judgmental departures from the figures shown by first-stage calculations. However, the budgetary standard rests on commonsense presumptions about resource needs in relation to work-load or activity rates, and these presumptions often turn out, on examination, to have incomplete justification.

In some cases, therefore, in-depth studies are made to provide deeper justification. Building maintenance standards, for example, have been studied to determine whether, at the historical rates of expenditure per square foot, buildings of various ages and construction types are receiving enough maintenance care to avoid the buildup of a backlog of deferred maintenance. A growing backlog indicates that the operating budgets of previous years have been understated.

Budgetary standards are usually, but not necessarily, stated as constant proportions or ratios. Statistical studies of the amount of general administration expense at various campuses of the University of California showed that, as a function of campus size, the percentage of general administration expense to total budget could be allowed to fall. This economy-of-scale finding could then be built into a declining-percentage budgetary standard for general administration expense budgeting.

Space standards are conceptually analoguous to the operating budget standards just discussed. Occasionally, external regulatory requirements impose the standard. An example is the set of regulations promulgated by the federal Public Health Service for the care of laboratory animals; these specify amounts of space and service requirements (such as airconditioning) for proper care of various animal species, and their effect is to set capital requirements on animal care facilities.

Some states have set space standards for various academic and administrative facilities. These may be based in part on human engineering considerations and in part on experience. One important purpose of such standards is to check the scope of a proposed building project against the estimated size of the set of activities to be accommodated by multiplying the size of each by its pertinent standards. Another purpose, in capacity studies, is to show how much additional activity can be accommodated in existing facilities.

The technologies of academic activities differ substantially from field to field. The rule of thumb standard per faculty member in the physical and biological sciences at the University of California is approximately 500 assignable square feet, including laboratory as well as office space. By contrast, faculty members in the social sciences or the humanities are expected to need about 100 assignable square feet. (Part of the gross square footage of a building consists of corridors, storage areas, and so forth. Only the space immediately usable by building occupants is assignable square feet.) An even larger differential is accorded the laboratory sciences graduate student, chiefly because of laboratory requirements.

Space standards embody educational policy. If a field of academic activity has historically justified a large amount of space per person, the implied capital costs are gradually built into the institution's cost structure. Actuals may, of course, deviate from the standard. During growth periods there was a tendency for staffing and enrollments to outpace the completion of space to house them. Fields that experience declining enrollment and activity are rarely penalized right away for occupying excess space. Their spokesmen usually argue that enrollment and staffing declines may soon be reversed. And often the physical location or functional characteristics of the excess space would be inappropriate for other uses unless heavy renovation and relocation investments were made. Thus, space standards may have very real importance in an institution, but deviations from them may be prolonged.

Budget Concepts and Categories

Traditionally, operating budgets in public agencies (and in most educational institutions) were laid out according to *line items* or *object classes,* such as the number of personnel in the various categories and their budgeted salary costs, equipment purchases and maintenance, purchased supplies, travel expenses, and building maintenance. A line item was any separately labeled category. Object classes were the standard categories for each type of budgeted resource. The dollar total in each of these categories could in turn be broken down into the allocation for each unit. Because each new building is a large, one-time investment, the capital outlay budget is typically a line-item budget, with each fiscal-year phase of design, construction, and equipping of the building a subitem. Only for deferred maintenance and renovations might there be a pooled capital budget total without prior designation of the amount to be spent on each project.

Traditional budgets are focused entirely on the various categories of input. A next step, and a valuable one, is to relate the change in inputs to the change in activity or workload. When this can be done, via agreed budgetary standards, two further steps are enough to produce a plausible and enforceable expenditure budget. One is to correct for year-to-year changes of the unit prices of inputs. In an era of inflation, it is important to do this carefully, but academic institutions have had difficulty using or constructing the appropriate price indices and still more difficulty predicting price changes. The income or revenue side of the budget also needs to be constructed, showing income by category, indicating how carryovers will be treated, and dealing with any intentional gaps between income and outgo. These steps, together wth the breakdowns to organizational units, are sufficient to produce an enforceable budget—presuming, of course, that the budgetary pattern reflects plausibly the conditions of operation and that no strong shock, to the income or the expenditure expectations, occurs from the environment.

The trouble with the object-class budget is that it is almost completely devoid of any conceptual representation of what the institution is doing. A better concept is what may be called the function and performance budget. This budget is cut into significant areas of functional operation, such as instructional and departmental research, organized research, libraries, organized activities, public and community service, maintenance and operation of plant, student services, and general administration. Activities or performance areas within each of these headings are broken down into finer categories. The library budget, for example, may be divided between two functional areas, acquisitions and acquisitions processing, and circulation and services. Wherever possible, agreed budgetary standards provide a basis for determining the amount of change in budgeted expenditure that is justified, according to a pertinent measure of workload, between the current year and the next. From the point of view of budgetary administration and control, the function and performance budget gives an improved basis for focusing budgetary responsibility on organizational units and for determining whether deviations between the budgeted expenditure rate and the actual rate are justified by unexpected workload changes or changes in other conditions.

Program Budgeting

Object-class budgeting is based purely on inputs. Function and performance budgets are based on areas and rates of activity. Program budgeting is a conceptual schema for directing resource allocations according to the objectives of the institution. This is a praiseworthy aim. The first step toward it in higher education institutions was to rearrange the format of the operating budget to divide the areas of functional activity into major programs and supporting programs and to work out reallocations of some functional budgets among the major and supporting programs thus identified. Even this modest step requires a great deal of exacting effort in any large-scale institution. In one university, for example, it was done by working out the definitions of programs and then writing a cross-over computer program that would redistribute the magnitudes of various budgetary components in the function and performance budget under the headings in the program classification.

An extensive review and critique of PPBS in higher Education was made by G. B. Weathersby and myself (Weathersby and Balderston, 1972). In the early 1960s, PPBS held out the promise of imparting a new degree of rationality to public-sector resource allocation and management. The experience of the Department of Defense under the leadership of then-Secretary McNamara and, especially in this area, of Charles J. Hitch, then assistant secretary and comptroller, provided the widely-heralded first example. Hitch emphasized that the implementation of a planning, programming, budgeting system in the Department of Defense did not mean that object-class budgeting was entirely abandoned. The old and the new had to be carried forward together, partly because congressional committees insisted on continuing to receive the traditional layout of resource commitments. The implementation of PPBS in the Defense Department depended on a large accumulated background of quantitative and qualitative analysis of defense programs and problems. This analysis was carried out mainly at the RAND Corporation. Other executive agencies attempted to follow the lead of the Department of Defense, in response to President Johnson's 1965 executive order mandating PPBS in federal agencies, and many state governments soon followed. Implementation proved frustrating in many areas of government, and there was eventually a pullback from the mechanics of PPBS in the federal budgeting process. State agencies, including public universities, also experienced difficulties.

One problem that soon developed was the lack of quantitatively definable objectives in many areas of government service, including higher education. There are broadly definable aims for a university and elements of university mission; but the specifics of measurement of the quantity and the quality of results achieved are not very far developed. Until there is reasonably clear agreement on what the accomplishments (or outputs) of a university are, it is not possible to deal conclusively with the results side of budgeting for results. Also, there is still much work to be done in identifying the processes of activity and to show what organizational units or combinations of units are responsible for the work, how the organizational units and processes are affected by a richer or more scant allocation of resources, and how the processes contribute to the attainment of objectives. A university abounds in multiple processes, and the analysis of costs and results in the presence of substantial jointness and interdependence is difficult.

But even if adroit compromises are reached on the use of substitute measures for the ideal ways of measuring results and on rule-of-thumb approximations for the problems of jointness, the remaining problem of time horizons has proved to be, politically, the most serious of all. One basic idea in PPBS is to specify what is to be accomplished in each program in each future year and then to calculate how many resources will be needed for the program and to specify when these resources have to be acquired and at what cost in order to meet the schedule for the program. This system forecasts the cost of the program over a series of years and sets forth the timing of these costs, thereby avoiding seemingly innocuous first-year commitments to programs that eventually turn out to be far more costly than originally contemplated. It is still quite possible to make a poor choice of program or to underestimate its costs, and PPBS did not altogether solve the problem of mistaken and misunderstood commitments, even in the Department of Defense. But it was certainly a far more sensible conceptual approach than the political jockeying that got programs started on false promises and then built them into unstoppable and large claims later on.

. Universities found that, although they tried to show the multiyear budgetary implications of programs, their funding sources were unwilling or unable to look beyond very short commitments—typically, the single budget year. Administrators were very much aware that most of what they were trying to sustain in existing programs or to initiate in new ones had implications for costs and horizons for results that stretched far beyond the immediate arguments of the up-coming fiscal year. But they have generally not been able to deal with the multiyear horizon except in terms of very contingent internal planning or by announcing noble hopes whose realization would be heavily dependent on future decisions of outside funding agencies. The most enduring legacy of the program budgeting experience of universities has been the development of a much more sophisticated analytic spirit, both within the university and in state and federal agencies.

Budget-Making Mechanisms

The two conceptual extremes of the budget-making process are to go from the top down and to assemble the budget from the grass roots. The president and other senior executives of a university have advantages and responsibilities that make the control of the budget-making process important to them. They know what the overall resource position of the institution is and what it is likely to be in the forthcoming fiscal period. In a public university, they have to negotiate with the agencies of state government for basic institutional support. And in a private university, they have the obligation to bring to the university's trustees the prime recommendations concerning allocation of endowment income and reserves, tuition income and tuition increases, and other estimates of the institution's income-base.

The senior administration and faculty leadership have whatever there is of a general vision of where the institution is and should be going—in other words, a sense of institutional priority.

They are aware of what is needed for academic development and in response to important pressures and opportunities facing the institution. Individual academic and administrative units, properly enough, see first and foremost their own domains of concern and not those which may cut across all features of the institution. In addition, the senior administration has or can get significant information for monitoring, comparison, and control. From the central campus source of enrollment and registration statistics, the work-load variations among departments and schools can be calculated. From the space inventory files, the allocations of building space to various academic and administrative uses can be monitored. Such judgments as there are of the general vigor and quality of important academic and administrative operations are generated by, or flow to, the central administration. Finally, and most important, the senior administration will have to assemble the final budget by reconciling competing claims and fitting them into the foreseeable resource situation.

Individual academic and administrative units also have important contributions to make to the budgeting process. They know what problems they face and what aspirations they have. If they are simply handed the budget as a *fait accompli,* with no opportunity to speak to their needs, they are likely to take the view that the constraints of the budget are not of their making. And they may feel free to circumvent the budget, if they are able to, rather than support it as the document that accurately describes the institution's fiscal position and commitments. I return to this issue in the discussion of resource management and incentives.

Each unit is likely to make expenditure requests that reflect aspirations and hopes much more heavily than considerations of efficiency. As any budgeteer knows, the first round of a purely grassroots budgeting process reflects the sum of hopes: the amount of money that it would take to go as rapidly toward goals as one could imagine, without winnowing out anything unnecessary, questionable, or obsolete. If the first round of budget-making simply answers the question, "What would you like to have?" then the second round— scaling requests to manageable proportions—is likely to be all the more traumatic on account of the hopes that have been aroused and the need for adjustment.

Kaludis (1973) makes the argument for an open, decentralized, budget-making process guided by a conception of institutional objectives and supported by an adequate system of financial information. What is needed, then, is a dialogue between the two valid perspectives: those of the decentralized operating units and of the central administration. The mechanism needs to include at least one round of responses from the other level of decision, no matter which does the initiating. One way to start from a semblance of realism is to have the central administration issue— for the forthcoming fiscal period—budget guidelines that include the preliminary forecasts of work-load changes, for each unit to use as a starting point in assembling its request.

The guidelines can also include, if necessary, an allocated amount of economizing adjustment that each operating unit is initially expected to absorb. Then each unit is free to assemble its expenditure request and its justification for the request, either accepting the guidelines or deviating from them.

Generally speaking, the budget-making mechanism needs to include at this point, or after another iteration, a discussion between the budget officer and senior administrators responsible for the area in which the unit operates and the head of the operating unit. This discussion can be well focused if the issues of concern have been worked on carefully by both sides. Program and efficiency questions will be raised by the budget director and senior administrators, and questions of program opportunity and unmet needs will be raised by the operating unit head.

The process can proceed rapidly if there are no serious cuts to be absorbed or serious questions of program goals and efficiency to be hammered out. But the latter kinds of questions deserve more attention than they often get. Such matters are often ignored or very incompletely addressed because they are difficult and sensitive questions. Some are put off for more leisurely attention at the time of periodic multi-year performance review of the unit and are not dealt with during the annual budget cycle. A budgeting process that relies very heavily on the current year as the base year—with only very infrequent reopening of the questions of program goals, performance, efficiency, and budgeting standards—is bound to reinforce the status quo and more or less proportional expansions of it (with, for example, workload adjustments for enrollment increases). Innovation in any institution that emphasizes this budgeting mode is likely to be confined to incremental change within the existing terms of reference of each academic unit. Significant departures from established goals or performance standards cannot usually be accommodated within the narrow limits of work-load budget adjustment, and significant changes are not stimulated as they would be by the necessity to react to more drastic shifts of resources.

Arthur Geoffrion, J. S. Dyer, and A. Feinberg of UCLA, have developed a mathematical programming approach (1972) to the iterative process of budget adjustment between a departmental unit and the central campus administration. Using iterative decomposition methods of mathematical programming, this approach enables a department to indicate what it would do if permitted to make changes in the amount and composition of resources provided, and it enables the central administrator to ask various kinds of "what if" questions about response to resource changes. The goals of the department and the goals of the central administrator are implicit. The relative importance of various activities is discovered through the steps of adjustment. The process is an effort to harmonize goals and the resource constraints of the situation. In 1972–1973, a pilot test was begun of the practical usability of Geoffrion's budget-adjustment concept in one substantial operating unit on the Los Angeles campus of the University of California.

The most onerous dialogue between central administration and operating units concerns *zero-base* budgeting, where each operating unit is put on notice that it should justify, from the ground up, all elements of its current expenditure pattern as well as any upward adjustments that it advocates. If it is not actually a realistic possibility that the forthcoming budget might be reduced to zero (that is, the department's claim to budget would be eliminated), then the zero part of zero-base budgeting may simply be an agonizing charade and not worth the trauma that raising such questions would entail. More sensible would be to divide the problem. Only occasionally, but more frequently than never, raise—in a full-scale performance review—the question of continuation of the activity. But in the annual budget cycle, use both the work-load guideline approach and a requirement that the operating unit show what it would do if it were to receive an absolute cut of some more or less tolerable magnitude, such as five, ten, or fifteen per cent. The responses to this would probably be in a continuum, from "burdensome inflexibility" to "cut in service delivery and quality by such and such degree" to "strictly infeasible (in view of contractual employment and other commitments) in one year." As we shall see, the pattern of resource use in most operating units is far more flexible upward than downward at the margin in short periods, and the opportunities to accommodate budget cuts by reducing the quality of work done are often held to be minimal in the very short run.

The annual budgeting cycle deserves some comment. An iterative budgeting process consumes both manpower and elapsed time and moves slowly toward closure and elimination of uncertainties. The calendar for the University of California's 1974–1975 budget illustrates the process. Initial budget instructions to the campuses were issued in December of 1972 (halfway through the 1972–1973 fiscal year) and were followed by guidelines for critical academic resources (estimated enrollments and staffing standards) in January 1973. In March of 1973, campuses submitted issues and problems relating to 1974–1975, and in May of 1973, they submitted full financial budgets for review by the office of the president. The proposed allocations to campuses were sent out in July 1973 for comment; reactions were received in August; the preliminary 1974–1975 proposed regents' budget was sent to the finance committee of the regents in September; and in October 1973, the regents' proposed 1974–1975 budget was approved for submission to the state government.

State budgeting calendars and procedures differ, and some work on a biennial rather than a one-year budgeting cycle. In California, the governor released the executive budget for 1974–1975 to the legislature in late January of 1974, for its consideration in budget hearings during the months following. Legislative action was not completed until June. Then there is often a flurry of activity as the governor vetoes some items (in California, the governor has a powerful form of veto that enables him to reduce by any amount any one line item of the budget). And finally, in late July or August, the legislature attempts to override some budget vetoes and restore cuts with which it disagrees. Meanwhile, the fiscal year that was the object of budgetary scrutiny had already begun on July 1, 1974.

In this setting, the senior administration and budget office of a university may have to keep track, simultaneously, of up to four fiscal-year budgets and their interrelations: (1) the most recently completed fiscal year, as a fully known and completed base; (2) the current fiscal-year budget, for control and administration in its own right and as a base for the following fiscal-year budget; (3) the preparation and defense of the following fiscal-year budget; and (4) the earliest indicators of developing issues for the second-following fiscal year. In a complex university, with dozens of budgetary standards, hundreds of activity centers of identified functions, and thousands of line items, it has been necessary to develop aids to budget accounting and control and methods of partially automating the budget accounting and its interyear ties. Given the level of complexity and detail, and the demands of reporting and justification, the budgeting process is always in danger of bogging down in detail and mechanics. Thus, it is necessary to apply very conscious pressure to save time for issues of policy substance.

A private university does not have to run the gauntlet of master negotiation for its basic support budget. Some steps in the process are eliminated, because negotiation with the state is not required. But the private university faces two other requirements that are more demanding for it than for the state institution. It relies proportionately more on extramural research funding and foundation grants than does the state-supported institution, and it is also more sensitive to variations in the income yield from endowments and in the income from tuition. Its revenue forecasting must therefore be very exacting. Also, the private university—because basic institutional support for its administration, academic units and faculty, library, and other basic operations are not underwritten from a (hopefully) stable state source—may have to react quickly to cuts in research funds or other extramural funds. It must preserve capability for quick within-year adjustments.

Budget Adjustment Strategies

Fiscal stress in universities—the causes of it and contemporary evidence about it—was discussed in Chapter Eight. Here we are concerned with the problem of budgetary control and an examination of four well-known strategies of budgetary adjustment.

Universities pass through phases of ebullient growth, managed stability or drift, slow decay, and, occasionally, sharp financial crisis. Whatever the phase, budgetary control has to be exerted. Aspirations for new work and the hankering for a higher institutional living standard produce a continual gap between expenditure aspirations and fiscal realities. Besides these pressures for program, amenities, and experiments (a worthwhile motivating pressure, in principle, and one whose absence would indicate serious institutional illness!), a specific feature of institutional organization gives rise to needs for budgetary control. General institutional resources are always at a premium. Demands for them come from three different sources: induced or required matching of special and restricted funds; the underwriting of direct academic programs that are valid old or new commitments of the institution but do not have any extramural support; and, most important, the budgetary support of core activities that are indispensable but unloved. The sum of these demands on general funds of the institution is invariably more than can be comfortably met within available general fund revenues, and so rationing through the budgetary process is required.

Close observers of higher education have noted that institutions often behave as if they were seeking to maximize expenditures —the larger the budget, the better. Many of the indicia of quality and vitality—high faculty salaries, generous allocations to the library, ease of funding new academic ventures—are associated with a high and rising expenditure rate. But this puts all the more premium on the careful assessment of revenues and the planning of revenue growth to support such a pattern of intended expenditures. The president of a private university needs to worry about money-raising and tuition policy. The president of a public university must worry about keeping the confidence of the state's governor and legislature, because the state's appropriation is the most crucial element of the institution's general funds.

Control and adjustment of the expenditure pattern can have positive or perverse effects on incentives and efficiency within the institution, depending on the manner in which the signals of control are designed and interpreted. A classic device in governmental budgeting, for example, is withdrawal of unspent balances from an agency at the end of a fiscal year and, often, reduction of the following year's allocation to reflect the excess in the previous allocation. This approach causes agency heads to spend all of their current fiscal-year allocations, even if they must make last minute commitments for equipment and supplies purchases or other expenditures that may have dubious merit. (In order to control this, still another layer of restraint is sometimes added—a bar against new commitments after a cutoff date late in the fiscal year.) The budget managers of a university create the same incentive if they require the return of unspent balances to a central, budget-balancing pool. Yet they may have to do so to balance out the fiscal year's total expenditures against total revenues and avoid budget overruns.

The budgeted expenditure pattern reflects the priority status of programs and functions. Year-to-year changes in the allocation for a given activity may be made because of shifts in earmarked revenues (control of the volume of an activity by the funding source), to offset price inflation that is eroding the real basis of support (influence of market events), because enrollment interest has shifted toward some fields and away from others (influence of student demand), or because an activity is assigned a changed priority (control according to institutional objectives). What is at stake, then, is the type and direction of control exerted over what the university is doing.

The expenditure pattern and the revenue-getting capability of the university are linked by demands for accountability. Donors to the private university may be reluctant to give if they perceive gross waste or if they are dissatisfied with the direction the university is taking. State governments are concerned about efficiency issues and also about the university's success or failure in adhering to numerous policy constraints imposed by the state.

These are some of the concerns about the focus and style of adjustments of both revenue and expenditures. The size of the swings to be dealt with, upward or downward, also affects both the type of budgetary adjustment strategy that can be used and the intensity of the response required. Universities are usually held to be far more capable of accommodating growth than of absorbing the pain of retrenchment. For retrenchment, both adjustment time and the absolute or percentage amount of reduction must be considered. With these considerations in mind, we now turn to an examination of four budgetary adjustment strategies.

Enriching or Reducing Budgetary Standards. The other three budgetary adjustment strategies all focus on programs, activities, or organizational units, and on different ways to arrange related budget adjustments. But a different dimensional view can be taken: namely, to adjust—upward or downward—a budgetary standard that is important enough to affect most facets of the university's operations and have important effects on the budget. Two illustrative problems are adjustments in the student-faculty ratio and in the standard for building maintenance.

A change in an important budgetary standard can produce substantial dollar impact on total budget because the budget components for many units of the institution are affected. Raising a question about a budgetary standard, such as the student-faculty ratio, defines a different domain of argument than does raising a question about a particular program or activity. The student-faculty ratio, after all, is based on a rough judgment of average academic staffing needs across many departments, with different compositions of undergraduate and graduate enrollment, different scales and styles of work, and different stages of development. Once such a question is raised, say, about increasing the ratio by enough so that enrollment-induced entitlement to more faculty positions will not be permitted, then the institution's president and the academic deans and department chairmen have trouble constructing an opposing argument. They may take the position that other institutions, similar to theirs in character and quality, have a richer academic staffing standard than the one proposed, and that, therefore, raising the student-faculty ratio would harm the university's quality. But this argument lacks concreteness. Or, alternatively, they may undertake a detailed analysis, to show adverse consequences, department by department and program by program, of the proposed change. But the use of a generalized standard such as the student-faculty ratio is in the first instance designed to avoid issues of detailed academic judgments which, if discussed at all, will put those who raise questions (whether they are private university trustees or state budget officers) in the position of offering counterjudgments about the merits of academic programs and their staffing requirements.

Thus, it is easy to see why budget cutters may choose to

attack the existing budgetary standards and why it is difficult for institutional spokesmen to counterattack.

Proportional Adjustment of Dollar Budgets. Suppose that a specific budget increase or decrease is determined to be necessary. Those concerned with internal administration of the university may simply distribute to every relevant unit the same percentage magnitude of upward or downward adjustment. Such a rule of simple proportionality seems fair, since all units share equally in the pain or gain. Especially in the early stages of budgetary retrenchment, or in response to what appears to be a temporary or one-time adjustment need, the institution's budget administrators often adopt this tactic. It is politically safe, because it avoids invidious distinctions between the contributions of various units. It is easy to calculate and enforce.

An alternative to simple dollar proportionality is work-load proportionality. For example, projected FTE enrollment for the fiscal period could be used as the basis for distribution of the given dollar change in the aggregate budget. If the budget allocation has customarily been made in accordance with a work-load standard, this method has internal plausibility throughout the institution and contains the presumption that resource needs change in accordance with changes of work load. However, it equates the average work-load requirement with the marginal requirement, which may not make much sense. Also, the distribution of resources within the institution is then governed, in the case of enrollment work loads, by shifts of student enrollment interest in programs. Carried far enough, this approach may compel the crippling or even closure of departments that, from the standpoint of compositional balance and longer-range institutional commitment, are regarded as worthwhile to the institution even if they temporarily would not qualify for resources according to an enrollment work-load standard.

Although a scheme of dollar proportionality or work-load proportionality may work for a time, persistent budget adjustment pressure must eventually arouse doubts. The short-term advantage of proportionality adjustment is precisely in avoiding questions about objectives, efficiency, and quality of performance. Nevertheless, there are implicit views in any institution concerning those aspects of its academic operations that are most important to it. There is also an internal distribution of power and influence in the academic leadership. Even during the early stages of application of a proportionality adjustment rule, some affected units may demand partial or full exemption from the cuts. Some of these, backed with cogent arguments about consequences at the margin or lack of adjustability of the unit's budget, may indeed be persuasive. But the granting of exemptions then increases the adjustment burden to be shared among other units.

Eventually, some units and their spokesmen may suggest that selective choices (presumably, in their favor) should be made, even if these must be based on the primacy of some objectives at the expense of others or on hard judgments about efficiency and quality. Meanwhile, however, repeated application of proportional adjustments has had two bad effects: the gradual weakening of performance and morale throughout the institution, among strong units as well as weaker ones; and the loss of time. If the issue of selective priority arises late, it arises as an emergency question. The response under these circumstances is unlikely to be sound and coherent, because substantial lead time is needed for adequate investigation of the merits of one scheme of selective priority over another.

"Every Tub on Its Own Bottom". Proportionality rules need to be administered centrally to distribute expenditure reductions. "Every tub on its own bottom" is a way to avoid even this degree of central administration responsibility. The concept is an old one, but its modern use and its nickname were popularized by former President Nathan Pusey of Harvard University. Each decentralized school or major program ("tub") is made responsible for generating its own operating revenue ("bottom") through extramural grants, contracts, and gifts; and sometimes the tuition income generated by enrollment in a program is left with the program to finance its budget. The essence of it is: let the market rule. If the program attracts funds and students, it can survive and even grow. If not, it may be given a grace period for a dignified passing instead of a sudden one, but the presumption is that it must die.

Fixing the responsibility for program survival on the program's entrepreneurial leadership provides strong motivation. The scheme has a measure of quality control built in, provided that funding sources use expert panels to place contracts and grants where scholarly reputation and the prospect of excellent work are highest. Funding agency and donor judgments are not, however, valid indicators of academic quality in programs where success is gained by doing applied work according to terms imposed by the fundor. If tuition revenue is left with a program, and if it has de facto control over student recruitment and admission, the program may pump enrollment for the sake of income, without adequate concern about the qualifications of students. It may also tolerate class sizes that are too high.

This allocation policy cannot be applied individually to academic areas that are strongly complementary and interdependent, as they are in the liberal arts undergraduate curriculum of a university. At Harvard, the main reach of the policy is toward the professional schools and some graduate programs—it does not extend to Harvard College. The policy would defeat most infant programs in an expanding university; these need seed money for the early years of development.

Even if the hazards of interdependence and of choking off young programs are avoided through judicious application of the policy, two deeper problems remain. The policy assumes that decentralized coupling of revenue and expenditure works to the institutional interests because funding and enrollment market signals are valid. But these signals may not be fully valid as a basis for institutional policy, and they may change much faster than the adjustment capability (particularly, the downward adjustment capability) of the program.

The mechanics of operation under this form of decentralization also pose problems. Most decentralized programs are not totally freestanding. Students often need to circulate among them. Faculty may need to be borrowed back and forth. Services of the central administration in business management, accounting, and other functions are generally characterized by economies of scale. If decentralized units perform these services, costs are high; if they use centrally provided services, careful cost accounting and recharge billing need to be done to allocate costs to the locations where revenue is. Similar observations can be made about computer centers, libraries, and major laboratories. The "every tub" philosophy may only too easily be taken as a mandate for excessive, autarchic decentralization of some functions, and it may weaken the quality of central administration and centrally provided academic support services. The decentralized resource policy may also inhibit the responsiveness of units to institution-wide policies and requirements —for example, for affirmative action in hiring—or even to demands for sufficient information to enable the central administration to understand, interpret, and defend the institution.

The positive appeal of this decentralized revenue-and-expenditure control policy—aside from the opportunity that it gives the central administration to escape the onus of adjustments—is the appeal of decentralization in any organization: authority and responsibility are firmly coupled, and the entrepreneurial capability of the leaders and members of the decentralized unit is both stimulated and tested. The question is whether this very great virtue is more than offset by the hazards and defects that have been pointed out.

Budgetary Adjustment According to Selective Program Priorities. This policy requires assessment of the program commitments of the institution and comparison of the resource costs and apparent efficiency of each one with what it delivers, quantitatively and qualitatively, toward the objectives of the university. On the basis of this assessment, differential treatment is accorded to different programs and areas of activity. Some may be permitted to remain at stable size and resource commitments; others are given targets of resource reduction while remaining at the same scale; still others are permitted work-load growth and resource allocations accordingly; and still others may be provided resources to do new things or improve quality of performance. Some programs may be determined to be unnecessary and may be phased out, with more or less time given for this painful process. The selective priority approach may also entail plans for reorganization, use of a different technology or style, and consolidation of activities.

This approach is by far the most upsetting, among all those discussed, to the organization and decision-making style of a university. At each stage—from funding, to program operation, to goal contribution—what goes on in a university is perceived by many of its actors as exhibiting properties of independence or complementarity. Cost analysis is made difficult by the existence of strong elements of jointness in the sharing of resources by several activities and jointness in contribution toward objectives. These factors make it difficult to assemble the evidence that is required to make selective decisions appear fair to the institutional community. When a program may be dropped, neither the faculty, staff, and students immediately affected nor an interested support-clientele in the outer community can draw much balm from the outcome of the decision process if it is adverse to them. The most that can be done is to show that the decision was reached only after careful and fair-minded inquiry, with use of a legitimate institutional process and with opportunities for fair hearing by the affected groups. Softening the blow to interests and pride by putting the phaseout in the form of reorganization and amalgamation sometimes makes a phaseout decision more palatable. Showing clearly that the fiscal circumstances or approved mission of the institution require drastic action can engage the sympathy, or allay the alarm, of other parts of the administrative and academic leadership—those who must at least be persuaded not to oppose actively what is done and if possible should share responsibility for it. Sometimes the blame for the decision can be exported to an outside funding source whose support has been withdrawn, or to a level of decision in the institution or the superstructure of coordination that is beyond the reach of the internal constituencies.

Precisely because it is costly in time and institutional energy, a selective priority scheme for retrenchment can accomplish only a modest number of major changes in each fiscal period. This cost is unlikely to be borne under ordinary circumstances. Selective priority usually becomes acceptable to constituencies within the institution only after repeated experience has been gained with fiscal and program tightening (as one governor has called it, "cut, squeeze, and trim"). But the case for selective priority is that the alternatives are worse. During a period of institutional expansion, selective approaches are needed for otherwise uncontrolled and ad hoc proliferation of programs, some of which will likely weaken instead of strengthen the institution. Selective priority is equally necessary during a period of retrenchment, for the alternative is some form of proportional budget-cutting that would produce anemia everywhere, weakening strong and essential programs in order to keep less important programs alive, even though these cannot be accorded enough resources to overcome performance difficulties.

A scheme of selective priority cannot work without the following ingredients: (1) a technical capability to analyze costs, interactions, and goal contributions of programs, and access to comparative data to buttress the findings; (2) a way of joining credible and expert academic judgments with fiscal information; (3) an institutional process that meets conditions of fairness; and (4) a quality and range of academic and administrative leadership that can reach and enforce decisions without losing the ability to function in the future.

Budgetary Controls, Internal Pricing, Incentives

As we observed in Chapter Three, the many units of a university operate according to their perceptions of what they should be doing individually, and they also acknowledge interdependencies and their obligation to contribute to the larger purposes of the institution. Administrative units, as was discussed in Chapter Four, are sometimes self-funded parts of the institution, seeking to confine their expenditures to the amount of internal revenue they can gain by billing their customers in the institution for services rendered. Other administrative units, such as the accounting office and the personnel office, are budgeted from institutional funds.

All budgeted units, academic and administrative, derive signals from the scheme of controls through which the annual budget is administered and from the budgetary adjustment strategy that is used. Some major consequences of the university's resource-allocation policies can be summarized by examining the specific incentives released by these signals and strategies.

Brief mention has already been made of the end-of-year recovery of unspent balances—a classic device of governmental budgeting. At the very least, this policy produces short-term incentives to spend the whole of the budgetary allocation. The disincentive to economical management is compounded if the following year's budget allocation is based on the *expenditures* made in the current year. If this is done, any savings and resulting unspent balances actually penalize the unit's future budget. (The perverse effects of this sort of budgetary control—which may be forced on a public university by state budgetary rules—can be reduced by making it clear that future budgets will not be reduced when unspent balances are reported, and reduced still further if a unit that makes economies is permitted to carry over or apply in a discretionary way some substantial part of the savings.)

The budgetary strategy of proportional adjustments also conveys perverse managerial incentives for both short-term economies—because all units receive the same budget cut regardless of whether they manage well—and for longer-term efforts to contribute to institutional aims. It is true that economizing pressures are applied throughout the institution when proportional cuts are made, and that clever management can offset some of the negative consequences. But no differential reward is given for exceptionally efficient or effective performance. Also, some units can absorb a given percentage cut in budget with relative ease, whereas the same percentage reduction might be devastating to other units—and a rule of proportionality fails to consider these differences.

The manager of a self-funded unit has clear responsibility for keeping expenditures within the boundaries of revenue from recharge billings. However, this does not guarantee that the unit will be operated at the highest possible level of efficiency, because the prices it charges may simply cover costs—even if costs are higher than they should be. Frequently, self-funded units are authorized to set their own recharge prices for cost recovery and to do their own cost accounting within general rules (such as the federal rules that are intended to prevent price discrimination against federal grants in the pricing of computer services). Also, the campus administration may prohibit the use of outside sources of similar services. This would give the self-funded unit *de facto* monopoly within the institution.

It is true, nevertheless, that a system of prices for services rendered to individuals or organizational units makes such customers consider carefully how much of the service to buy and—if several qualities of service are available at different prices—what quality they find appropriate. Whether it is a personal budget or a budget of an organizational unit, a decision to economize on the service leaves more funds for other needs. The alternative to charging a price for a needed service that costs something to produce is to allocate it among users by means of administrative decisions. Some rationing takes place—by making people wait in queues or by classifying some users as eligible and others as ineligible—but it is rationing by administrative choices rather than by allowing users discretion to make their own decisions.

An industrial corporation that has several decentralized operating divisions often uses a system of internal prices (sometimes called transfer prices) to focus responsibility on each division manager for contributing to the overall profit performance of the corporation. The division receives revenue credits on the books of the corporation for the volume of components, subassemblies, or other items that it produces and sends to other divisions. The division that receives these items has to recognize their cost to it (the number of units multiplied by the transfer price). If the transfer prices are set correctly, the contribution of each operating division to the overall profits of the corporation can be determined. The manager who contributes most can be rewarded, and the manager who does poorly can be penalized.

Such internal pricing is an approximation of the invisible hand of a market system as an alternative to the visible hand of administratively determined allocations. There is considerable interest in using this device in universities to stimulate managerial rationality in both the producer and the user of services. There are many possible designs for such pricing schemes. Pricing approaches are also potentially suitable for allocating some scarce resources within a university, but it might well be a mistake to try them for other allocations when higher-level coordination and guidance of the institution as a whole are directly involved. The opportunities and the problems, including some of the practical difficulties of implementation, are discussed by Breneman (1971a).

Summary

We have now completed the discussion of mechanisms and procedures for university budgeting, of analytical questions about budgetary choices, and of budgetary strategies that a university can pursue. In Chapter Ten we look at data systems. These are important not only as informational support to the process of resource allocation but also for a wide variety of other institutional purposes.

Chapter 10

Institutional
Data Systems

The organization of a university is complicated because there are several classes of internal participants. Each individual within each of these classes has to connect with different units of organization for different purposes. And the university has to maintain relationships with numerous external constituencies. Given these attributes of the contemporary university, it should be no surprise that the data systems of such an institution are large and costly.

Those in official roles—administrators, faculty, student spokesmen, and members of the governing board—have different concerns about information and who gets it. They need information to operate in their own roles. They generate (or resist generating) information for others in related official roles. And, because they often have substantial direct or indirect dealings with the various groups of people who care about the institution, they supply or filter information to these people.

One crucial distinction must be made clear: that between *data* and *information*. Raw data—individual entries in the ledger, lists of names in a file cabinet, notes in an envelope in the president's coat pocket, or a record that Andrew Green got a B- in English 103 in the fall quarter—scarcely qualify as information. Information is a set of elements needed for a current or future decision. Raw data always need to be aggregated, transformed, interpreted, and appropriately conveyed to serve as information for a decision.

An ideal data system for a university would contain, in accessible form, all the raw facts necessary to supply the pertinent information—no more and no less—to a decision-maker having a valid need for it. The system would draw these facts from all the scattered sources and combine them in just the right way. It would translate the information into terms convenient to the decision-maker. It would deliver the information instantly, and it would operate at zero cost! Such a data system is not of this world, and this chapter is thus concerned with the burdens and hazards of arriving at tolerable compromises.

Data Files for Operations, Management, Planning, Evaluation

Several broad categories of operating data are maintained for the high volume of activities in a university: accounting, financial, and budget; students; employed personnel; facilities and equipment; and inventoried supplies. Within each of these categories, there is further subdivision. The breakdown of subfiles is standardized for accounting and financial record files in accordance with the standard manual of college and university financial accounting. Many of the other operating files are separated according to the scale, complexity, and mode of organization of the institution. Accidents of institutional history, for example, may determine whether the records of student financial aid are regarded as student files and kept in acordance with the style and tastes of the student affairs offices, or are regarded as accounting and business files and kept in those units.

Systematic work on the development of manuals in areas other than accounting gives guidelines for definitions, classification, and recording of transactions. The form of the record-keeping system for personnel is often mandated by state civil service regulations for state-supported institutions. Personnel data systems in other institutions have been developed along lines that were convenient and were considered appropriate by administrators, and there is a great deal of variety in the form, substance, and degree of detail across institutions.

But most data systems for operations have generally been products of administrative evolution and higher-level neglect. After all, there used to be no more searing insult to an academic leader than to call him a great administrator. It was all right to be known as a chooser of good people and important ideas in addition to being good at the eternal hustle for resources. But to be intimately concerned with choosing systems and knowledgeable about their details was no encomium in the universities.

When the customary operating data systems of an institution are studied to modernize them and to convert them to computer processing, several issues are likely to arise: How can definitions and categories be made sufficiently precise to permit standardized treatment? What provisions should be made to permit cross-referencing between files (for example, between the payroll file in the accounting system and the student status and financial aid files in the student record system)? Can the modernization of each data system be accomplished with the present scheme of administrative organization, or is a reshuffling of units and their responsibilities called for? Can each data system be left with the relevant operating unit, or is it necessary to consolidate the files and transaction-recording functions in one place, with the operating unit responsible for determining what to put into the system and then responsible for using it, while a data-processing center takes care of storage, processing, and data management? Many similar questions arise when data systems are modernized to support day-to-day operations. But at the next higher level, a manager who supervises operating units wants the data system for daily operations to provide ready summaries and indicators for purposes of managerial control. He or she also wants the system to provide the material needed for standard reports to external agencies.

First-level managers generally act within existing policies of the university, perhaps with some discretion in applying these policies in particular cases. Administrators at the policy-making level want the data system to provide them with indicators showing whether subordinates are adhering to existing policies, and they also need data in order to consider whether to make changes in existing policies. Those who are responsible for institutional planning have still another set of needs for data.

Data files and data controls for daily operations are not easily adapted to these other purposes. The manager who supervises operating units needs summaries and indicators showing whether each operating unit is performing properly and may also need cross-referencing between the data files of the one unit and those of another to assure coordination. For purposes of policy enforcement, the manager's transactional summaries are not enough. The data system may need to be used for spot checks to assure conformity with existing policies.

Studies leading to possible policy changes and analyses for planning require that some data not in the day-to-day flow be maintained. The operating data files may also need to be organized differently for these purposes. Finally, policy analysts and planners frequently have to explore new questions which could not have been anticipated when the data files were originally designed. To do so, they may have to extract data from numerous scattered sources, and the cost and convenience of doing so depend on whether a flexible data system exists.

Here are two examples to illustrate the problems of creating data systems that are responsive to needs at several levels of decision-making.

First, it is sufficient, in maintaining academic records concerning currently enrolled students, to know a student's address, major, accumulated academic credits, and whether he or she is still active. The system may have to provide transcript information for a student who previously graduated or one who withdrew or transferred, but there is no interest in adding more information to the file of a student who is no longer active. As we know only too well, however, evaluation of the academic impact of an institution includes attention to both the reasons for and the fate of dropouts and to the careers of graduated students. For much shorter-term planning and budgeting purposes, student records may be a source of estimates of the numbers of continuing students and their expected presence in various courses. The operational files are usually not organized to permit such estimates to be made directly. (In the case of dropouts, there is a hole in follow-up that limits the usefulness of the file for evaluation; in the case of course enrollment, organization of the data impedes its use as direct input for short-term planning.)

As another example, university accounting systems are designed as fund accounting systems—to assure stewardship of funds (including adherence to any restrictions on the use of a particular fund), to record transactions accurately, and to maintain control against overspending of each fund account. The budgeting system, and budget accounting, are overlays on the financial accounts. Academic department heads, research directors, and others who must assure themselves that their areas of responsibility are in control often cannot get current information from the accounting system concerning the amounts spent relative to the total amount budgeted or available, and they therefore have to maintain supplemental accounting schemes. Also, the financial accounting system contains great amounts of transaction data, but these are usually inaccessible for cost-accounting purposes, and a cost-accounting capability that will extract usable parts of the data base and supply cost-accounting information to managers has usually not been incorporated into accounting systems.

Although we now have data systems that allow systematic attention to the problems of management control and planning, we need to make decisions about what features to incorporate to provide information for the higher-level decisions I have just described. Beyond this, institutions find now that they must deal increasingly with demands from the growing state and federal superstructures concerned with higher education for reports and justifications. This increase of attention toward superstructure also increases demands on institutional administrators to function in new ways as institutions become vulnerable to resource constraint.

The Emergence of System

The architects of superstructure have had to learn what questions to ask about what is going on in institutions, so that they can determine what blueprints for operations to put forward and what notions about priorities and direction to advance. One of the main pressures toward system has thus been the appetite of state budgeting agencies and coordinating bodies for information. The responsibility to provide this information devolves first on the institutional spokesmen and their administrative cadres, who react to their initial embarrassment about being uninformed by insisting on concrete and detailed information from individuals and operating units.

The superstructure operators need, for various kinds of analysis and comparison, information that they can rely on and that is expressed in standard form. And so their demands are for form as well as substance. A lexicon is emerging: FTE students; FTE faculty and employees; workload measures; and the rest.

The National Center for Higher Education Management Systems (NCHEMS) at the Western Interstate Commission on Higher Education (WICHE) has become the major interlocutor for determining the appropriate definitions and details in many areas of measurement and reporting. In 1968, a planning and management systems project at WICHE was initiated by representatives of several western universities. These administrators saw needs to cooperate by pooling efforts toward the design and use of information-gathering tools. They felt that these tools were needed so that they could cope better with their institutional problems and with the rising pressures for better information coming from state budget offices and coordinators. The early idea has had all but outrageous success in spreading to include all types of institutions, becoming a nationwide effort, and engaging the participation and backing not only of state agencies but of the federal establishment, which now provides most of the funds for the work of NCHEMS.

This burgeoning development has emerged as so consequential that many alarms are now being sounded. Cheit (1973) poses the issue of "The Management Systems Challenge: How to be Academic Though Systematic." He provides an interpretive survey of the many motivations that have brought the NCHEMS effort to its current state. He raises doubts about whether it is likely to mute the external critics of inefficiency in higher education, and he offers a guardedly positive evaluation of its likely impact on most institutions that adopt NCHEMS tools for management and planning. In a discussion, below, on features of several subsystems, I offer some comments on the uses, current limitations, and future prospects for NCHEMS measurement tools. First, however, it is necessary to turn attention to the various kinds of clients (and critics) of academic institutions who see needs for answers to their questions and who, therefore, have much to say about the agenda for institutional data systems.

Who Cares? About What?

Academic institutions serve a generalized public interest and are entitled to say so. However, many individuals and organizations have a "need to know" in order to evaluate and decide: the prospective student—whether to come; the alumnus—whether to support the institution with concern or money; the seller of supplies—on what terms to sell what to the institution; the well-known faculty member at a sister institution—whether to send a student, recommend a candidate for a faculty post, or accept an offer to come in as department chairman; the accrediting organization—whether to accord good standing to the institution or to an important program within it; the trustee—whether to be pleased or alarmed or both; the current student—whether to work harder, change major, participate more as a citizen of the institution, or perhaps leave for study elsewhere or for employment; the current faculty member— whether to push for better pay, take on an extra course, or press harder on research interests; the current member of administrative staff—whether to keep on as is, make changes, aim toward advancement in the administrative hierarchy, or consider other jobs; the legislator—whether to believe the claims of need for student aid, and institutional support, and the claims for freedom from legislative influence or control; the foundation or research agency—whether to accept and fund a proposal for research or institutional improvement on the basis of the capabilities of the proposers and of the institution.

All these sources of evaluative judgment and their characteristic concerns have been with us for a long time. These individual judgments sum up to determine the conditions for survival, in terms of both internal cohesion and marketplace viability for enrollment and funding. American colleges and universities have always had to face a rough form of accountability. Several new factors make the evaluative judgments sharper now and increase the importance of information:

(1) The total enrollment market has grown enormously; the right to college opportunity has broadened; and more institutions, programs, and students are participating. Information—to show what the institution is like, to help attract the students it seeks, and to show how well it serves—has become far more sophisticated.

(2) Most institutions are more complicated than before. There are more competitors (and more possibilities for symbiotic cooperation) than previously, and each institution has more interest in comparing its activities and performance with those of other institutions.

(3) Higher education is more important in the public mind; policies toward it have become more urgent business for legislators, Congress, commissions, and assemblies; blue-ribbon panels have announced solutions at a rapid rate; and higher education also has tougher competition among public-sector activities.

(4) Inflation and productivity problems, together with the willingness or proneness of institutions to take on additional programs and responsibilities, have tightened the budget squeeze each faces, reduced fiscal flexibility, and created new struggles about academic and institutional priorities.

(5) Shifts in manpower markets (national, regional, and local) and shifts in other major features of the market environment for educational services (including the results of research and scholarship) have become more frequent, and several of these factors shifted adversely at the end of the 1960s.

Stresses Created by Information

Determination of the right course of action has become more difficult, and individuals now call for more information. Organizations impinging on educational institutions face a great variety of pressures and claims, and they want more and different information than before. Academic institutions face more urgent problems of adjustment, viability, and even purposes, and they must have more kinds of information, in new frames, to find their way and settle their problems. If more information is not forthcoming, people will make snap decisions or power decisions, neither of which is desirable. But the amount and variety of needed information are also alarming: educational effectiveness and payoff; program scope, quality, and interdependence; fiscal responsibility and institutional efficiency. No wonder there is increasing stress over questions of reporting, measurement, and evaluation!

Another factor that increases stress is the erosion of old distinctions between what is external and what is internal. Both the members of the internal institutional community and the external supporters or questioners share overlapping interests in evaluative questions, but they have differing perspectives about these questions. An old tactic of the working politician was to make different speeches to different groups of constituents, and the institutional balancer of forces—usually the president—may at least shade the story for each audience. But his different audiences communicate with each other, and all have access to most of what he says. Reports and estimates quickly become common property, even though they might have been produced with different assumptions for different purposes. To the extent that adversary relations, debate, or hard conflict may be generated around an issue, information is by no means neutral, and seeming inconsistencies in the information provided can arouse strong feeling. Ordinarily, most of the interested parties are benign, if not passive, most of the time; but a seemingly routine estimate (for example, that of the unit cost of instruction per student year) may suddenly come to the front of attention simultaneously for budget consideration, changes in tuition or fees, and arguments about faculty compensation.

In an atmosphere of concern, interest, and incipient contention about many matters, control over the data systems of the institution and over the statistics that they produce may also become a lively issue. Data systems need to be reliable instruments for analysis and for providing evaluative information, but these data systems are necessarily compromises because they must serve so many masters. These inevitable compromises cause any data system to be less than perfect for some of its users. And, because it is costly to build in flexibility and rapid response, a data system seriously constrained by budget limitations is likely to be especially criticized by its users.

If the hazards of inflaming controversies by providing additional information are perceived as serious, it would be tempting to avoid producing the information or to try to regulate access to it. Some data—about pending transactions or about confidential relations between the institution and individual persons—can be protected. Increasingly wide disclosure of most aggregative reports and measures has become the trend, however, and it is necessary to assume that reports on almost all topics—budgets, student persistence and attrition, accreditation and reputation ratings of academic programs, faculty salaries, to name a few—are likely to become grist for everyone's mill.

A traditional source of power in the senior administration has been a monopoly of crucial information, or at least a substantial lead time to cope with particulars and a near monopoly on the ability to correlate and coordinate information from a variety of external and internal sources. For the most part, this power remains for most pending negotiations, but the senior administrators cannot withhold most important information from interested constituencies. In an adversary climate, the widespread availability of information reduces the latitude of senior administrators in doing the balancing act.

A sense that there are problems, heightened appreciation of the problems as a result of more knowledge about them, and the frustration of contending groups—all lead to tensions that can either paralyze action or result in the creative release of institutional energies. The task of a college or university president and of other key spokesmen is functionally different now, when interested parties feel eligible and equipped to debate their claims and concerns.

University leaders need to assure that more information is provided to the larger number of participants in the institutional dialogue. Pending issues need to be stated clearly, and enough information must be provided to heighten the prospects of responsible advocacy. Thus, data systems and reporting must develop information flows that increase understanding and facilitate decisions toward good institutional ends.

Many individuals in the complex environment of academic

institutions perceive themselves as powerless, lacking ability either to contribute or to pursue their own interests. If the institutions cannot be made simpler—and this is seldom possible—the only remedy for this spreading anomie is to provide an understandable conceptual picture of the whole, so that individuals can relate their local perceptions to it. To determine their immediate actions, individuals usually need more precise and timely information than has traditionally been delivered to them. But the information they need to gain broader perspective about the university is even more important, and the institutional leadership has a responsibility to help people toward such perspective. This responsibility goes far beyond providing data. Ways need to be found to discuss institutional aims and organizing concepts and to relate what the university is all about to what society is and will be like. Only limited progress with these difficult responsibilities is being made now in most colleges and universities, but they may be the most important eventual product of the interpretation of and inferences from information gained through data systems.

Institutional Style

These comments flow from my views about the preferred style of operation and policy-setting and the handling of decisions and disagreements in colleges and universities in the contemporary American cultural setting. This preference is based on the proposition that the most important things that happen in these institutions are the learning efforts of students and creative scholars, and that this learning is most powerfully elicited under voluntaristic conditions of personal commitment.

Defense of the institution as a legal entity is essential. The administrative operations of the institution need to be well designed, well manned, and capable of providing a strong enabling frame for learning. The political defense of the institution against its detractors and enemies, wherever situated, is a hard responsibility of its leadership. But I believe that important consequences flow from the voluntaristic and self-propelling character of the process of learning by individuals and groups of scholars.

According to this concept, each member of the institution feels obliged to pursue learning and encourage others. Students, faculty, and staff are able to get the information that they need for their actions and to use it to make up their minds about what to do in most situations, subject to known rules and good access to advisory judgments. There must be an open process within the institution for matters of interest to all institutional citizens.

Once all these conditions exist, the task the institution has of dealing with its many publics is highly dependent on its ability to convey and interpret information about its operations and its policies. These, too, must be open processes.

In this situation, to be sure, sanctions are available and enforced. People have to pay their bills and meet their commitments. Units of the organization are held to their budgets. Plans are subject to open consideration and debate, but then are adopted and enforced as institutional guides unless or until circumstances warrant changing them. In this perspective, access to information is an important precondition for understanding and personal responsibility.

There are other, competing concepts of the best way to function. One is the legal-bureaucratic concept from the governing board on down. Another—the political concept—consists in mobilizing power through the use of money, organizational position, and political alliance. These considerations are never absent from any working organization.

The ongoing, institutional style is actually some mixture of the legal-bureaucratic, the political, and the voluntaristic schemes that rely substantially on individual initiatives and on widespread information. The other competing styles tend to impose barriers against the propagation and accessibility of some information. Because of the relevance of both the legal and the political concerns to the survival of institutions and the risks faced by key people in their jobs, there is a case against the concept of voluntarism and generally open information. Nevertheless, I argue here that, in the interest of fundamental efficiencies—namely those having to do with learning—these risks ought to be borne.

Information for Planning

The modernization of data-handling systems within colleges and universities almost always has to start with the operating data areas. Computerized data systems are usually developed first in those areas having high transaction volumes and frequent routine updating—payroll, ledger accounting, sometimes budget breakdown and budget control, and student records and transcripts. From there, the modernization of data systems proceeds both laterally, to include more areas of operating concern, and vertically, to accommodate cross-referencing between operating files and the integration and interpretation of material for management and planning purposes.

Operating data systems have as their primary initial users and operators the people responsible for particular administrative units of the institution: the chief accounting officer, the dean of the engineering college, the manager of business services, the registrar, the chairman of the math department, the director of the physics laboratory, the head librarian, and so on. To the extent that these administrators need anticipatory information (for example, projections of budgeted expenditures for the remainder of a fiscal period), prompt summary reporting and some projecting capability are needed, even for informational support for operations. And to provide these is no small step.

The kinds of regular operating reports that depend on these operating data include the following: quarterly financial summaries and annual reports of the sources and uses of funds; the annual budget document, divided into operating and capital budget sections, and a comparison with the previous year; a report of course enrollments and instructional loading on academic departments; reports of persistence, attrition, and degrees granted, by major and level of degree; reports of the assets and liabilities of the institution, including investments and the returns on them, and of the debt structure. These reports are often published and are surely made available to the governing board. In addition, the administration may require performance and activity reports from the heads of organizational units, either in conjunction with budget review or in addition to it.

For management control and planning, data in operating files must often be brought together and reorganized because the boundaries of the individual areas of operating responsibility (which determine how the data are collected and kept) do not usually conform with the boundaries of management and planning problems. Just as important is the ability to supplement operating data with other information—longitudinal follow-up concerning students, comparative faculty salary information from other institutions, estimates of future price trends on purchased supplies.

NCHEMS has developed a series of measurement techniques for management, planning, and institutional comparison. This Resource Requirements Prediction Model (RRPM) is intended to provide estimates of the direct instructional cost per student by type of program and level and the allocated full instructional cost per student. It requires use of enrollment distribution data and other data from operating subsystems, and it requires that the institution utilize some standard data definitions and fit programs into a defined classification structure. Information is also needed on the allocation of faculty effort and the distribution of faculty teaching assignments. For part of this task, information from course schedules is sufficient, but NCHEMS has also developed procedures for faculty activity analysis.

RRPM has been tried in a number of institutions. The approach permits fine-grained estimation of resources used in instruction. It does not as yet treat problems of joint processes and joint products, and research universities can therefore make only limited use of it.

As we saw in Chapter Seven, there are many uses for cost analysis, and different cost concepts and measurement methods are needed for each use or decision on which costs have a bearing. There are numerous other techniques and models for costing, some developed for their own convenience by institutions and some by consulting agencies.

In Chapter Six we discussed some market indicators on which a university can rely. These pertain to the markets for incoming students, the markets for students leaving the university, and the indicators of reputation and quality. If this information is to be used systematically in the planning process of a university, its data systems have to make provision for them. In its budgeting and planning, a university faces significant issues of internal priority, assessment of the extent to which it is meeting the goals implicit in its mission, and assessment of the quality of education and new scholarship that it is achieving. Here is where the planning process of an institution must include difficult judgments on academic issues.

Evaluative information from accrediting organizations and panels of external evaluators may help to reinforce the kind of internal assessment that the institution carries on. Many colleges and universities, in the search for ways to assert priority, are now engaging in careful efforts at program analysis and examination of the effectiveness of what they are doing (CED, 1973).

Because the questions of assessment, priority, and planning shift from issue to issue over time, it is difficult to specify the ways in which analytical effort in the planning process may all depend on operating data files. Information that is not incorporated in standard operating files may also have to be collected for special analyses. Thus, the relation between operating and line-management data needs and the needs for longer-range planning is unlikely ever to be completely resolved.

Design Options for a Data System

Design of an institutional data system needs to be considered in several dimensions, and each important dimensional combination is considered a design option. The first dimensional issue is that of concept—should the system be considered as one integrated whole or as a series of partitioned subsystems with actual or potential links built among them? In the early 1960s, proponents of corporate information systems sometimes argued for the integrated, whole-system concept, on the appealing basis that such a system was necessary to exploit the power of information for higher-level purposes and to avoid duplications and patchwork interties. This approach has run into all but insuperable practical difficulties in most large-scale, complex organizations, and the reasons are of specific interest here. The whole-system concept requires that everything be understood before anything can be accomplished. It requires one large-scale implementation; all the parts have to be finished before any of it will work for anybody. It is vulnerable to blockage by any one constituency. And, finally, it requires a long development time, during which there is no apparent payoff to the organization. For all these reasons, a partitioned, subsystem approach is preferable. However, if this approach is used, a good strategy of partitioning and the careful provision for links between subsystems are major requisites.

Centralized system development, as against decentralized development, is the second dimensional issue. The existing degree of decentralization in the structure and in the decision process of the institution is the starting point. There has been much talk about and some evidence confirms the centralizing influence of modernized information systems in large-scale organizations. The fear of loss of autonomy, whether intended or not, can cause strong local resistance to system developments.

This issue, in turn, can be subdivided. If the initial, main clients of the system are the existing operating units, their priorities for information for operating and localized management purposes need to be immediately reflected in each subsystem design, and the key people in each operating unit have to be involved in strong roles, together with the technical design groups. Higher-level monitoring and managerial needs—for example, those of the president's office— are then grafted onto the subsystem characteristics. In order to provide for these higher-level uses, controls on data definitions and identifiers must be exercised, so that aggregating and cross-referencing eventually are done for higher-level purposes.

A third dimensional issue is that of timing and scope. Should the effort be undertaken on an all-at-once, all-or-none basis, or in incremental stages? Budget limitations, scarcity of design personnel, and the exceptional pressure on operating people for their cooperation in a big push—all argue against the all-at-once approach. Modules that are completed early in a slow incremental development are, however, likely to be based on an inadequate conception of general institutional needs. Slow development may also imply low priority to the cross-referencing and data standards that are important for higher-level applications in the later stages.

Finally, each subsystem needs to be considered in terms of the nature of its response capability. Should the subsystem be geared to standardized data-handling and response, or must it accommodate a variety of responses flexibly? Must it be automated, or can it be kept as a manual system? If it is automated, does this require continuous, interactive response, or are periodic input and delayed response sufficient? Is the information or estimate that needs to be secured from the system historical (some set of factual items or a summary of them) or is it anticipatory or prospective?

The first level considered in the development of operating and managerial data handling is a formal organizational unit, such as an academic department, the accounting office, or the storehouse manager's office. At this level, many evaluative decisions are made about the operations of the unit and its relations throughout the institution. But at this level the individual student, administrative staff member, or faculty member is already regarded as a data provider and not as a user. To the extent that efforts are made to keep the design humane, the idea is to minimize the pain of coughing up information that the organizational unit will use. However, it is a mistake to regard people only as data providers and not as data users. The individual needs to find out many things in order to decide what to do. By building in a capability to respond to these needs, a data system can improve considerably the ability of individuals to take care of their own destinies in the institution. This issue is only partly related to data files, although they often need to be consulted because individuals usually need to ask other people for both facts and judgments.

Those in the senior administration, the student and faculty leadership, and the governing board (whose tasks include goal-setting and whose locus is in the markets for funding, academic reputation, and public acceptance) all make demands of different kinds on the institutional data system. They need information about program activities, accomplishment, quality, and resource use, and they need to gauge this information against comparative standards and environmental opportunities. They also have to serve as interlocutors for policy changes to meet new pressures—for example, for affirmative action concerning the status of women and minorities. When these pressures arise, the first, urgent call is likely to be for information that operating data systems were not designed to provide.

It is helpful, therefore, to have some capability for probing needs and opportunities and assessing emergent forces in the environment ahead of a crisis. American colleges and universities—like other stable, complex organizations in the society—often appear to be reactive rather than creative in their responses to opportunities and pressures because they have not previously bought themselves lead time to work out sensible policies.

Close to the academic heart of an institution is the problem of anticipating curriculum and program changes in accordance with the needs and future career interests of students. In many institutions, the departmental processes of curriculum and program adjustment are not assisted by systematic information and forecasts. The number of college age men and women is already known to about 1990. The profile shows a pronounced decline in numbers commencing at the end of the 1970s. How many institutions are consciously bracing themselves, in the plans they are now making, for this clear forecast of the environment? How many are doing so, but in a way that assumes that they can successfully export the problem to other institutions by gaining an increased market share?

The spokesmen for an institution must often involve themselves in negotiating with its environment—with other institutions where cooperative or competitive relationships occur and with state coordinating agencies and the federal establishment. If the institution is to execute these functions of spokesmanship effectively, some systematic work often needs to be done to identify interests and to demonstrate what ought to be advocated. The spokesmen also need to have the evaluative and comparative information that becomes pertinent to the negotiation. Although this effort to support institutional spokesmen draws on the institutional data systems, the prime need is for good policy analysis.

Summary

The data systems of the contemporary university are relied on by its many participants for a great many different purposes. Universities are struggling to assimilate modern information-processing technologies. They face significant problems of cost and conceptual design in reshaping their data systems. Whether university data systems of the future will reflect a philosophy of openness and assistance to students, faculty, and staff or will make most individuals feel helpless while serving mainly to tighten managerial control is a major issue. The demands for external reporting and accountability are expanding the demands for information of many types.

Chapter **11**

Toward Survival, Stability, and Excellence

Most significant actions within a university have consequences for survival, stability, and excellence, and many policy decisions require striking a balance among competing and complementary considerations. Perhaps it is unfortunate for the science of managing, and perhaps it is just as well, that there is no substitute for wisdom in this process.

Managing for Survival

By the *survival* of a university I mean its ability to maintain the essentials of its mission and charter in institutional, academic, and fiscal terms, without having to change its qualitative program character out of recognition and without having to accept a radical and involuntary change in its mode of governance. The essential threads of continuity must be maintained. This definition tolerates closures of individual academic departments, internal reorganizations, mild adjustments of governing board composition, and fiscal retrenchments.

Perhaps it is easiest to illustrate the definition with a few cases of nonsurvival. The closing of an institution, dispersal of its staff, and liquidation of its assets is one type, and a few colleges in fact do this every year. Another kind of nonsurvival is the institution that is involuntarily absorbed into another college or system. There are several well-known instances of significant changes of status—for example, the conversion of the previously independent University of Buffalo into suny-Buffalo, the change of the University of Pittsburgh and Temple University from independence to state-related status in Pennsylvania, and the change of the University of Houston to a unit of the state university system in Texas. In all four cases, the name and the span of academic functions continued, but the previous autonomy was lost. If the change was actively sought and desired and if it did not result in a change of mission and character, then it would not qualify as a case of nonsurvival under our definition. The outsider can seldom know whether the institutional transformation was desired and voluntary or feared and involuntary.

Fiscal emergency in a private institution is signaled by rapid depletion of financial resources, including investment assets in its endowment, and the sharp increase of bank borrowings or other short-term debt in order to meet immediate working-capital depletion and operating deficits, often accompanied by heavy layoffs of core personnel. In *The New Depression in Higher Education,* Cheit (1971) found it necessary to define an institution "in financial trouble" as one that faced severe financing problems *relative to its self-defined mission* (p. 36). Cheit found that, because academic institutions customarily try to break even, the mere presence of an operating deficit (if the institution is permitted by law to have one —many public institutions are not) is not a sufficient test of trouble. As was discussed in Chapter Eight, it has been difficult to find a practical definition of financial distress that would guide allocations of rescue money only to institutions that would otherwise go under completely or be subject to functional damage that would seriously impair their ability to serve. This is apparently why the section of the Higher Education Amendments of 1972 authorizing the creation of a fund for such emergency allocations has not been implemented by Congress with appropriation action.

To avoid impending closure or an unwanted (or unavailable)' transformation of status, a university can make severe expenditure reductions. These entail radical retrenchments of academic programs, layoffs of core personnel, and attempts to dispose of what had been considered permanent facilities and assets. Saint Louis University faced its severe problems this way, by closing a dental school and undertaking other retrenchments. New York University sold its uptown campus, closed its engineering program, and made other very painful adjustments.

Unless the state government is in basic financial jeopardy, and that has not happened since the 1930s, it is difficult to claim that a state must close a state-supported institution because there is no money available. State governments can determine expenditure patterns within the available tax revenues, and the tax base can be increased unless there are constitutional limitations that cannot be overcome in the time available. A state government could, however, decide to reduce budgets for operation of state-supported universities, terminate programs, or even close institutions. The state's governor, legislature, and administrators of higher education are, after all, obliged to justify to the state's electorate the expenditure for higher education and what that expenditure buys. One signal of distress is a serious decline of enrollment at particular campuses or in some types of institutions or programs, either because state population shifts or because some educational programs lose market attractiveness. Another signal is different in character: a public policy decision to alter the conditions of access to higher education by raising tuition sharply (thus depressing enrollments) or by reducing the number of locations at which education is offered, on grounds that state fiscal and program priorities have shifted. A particular campus may be "elected" as a candidate for closing under these circumstances, perhaps because of a misfortune of location or program emphasis in a field of declining state need or unpopularity with key decision-makers at higher levels.

Few state systems of higher education have as yet had to select campuses to close. When they do, in the coming period of enrollment decline, the smaller, limited purpose, and less conspicuous institutions are more likely to be closed than are university campuses. An institution that is closed in these circumstances will not, strictly speaking, be a victim of fiscal bankruptcy but of decisions made in the context of the organization and politics of higher education in the state.

Deep institutional crisis—of governance and the ability to function—is a second type of risk to survival. The Carnegie Commission's report, *Dissent and Disruption* (1971), reviewed the crisis problems that arose in many institutions in the 1960s and recommended guidelines for institutional, student, and faculty responsibility and conduct. Dissent and disruption, rooted in the growing consciousness of young people, followed a pattern: arousal on an issue; confrontation with the university either over the issue or over the means advocated or used to focus attention on the issue; escalation, sometimes to the point of physical violence, property damage, and injury and loss of life; and catharsis, negotiated settlement, or suppression of the issue or the movement. Universities all over the world are no strangers to this phenomenon, which has created many crises. What was unusual for the United States, though it has been part of the tradition in many countries, was the joining of larger ideology and power interest with issues of policy and the structure of power within the university.[1]

In the relative quiet that has descended on universities during the past few years, it is difficult to remember the inflaming passions that were occasioned by moral indignation about the war in Indochina, the position of the poor and Black, and the ideology of youthful frustration and protest. Universities were the available symbol of a repressive and wicked establishment. They discovered how very vulnerable they were to crowd behavior and to determined physical onslaught by even a handful of people.

When an issue produced confrontation, university decision-makers—through hard experience—discovered several things. It

---

[1] Among the numerous assessments made by public bodies of the protest movements of the 1960s are those of the National Commission on the Causes and Prevention of Violence, and, with particular reference to campus disturbances, the report of the Scranton Commission. There was an outpouring of academic literature. See, in particular, Lipset (1970) and *Daedalus* (1970). Searle (1971) provides an extended analysis of the philosophical and psychological basis and the institutional dynamics of this kind of crisis.

was important for the university to have explicit rules and procedures, both for discussion of precipitating issues and, in disciplinary proceedings, for arriving at sanctions on students, staff, or other university members who broke the rules. One objective of dissenting groups was to produce disputes that were too large to be handled by campus police. If law enforcement people from the surrounding communities were brought in, the prospects for violence and for enlargement of the issues and the crowds were heightened. Universities did not and could not stand apart from the surrounding community. If a sufficiently large outbreak occurred, the outside authorities could by law, and did by discretionary preference, step in.

People talk of *crisis management*. It is true that many episodes were dealt with patiently and skillfully; grievance issues were defused and the escalation risks were avoided. In most cases, those who made themselves the focus of protest and broke rules or laws were not followed by a larger crowd. University presidents, administrators, faculty, and students learned to their sorrow, however, that some people and some extreme behavior could not be coped with by accommodation within the system. Part of the remedy had to be tightened, more professional, and much more expensive security within institutions, and an increase of liaison with sophisticated law enforcement agencies.

The episodic intensity of grievances died off, in part, because both the general community and the university became more responsive and tolerant about the desires of young people for recognition and participation. Two major general measures—one giving voting rights and adult legal status to eighteen-year olds, and the other phasing out the military draft—were important. Changes adopted in many universities included the elaboration of due process for students and the increased involvement of students in the decision process—including representation on many committees concerned with academic policies and in consultative bodies concerned with governance. In most American universities, the transformation was not nearly as shocking and did not go as far as it did, for example, in the Netherlands, where parliamentary action in 1971 provided for a multipartite, elected university council—

including a substantial number of students elected by students—that became the legislating policy group for each university.

Far from being a disaster, as many academic conservatives predicted, broadened student participation in the processes of American universities has often been salutary. Student participation in major policy areas is handicapped by rapid turnover and because—like much faculty participation—it is representation by part-time people who cannot match the expertise of full-time administrators. This makes the new consultative arrangements both cumbersome in structure and uneven in results.

One can predict that some future crises will center on issues for which the immediate interests of students, or faculty, or employed staff, will clash with what the administration and governing board conceive as the best long-term interest of the university. In some institutions, faculty collective bargaining and unionization of staff already provide a power base for interest-group pressures. Student organizations within the individual institution and in contact with state legislators, may well increase the leverage of students in such areas as students fees, financial aid, and housing. In the future we may see strident dispute, based in interest-group organizations (such as faculty unions, staff unions, and student lobbies), over academic priorities, programs, and standards—matters that are not at all likely to be soundly treated by interest-group conflict.

Two other sources of crisis pressure—the local community surrounding the university and the bureaucratic and political constitutencies with which it must negotiate—also deserve mention. The quality of normal relationships and the competence and goodwill on both sides affect the chances of crisis. But crisis there can indeed be—over attempts of a university to expand its land area and engage in development opposed by neighbors, over demands for more or differently distributed health care services to local residents from a university's teaching hospital, and over other issues that can range a significant constituency and its spokesmen and political allies against something that a university is doing or proposes to do. A university facing such issues cannot afford not to have well-placed in its administration the kinds of talent that are required to maintain effective relationships and solve most problems before they balloon to crisis proportions. Universities have customarily expected that among their trustees would be some who could maintain effective linkages with the various parts of the establishment that are important to the survival of the institution. But they have often been caught short in recent times, without either trustee or administration liaison and leverage with new constituency pressures that impinge on them.

Four long-range aspects of survival need to be discussed: the preservation of autonomy; the preservation of viable governance; viability through fund-getting; and viability through prudence and efficient management.

Autonomy, as we have seen in the discussion of interinstitutional cooperation and of community and political relationships, does not mean going it alone. Most universities are now "in the world," even if they are organized as private, nonprofit corporations. The most important long-range problem is to maintain the kind of independence that is associated with academic freedom: to maintain the conditions of pursuit of truth even where this is unpopular with or uninteresting to substantial constituencies that have the power to press their claims on the institution.

From within the university, one source of risk is the imposition of some absolute about what *consequences* of discovery are tolerable, instead of the consistent willingness to defend the *process* of scholarship so long as it is conducted competently. Another hazard is impatience with standards or doubt as to whether they matter enough to be defended. If faculty members are unwilling to discipline a colleague, after appropriate due process, for gross incompetence or for academic malfeasance, they weaken values essential to the institution. Students do the same if they try to insist on the removal of positive standards of competent work. A university's leadership needs to be active and persuasive within the institution on behalf of these values and standards.

Historically, universities had patrons—kings or churches—on whom they relied not only for money but also for assistance in maintaining essential autonomy. The contemporary American university has as much establishment luster as it can get on its board of trustees. Besides exploiting its best friends among alumni, private donors, foundations, and corporations, a major university looks to Washington, D. C., where much of the money is; and increasingly, private as well as state universities have intricate dealings with state governments.

The survival of major universities is strongly influenced by the generosity of federal funding of research and some aspects of graduate education and by the terms on which funding is provided. The universities of the Association of American Universities formed a Council on Federal Relations in the latter 1960s in order to develop and share a better base of knowledge and a more vigorous presence in the formulation of research and funding policies. The National Board on Graduate Education has issued two major reports with accompanying recommendations on significant aspects of national and federal policy (NBGE, 1973, 1974). The higher education industry in the United States is no monolith, but rather a series of overlapping and partly competitive constituencies. Nowhere is this more evident than in Washington, where association representatives of many national and regional groupings of institutions and interests converge and, in violation of the public relations man's cardinal rule, speak with many voices instead of one.

Occasionally an administrative representative must carry a university's case to Washington. But the eminence, energy, and number of its faculty are the major factors in obtaining research funding. Paradoxically, this individualistic activity is so hard to organize that it is perhaps the best basis—so long as grants based on competence in basic research remain the rule—for maintaining the vitality of the major universities.

Universities are on sound long-term philosophical ground when they advocate, and gain understanding for, the functions of basic scientific research and of creative scholarship and original work in the humanities and the arts. In a democratic society in which the newest pressures are increasingly functionalist and egalitarian, the universities are more precariously situated than other institutions in pressing the politics of their case. One pressure is utilitarian: toward the applied and problem-solving in research, and the sure delivery of useful training to students. Another is toward assurances that everybody can benefit. At this point, there is no skillfully developed strategy for major universities to use in response to the egalitarian demand for the greatest educational good to the greatest number.

Resources are important for long-term institutional survival. The success of a university president tends to be measured by his ability to get money. A private university president is concerned with the amount of annual giving and the size and flexibility of accretions to endowment funds; the president of a state university is interested in the amounts and the composition of capital and operating budget that survive executive and legislative scrutiny. Both private and public have in common a concern about research funding from agencies and foundations in Washington.

Until tuition in private universities began to exhaust the ability to pay of upper-middle income parents, private universities raised tuition frequently (with some increases in financial aid) because they needed revenue to offset inflation. The state university administration faces a different problem: the portion of the state operating appropriation earmarked for instructional activities is determined largely by applying work-load standards to changes of enrollment. The enrollment-taking obligation of the state university and its generally more meager budget per student are the other side of the problem; it is quite possible for a state university to have a large budget, which in total dollars would be the envy of a private university, but to have a relatively poor budget per student. In this context, also, student fees are a politically-sensitive residuum of the funding actions taken by the state.

Thus, the administration of a public university has an intricate problem in the negotiation of operating resources relative to enrollment. It must seek the largest number of dollars and an operating budget that grows over time. And it must try to achieve these goals while avoiding decline in the purchasing power of budgeted funds per student (except in so far as economies of scale can be found and claimed). And, in order to avoid a decrease in student access, it must negotiate without triggering political demands for increases of student fees. Negotiation during a time of growing enrollment demand must consider the amount of additional enrollment that the public university should take and the standards of eligibility for admission that it should enforce.

The component of revenues related to enrollment will be subject to stabilization or (in the absence of a willingness to reduce admission standards) to an absolute decline in the latter 1970s and the 1980s. The small private universities that were highly selective in the 1950s and became ultraselective in the 1960s can at least maintain enrollment and that portion of revenue related to it simply by discreet broadening of admission eligibility. Larger public universities with official and published admission standards already take a wide cut of the ability distribution. They will have difficulty maintaining enrollment in the 1980s, unless they are able to recruit a larger proportion of the eligible pool or can negotiate broadened eligibility standards.

Major universities—both public and private—will face severe problems in getting funds in an environment of enrollment stability. The financing of research responsibilities is one major need that I have already discussed. Funds not related to enrollment are also needed to support overhead—maintenance of plant, maintenance and replacement of major equipment, and general administration—and such crucial academic resources as the library and the computer center. Major research libraries and major academic computing centers are an important national resource, and a new program of federal, categorical grants to support these basic investments would make sense. With or without such special federal funding, major universities may find that they must participate in regional or statewide networks or service systems.

As every university president is acutely aware, aspirations always do (and probably should) outrun resources. Institutions have a deep tendency to accumulate new program commitments whenever new resources become available to support new beginnings. Thus, long-term survival cannot be assured solely by increased funds. Control of what the institution tries to do is also essential. A long-term strategy for survival therefore must include two additional features: a prudential view and an emphasis on resource-efficient operation. Let us discuss the second of these first.

A resource-efficient university accomplishes powerful results without more wastage of resources than is inherent in the conduct of learning processes that are, of necessity, difficult to evaluate because of their many dimensions and because the outcomes are

uncertain. We have seen in the discussion of the problems of resource analysis that this kind of managing is hard, for the understanding of what is to be achieved is incomplete. The technologies
of academic activities are quite varied, are subject to jointness and
interdependence, and change over time; and a university's ways of
dealing with the allocation and combining of its resources are bound
by history and the typical modes of institutional organization. Both
students and faculty need substantial personal autonomy in organizing their academic tasks. This environment is essential to produce
the highest motivations for sustained efforts.

The problem is to evolve and, over time, adjust an organizing frame for these heterogeneous individual activities. Some kinds
of structure are necessary for it, and the framework as a whole can
be more or less efficient on both a short-term basis and a long-
term basis.

Where the pattern of instruction and the pattern of research and scholarship are reasonably congruent with departmental
organization, as they are in most foundational disciplines, the first
task is to achieve some alignment of the resources being used with
evidence of the level of activity and effort in each program area.
This does not mean avoiding all high-cost areas of academic activity
(or imputing value to them just because their costs are high).
Rather, evidence must be sought of the extent to which costs are
high because the program area is inherently a heavy resource-user,
or of the extent to which costs are high because the program is in
an early stage of enrollment-growth. The second step is to examine
the critical interactions between that program area and other academic activities. Some fields and programs operate in relative isolation, while others have such extensive interactions that a major
part of the justification for them is their contributions to effective
conduct of other programs. A third step is to deal with some of the
uncertainties by assembling a range of sensible evaluative judgments. It is difficult to predict either the quantity or the quality of
the results of much research. Effective administration needs some
expert judgments to buttress impressions and to gauge the claims
of importance by those who are pleading their cases. It is also a
good idea to record the claims made when research efforts are
initiated, to provide some basis for evaluation of achievements.

In some important areas, the discsipline organization is disjoint from a research problem area and the university is asked to help finance a multidisciplinary research unit. If skilled entrepreneurship can produce substantial extramural funding, this is a partial test of the promise, if not the achievement, of those who promote interest in the problem area. Some cross-disciplinary instructional programs emerge from the problem interests generated by research or from a new definition of a curricular objective. Here senior administration and faculty review bodies must decide whether there is sufficient good sense in the problem area and in the program design, and sufficient leadership for the instructional program, so that students involved in it, and the institution, will achieve gratifying results.

Short-term danger signals of ineffective resource use in research or academic programs are: heavy resource use without any progress toward reasonable growth of activity-levels; rapid and unexpected additional demands for budgetary resources, either directly or by pressure on other parts of the institution; failure of the program to achieve coherence; and failure of the program to provide interactive support to other programs on the campus. The longer-term problems of resource-efficiency in academic programs go to the deeper questions of quality and impact—impact on the faculty and students involved, on the institution, and on wider constituencies in the world of scholarship and the community. No academic program in a university should be exempt from periodic self-examination and periodic broad-scale evaluation on these criteria.

One test of resource-efficient management of supporting activities, including the departments of general administration, is the complaint level from clients within the institution or from outside agencies, but complaints (or the lack of them) are seldom a sufficient test. Universities have been slow to adopt proven methods of efficient administration. Periodic modernization and overhaul is necessary to keep administrative apparatus up to date. At the same time, the peculiarities of university organization prevent a one-to-one transfer of administrative techniques from industry to the university.

There are several reasons why a resource-efficient pattern is important to long-term survival. First, a poorly operated activity uses up part of the small margin of immediate discretionary resources in the institution, and it diminishes the performance of more successful programs. Second, every organizational unit and every program is likely to become a largely fixed commitment unless evaluated at regular intervals. Fixed institutional commitments, which must be sustained in an uncertain revenue-getting environment, endanger fiscal survival. And finally, an operation that is visibly poor and that continues to operate without constraints not only arouses complaints but discourages energetic and effective performance elsewhere in the institution. The grapevine is powerful, and the quality of what is done both academically and administratively is affected by the sense of standards—or the sense of a lack of them. Thus, the internal credibility of the choices made by administration and the senior faculty depends on the widespread impression that some standards of effectiveness exist and are being enforced fairly and firmly.

The prudent view requires a willingness to make choices that are sustainable in the longer-term. Prudence does not dictate avoidance of what is risky or uncertain; if it did, none of the daring, high-risk programs on which the future blossoming of excellence depends would ever be chosen. I am talking about a prudent view of the university's sustainable quality and vitality.

The prudent view requires, first, attention to the claims of the present as against the future. Two examples may suffice. A capital gift for construction of a new building is a very nice thing. Both the donor and the recipient institution ordinarily congratulate themselves about it. But the new building also increases burdens on the university's maintenance budget except in the unlikely event that it replaces an obsolete building. Prudence requires that if the university accepts the gift, it must either persuade the donor to provide endowment for maintenance of the building or else make appropriate provision for increased operating budget out of other funds. A second hard choice between present and future involves the rate of use of income generated from endowment funds. Some private universities, with nudging from the Ford Foundation, have in recent years decided to recognize as income not only the dividends and interest received from endowment but also all or part of the realized capital gains. (The total return on endowment funds, of course, includes unrealized capital gains as well.) What might have seemed plausible in the latter 1960s and is now urgently expedient in the 1970s may be a doubtful long-term strategy, however, because price inflation is eroding the purchasing power of the stream of income from endowment. A prudent offset is to set aside part of the income stream to increase the endowment or as an anti-inflation reserve for the future, but this would be very painful to do. So what is now happening is the reduction, over time, of the amounts of real activity that a given endowment fund can support, and many universities are making greater current expenditures from endowment income than they will be able to sustain for the long term. To what extent, then, does the future have to take care of itself?

Those who are concerned with the long-term fortunes of a public university in the mercurial political climate of state government face an important, though less well-defined, series of similar choices between the present and the future. The essence of the problem is to promote the concept of integrity and usefulness, even though, at the same time, many dimensional details of the budgetary process and priorities are subject to pragmatic negotiation. Further, at any one time dominant leverage on these negotiating issues may be held by one group of political actors and interests while others are less able to press their claims or exert much immediate pressure for the amount and composition of funds or the policy standards they consider important. For the long range, it is crucial to hold to essential principles of university jurisdiction, mission, and principles of operation and state relationships, even though in the short range this may complicate negotiation. For the long-range, it is important to look ahead to the time when the presently dominant political forces may be replaced by other leadership personalities and interests. A university is typically not well situated to play this sort of interest-group and power-jockeying game, but it is the game as political operators understand it. For this reason, it is also typical that one set of university spokesmen is periodically superseded by another that can deal more effectively with a newly dominant set of political forces in a state government.

A particular president may be expendable if the institution is to continue to be effectively represented.

Managing for Stability

Stability does not have the philosophical attraction associated with the struggle for survival. But managing for stability is an important *desideratum* for a university. By stability I mean an operation that is reasonably smooth, produces solid institutional results each year, contains enough flexibility to accommodate some response to new opportunities, and is steady enough so that crisis adjustments are not imposed on the rather delicate balances of the university's internal organization. This definition of stability implies a steady trajectory through time, not a static or steady-state condition. It became fashionable in the 1950s and 1960s to judge the quality and vitality of a university on the basis of a high rate of growth in resources, capital facilities, faculty, enrollment, number of programs, and even (in the case of public universities) number of campuses. Not only was managing for rapid growth more fun, but it was also a way to make new choices and commitments at the relatively painless margin of expansion while the fixed commitments of the institution took care of themselves. The opportunities for quality and innovation were enlarged because of this margin of growth. But if growth is not feasible, must innovation and quality suffer? Overall higher education enrollment growth will taper very soon and enrollments will very likely be static for some years in the 1980s. Because resources are to a large extent enrollment-based, budgets will be sharply constrained. Many universities are abandoning growthmanship for viability under steady-state conditions.

Stability, in the sense of a steady and sustainable trajectory through time, is much more beneficial to the long-term character of a university than is oscillation. An institution that goes through rapid growth intervals—particularly when mandated by state government—pays a price for it. The number of new junior faculty appointments per year is so large, in relation to the existing faculty leadership, that recruitment and quality screening become difficult. And promotions of nontenure faculty to tenure come too easily under rapid growth. An appreciable number of new senior faculty are required during rapid growth, and to get first-rate people a university must usually offer them both a salary premium and substantial nonsalary inducements, such as special laboratory equipment for the star scientist. Tapering off after rapid growth creates holes in the composition of faculty by rank and age, and these persist for a long time.

Stability facilitates careful consideration of the design of new programs and curricula. Both a rapid growth rate and oscillation make it difficult to evolve responsible institutional processes and generate loyalty to them. Finally the period of cooling out after rapid growth or an oscillatory upswing is functionally similar to absolute retrenchment, and a university cannot go through such periods without severe morale problems and hazards to its vitality.

There are two exceptions to the preference for small, steady growth as a trajectory. A university that is in a poor starting position may have determined backers (private or public) who are prepared to pay very heavily to put it on the map. If they are lucky in acquiring first-class entrepreneurial leadership, quality and prestige can be achieved faster by drowning the old state of affairs in growth than by letting the previous low quality of faculty and programs dominate a slower pattern of expansion. A second exception is summarized in the phrase "seize the time." The opportunities for doing many things are fleeting in terms of political support for improvement; when such an opportunity occurs, an institution might choose to gamble on the outcome and use up temporarily lavish resource increments as rapidly as they are provided.

Now let us turn to the broad problem faced by a university that is trying to defend its best prospects for the long run. Clearly it must survive short-term crises, but the stability of a continuous rate of assured strong performance is more than survival.

Both public and private universities are finding that they must cope with increasingly complex schemes of coordination and control of postsecondary education. Control standards are now being promulgated by executive agencies in Washington, to regularize the accounting and overhead costing relationships of research universities with the federal government and to regulate other aspects of university operations in which federal agencies and the Congress have an interest. Large-scale programs of federal financial support of students can hardly fail to bring controls. Universities are only one subset of postsecondary educational institutions, and a small one at that, and they are unlikely to get special recognition for many of their problems. In graduate education and research, they would be greatly assisted if the broad-scale recommendations of the Carnegie Commission and the detailed proposals of the National Board on Graduate Education were adopted as federal policy. Increased vulnerability to swings in federal policy, in the absence of adoption and sustained implementation of these policy proposals, means precarious and unstable conditions for the major universities.

At the state level, there is a need for vigorous attention to the interests of both public and private universities. Here, increasingly aggressive and sophisticated program controls are intended to constrain institutional self-determination and will likely have that effect. The coordinating role and the planning and measuring techniques of state agencies are often predicated on quite conventional views of what education is all about, and plans of such agencies are based on what is most easily measured. Universities are less tractable than other institutions from this point of view; one might even guess that the better a university is, the less well it will fit. Universities must press actively for better and deeper concepts of state planning and coordination. If poor concepts dominate, universities and what they stand for will suffer more severely than other institutions.

The university in a democratic society, whether organized as a publicly supported or a private institution, must overcome hazards and needs to cultivate many different constituencies if it means to keep to a stable and effective course. This requires not only a fundamental commitment to values and internal processes but also a continual effort to engage and intensify the support of a large number of constituencies. Some believe that it is possible to avoid the issue of accountability. I believe that the pressures for explanation and justification, and the validity or at least the insistence of these pressures, make it impossible to duck this issue. Stability in the broad sense will depend on meeting it, and meeting it credibly and firmly.

Managing for Excellence

The notion of academic excellence has its absolutes, but as a practical matter, it usually involves invidious distinctions. If there is a best, there is by implication a second best, a mediocre, and a worst. In the central functions of teaching and basic scholarship, the appreciation of excellence in each field almost always has to be the province of knowledgeable peers in that field. This makes the students, the senior administration, and the general body of the faculty prisoners of testimony and evidence from specialists within the university and—if their opinions are sought—specialists from elsewhere. The administration and the general faculty can make some assessment in accordance with generalized standards of academic performance, but these are not likely to carry to the fine distinctions between good performance and what is construed by experts to be outstanding.

Excellence, then, is represented by academic reputation, and this operates with lags: a quite short lag among the cognoscenti, longer ones for the peers in the discipline as a whole, and still longer ones for academia, for administrators, for most students, and for the general public. Because of these lags, a university is both the beneficiary and the victim of its past. Many of the things it does have only long-range impact on the impressions of excellence that it has of itself and that it conveys among institutions.

Some of the hallmarks of excellence do have an impact in a short time, and others that have only long-term implications are taken by competitors as significant signals of intentions. A university that is able to attract a star appointment—someone who has acquired wide reputation early and still has a substantial period ahead of intensive scholarly productivity—adds immediately to its reputation in that field. In addition to contributing his own productivity, the star is often a nucleating force for attracting grant funds, doctoral candidates, and junior faculty.

Short-term steps that have long-term implications include: institutional commitments of building space, equipment funds, library acquisition funds, and allocations of faculty positions and operating budget. One of the few certainties about academic work is that if the people are good, they are likely to achieve good results. Thus, tightening of admission standards, aggressive recruitment for outstanding students, and an effort to make the most promising junior faculty appointments are promises for the long-range and are taken as signals of intentions by the academic community generally. The real consequences do not become evident until much later, as students complete their thesis research and go on the job market and as junior faculty establish scholarly reputations.

Publishable research is the dominant vehicle of scholarly contribution in most conventional fields. There are exceptions, in the fine arts, in architectual design, and sometimes in law or medicine; in all of these, eminence may result from evidence of creativity in doing something rather than saying something. Published research generally has to survive peer-group screening by journal editors, and good work gets fairly rapid feedback in most fields. Qualitative originality, as distinct from a high general level of scholarly effort, which is worthwhile in itself, is hard to bring off and hard to predict. For this reason, a university that wants to assure itself of an exceptional scholarly reputation in a field must usually underwrite a fairly large number of scholars in that field.

In the traditional scholarly fields, impressions of excellence percolate from the cognoscenti to the journeymen in the field and thence back to the institution. When a nucleus of faculty at a university make a claim for a degree program or a research establishment—according to a new intellectual design or a commitment to a problem area for which they think interesting progress can be made —they seek sponsorship from the university (as well as, often, from extramural funding sources), and this confronts the administration and the faculty organization with a high-risk choice. If there is no defined peer group, there is no assured feedback, which is bad; yet, in some cases, a new design can be productive and influential, and the university that has underwritten a qualitatively new venture that proves successful gains reputation and a head start.

Appreciation of quality in curriculum and in the teaching process, as contrasted with research quality, usually starts out as local. There are a few direct, cross-institutional comparative measures, such as performance of undergraduate students in graduate school aptitude tests and placement of undergraduates in outstanding graduate schools. But the basis for a reputation for teaching excellence even within the local communication networks of one university, much less among universities, is often uncertain. Because the status quo is always less than ideal and the frontier of knowledge is changing, evidence of changes is often taken to be a correlate of quality. Such changes include overhaul of curricula, updating and redesign of particular courses, and experiments with new and hopefully more effective methods of teaching. The administration can stimulate such efforts by providing funds and time for departmental and individual faculty efforts. The faculty and administration, together, can increase the level of attention to teaching quality and innovations and provide incentives by assuring that good teaching performance is rewarded on the occasions of faculty personnel review and that there are penalties for poor teaching.

The enrollment popularity of a program, curriculum, course, or teacher is an indicator of success among students. But many factors unrelated to academic quality may be responsible for popularity, and there is the acknowledged hazard that some methods of gaining popularity—for example, giving high grades regardless of student effort, or pandering to demands for relevance—may actually be inverse to quality. I favor systematic student evaluations of courses as a partial and not definitive indicator of teaching quality, but more than this needs to be done.

Sometimes a program or a whole institution can gain celebrity for its styles of teaching and learning, or for standards of student achievement. This requires long-range rather than short-range attention by the administration and the faculty. A strong reputation for excellence of instruction, once achieved, is self-reinforcing because it attracts able students. At its best, a university conveys a special atmosphere of concern for learning that contributes to the quality of work done by both students and faculty. Faculty leadership is more important in creating this atmosphere, discussed in Chapter Three, than is administration action. If there are active and lively colloquia in a field, if scholars from other universities and abroad are welcomed and have an audience, if the library collection or the laboratory equipment are an excellent base for the exciting areas of discovery in the field—then, in that field, a university becomes a nodal point in the network of scholarship. This atmosphere is most apparent to faculty, full-time research personnel, and advanced graduate and undergraduate students; but if it is felt in enough areas of work, then the university generates special qualities as a good place to be.

The cultural, aesthetic, and communicative character of the institution and the breadth of opportunity for these forms of stimulus determine the quality of student life and bind together the academic community. Here, the administration and the general faculty organization are crucial forces. They provide facilities and funds for cultural breadth and assure that good things are done to strengthen this aspect of the climate of excellence of the university.

In allocating resources toward excellence, the leadership of a university has to rely more on developing and using good mechanisms than on the ability of a few individuals to make the crucial decisions. The process begins with academic appointments and promotions, for the standards of faculty appointments and the skill and insight with which they are enforced are crucial to a university's excellence. Pay scales and other aspects of compensation have to be competitive, but it is perfectly possible to have a high wage bill and a mediocre faculty. The important thing is to have positive standards of quality in all the significant dimensions, to assure that these are enforced firmly and fairly, and to propagate these standards as norms throughout the faculty.

Beyond this, the administration, sometimes assisted by the faculty organization or by other instrumentalities, needs to review the quality of academic operations and make courageous, discriminating choices. During past periods of rapidly increasing resources, improvements leading to excellence could often be financed out of the growth margin. As growth has slowed down, this has become and will continue to be a strategy that few universities can employ. The only alternative to selectivity will be to maintain in operation more programs and activities than the university can afford to finance at a high standard of excellence.

A deserved reputation for excellence improves the claims of a university on its loyal constituencies and on society. It helps to attract funds from those sources that pay attention to academic reputation or that grant funds to enforce quality. A university cannot afford not to be actively striving for excellence, just as an athlete must always be training and testing his limits if he is to do well.

But the policy of pressure toward excellence has costs and risks, and its pursuit sometimes endangers an institution's survival prospects. Some commitments to excellence are costly in resources. Many have long gestation periods before results are known and appreciated and entail significant risks that results will not be favorable. This is true of the bets placed on key areas of research and on faculty personnel. Because many commitments balloon in size over time, the university may all too easily discover that its aggregate of program requirements is unsustainable. At times it is necessary, on behalf of excellence and of academic principles, to embroil the institution in internal controversy or unpopular stands in defense of a program or an individual. This has happened repeatedly in academic history, both in the United States and abroad.

Putting It All Together

What any one university should do to find a balance among the criteria of survival, stability and excellence depends, of course, on its particular circumstances and on the outlook and values of those who are seeking a viable path for it. I can, however, suggest a way of looking at the problems and the opportunities and a way of using this approach to bring together the particulars of analysis that have led us toward this concluding chapter.

A set of institutional aims must be identified. These must be translated into guiding policies and program obligations. And all of the university's constituencies must be dealt with. The essential values of a university must be honored and supported while the institution does as well as it can in pressing toward its institutional aims. Some tests can be applied: compatibility of aims; effectiveness and mutual reinforcement of programs; and viability with the most important constituencies. Every university of consequence has existed for some time and has accumulated previous commitments. How can each university move from its past and present toward the future it considers most desirable?

Institutional aims can be chosen as points along each of a series of value dimensions, such as: broadly popular or highly selective; utilitarian or idealistic, critical and visionary; applied knowledge or fundamental; local concerns or national and cosmopolitan; spontaneous and immediate or sustained and long range; education for a basic start or education at the most advanced levels of scholarship and in the graduate professions; popular values and style or high-status values and style.

Suppose that only two of these dimensions of value commitment needed to be considered—say, popular versus selective, and local versus cosmopolitan. Then an institution that chose only one point in each of these dimensions would be located, according to that pair of values, at a point in a two-dimensional diagram. Figure 3 illustrates the position of a highly selective institution emphasizing cosmopolitan interests, the position of a popular and local institution, and the position of an institution having a zone of commitments instead of a point.

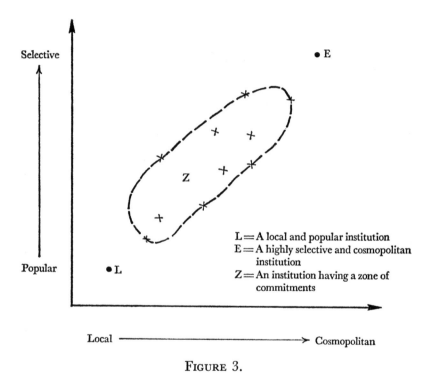

FIGURE 3.

But the problem has many more than two dimensions. Thus it is not possible to draw a diagram that actually represents the combination of value commitments (or "n-tuple") in the many-dimensional space. We can, however, suggest a crude visual approximation as a projection from the many dimensions down to one piece of paper, and this is done in Figure 4. Later on, we will locate the

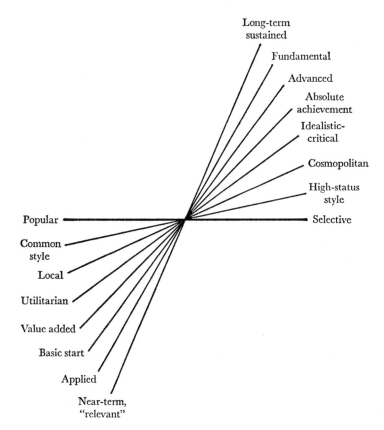

FIGURE 4. Projection of numerous value dimensions to the plane.

commitments of an institution separately in each of these dimensions.

We may now proceed to a few observations about these value dimensions and the kinds of constituency interests that are attracted to them. First, the faculty constituency: in order to connect with the worldwide community of scholars in a field, university faculty members in the basic disciplines emphasize the selective, the critical, the fundamental, the cosmopolitan, the sustained or long range, and the advanced levels of education. In the graduate professions this commitment is tempered by some emphasis on the utilitarian. Some faculty do have a commitment to education of students for a basic start, and some to a philosophical orientation or ideology that stresses, in these existential times, student interest in the spontaneous and the relevant. But often the claims they make for resources and curricular changes conflict with the interests of discipline-oriented colleagues. Problem-focused and value-focused curricular proposals challenge the conventional academic organization, whether the topic is social ecology, conservation and natural resources, women's studies, or Third World studies.

Both faculty and applied research groups in the health professions, law, engineering, urban planning, agriculture, and business administration have to span clientele, curricular, and problem-solving research interests that are often local, popular and utilitarian. At the same time they must deal with scholars in the basic disciplines whose work serves as background for their own. Some professional schools reflect an added tension—a desire for highly selective admission and the admission of high-status candidates into their professional curricula, and an emphasis on utilitarian interests.

Each external constituency has some points of attraction on each value dimension, some points of indifference, and some of active conflict or repulsion. A research funding agency that supports basic research in a scientific field may be positively interested in what the advanced students in that field can contribute to a project, but it will want safeguards against the diversion of grant resources to basic instruction or to applied or utilitarian research. The liberals in a state legislature usually welcome evidence that a publicly-supported institution is responding to the needs of young state residents for access to higher education and meeting the basic-start educational needs of students, but they are often very skeptical about admission of out-of-state and foreign students and about educational programs in exotic foreign languages, abstruse areas of both science and the humanities, and so on.

Where are the major universities located in these value dimensions? How can universities come to terms with the dominant themes of contemporary democratic society, particularly the egalitarian forces that are proving to be so powerful both in western Europe and in the United States? In the American context, there are two versions of egalitarianism. The Jeffersonians are believers in equality of opportunity, and in struggle for individual gain and growth on the basis of individual merit. The Jacksonians and the levelers regard justice in the society as requiring equality of condition and results. Unusual intellectual attainment is reasonably compatible with the Jeffersonian ideal, but to the Jacksonians, intellectualism is suspect. As Hofstadter (1963) pointed out in his brilliant book, *Anti-Intellectualism in American Life,* Americans have always favored lots of education but they have been deeply ambivalent about intellectuals and ideas. The rugged man of common sense is better, and more to be trusted, than the effete intellectual snob.

On another aspect of the egalitarian position, the question of the university's influence on the concentration or diffusion of power in the society, the responses of the modern-day Jeffersonian and the Jacksonian are not so clearly and easily differentiated. The Jeffersonians have always favored maximum diffusion of power. They applaud the university if it is shown to assist the diffusion process and inhibit power concentration. The Jacksonians and the levelers, on the other hand, are interested in what the system delivers to the mass of people and in closing the gap between those at the top and those at the bottom. They are willing to use the power of the state to accomplish these ends—for example, via income redistribution plans. If the university adds to the amount that society delivers and adds to the state's capacity to control the economy and equalize delivery, the Jacksonians may be more in favor of the university (as a supplier of facilitating ideas for their interventions) than the Jeffersonians are!

Some institutions have a cluster of commitments at one end of all of these value dimensions. A technical-vocational institution of postsecondary instruction might well classify itself as open admission, applied, utilitarian, local, organized to give its students a basic start and maximum educational value-added, providing a relatively short exposure to relevant training, and operating according to popular values and style. A community college that emphasizes general liberal arts education, on the other hand, prepares students to go on toward completion of the baccalaureate degree at a four-year college or university, and it may well give greater accent to fundamental learning, absolute achievement, and the idealistic-critical functions of education.

At the opposite pole from the technical-vocational institution are the most elite institutions, such as Oxford and Cambridge in the

United Kingdom, the *grands ecoles* in France (more than the French universities), and, in the United States, a relative handful of great private universities beginning with the Ivy League. Perhaps the purest cases in the United States are Rockefeller University, which has very few students, all at the graduate level, and the Institute for Advanced Study at Princeton, which has no students at all.

There is an appearance of easy compatibility in the value commitments and the educational programs to realize these commitments in the technical-vocational community institution at one end of the spectrum and the elite private university at the other. These two polar cases are illustrated in Figure 5.

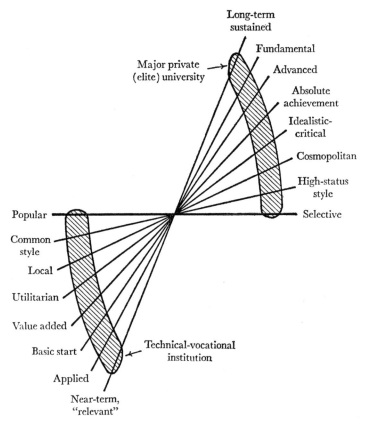

FIGURE 5. Comparing a technical-vocational institution and a major private university.

But where do the great state universities fit—Michigan and Michigan State, Wisconsin, Illinois, Ohio State, Minnesota, and of course, California? These universities can be shown to be operating *simultaneously* at several points in each of the pertinent value-dimensions, disposing educational, research, and service commitments to meet constituency claims. But, more than this, these public universities are reflections of a democratic vision that has for a long time combined, in some state of tension, the Jeffersonian and the Jacksonian themes.

It is clear that the local citizenry will give strong funding and community support to the community college. Constituency support for the major private university is also easy to characterize. The very best money is contributed by people already dead, the next best by foundations and agencies that finance basic research and scholarship. Then come tuition income and current alumni giving, and finally, support provided by the living rich and the great corporations. The great university is discreet in cultivating establishmentarian support, for it has to guard its independence. Its faculty, through the critical and humane scholarship, illumines and contributes to the high culture, and the high culture is inescapably and properly in a state of tension toward both the establishment and the mass society.

The great private universities have a vital role in American society. They seek the very best student and faculty talent wherever they can find it, thus approximating the Jeffersonian idea. There is a positive rationale for the contributions of these universities. The argument can be put this way. Fundamental science and discovery are essential to feed the applied and the utilitarian, which would soon atrophy without a stream of new basic findings. (Further, it is necessary to have fundamental discovery nearby, for lead time is essential in the game of application.) A shelter for idealistic, critical, and visionary scholarship is necessary to the body social and philosophical; otherwise, complacency, philistinism, and sentimentality will overtake both the establishment and the conservative mass of the population. High selectivity and emphasis on the most intensive and advanced levels of education are essential for those who will take the leadership roles. A relative handful of people at the top end of the distribution of talent and energy provides the driving force of a society, and on the quality of this aristocracy of merit the welfare of the mass of people depends. As a national and cosmopolitan institution, the university contributes to, is in touch with, and attracts the very best of what is happening all over the world, and it would be hampered in its tasks if it was provincial. The egalitarian critic can be assured that the great private university pursues its elite role without regard to race, creed, or sex, demanding only extraordinary talent in all those whom it accepts as students or appoints as faculty. The essence of such an institution is absolute devotion to academic excellence.

The elite university enhances the competitive power of a nation and the flowering of its civilization. For the mass of people, the proposition is that these elite functions produce essential results and positive effects on which the welfare of the mass of people depend and these results trickle down to them.

The great private university can promise to serve as a gateway to leadership and eminence for the ablest people, whatever their origins, provided that it is seeking them out and helping them to overcome barriers (including the financial and the psychic) to attendance and to success in education.

Public universities have a more diversified, more dangerous, and thus more interesting set of relations among their value commitments and programs than do private universities, and they have to elicit support from the democratic political process and from many publics in a much more direct way. The public university competes with other major universities in the United States and abroad and also stands in a symbiotic relation with them. Scholarly talent circulates, ideas circulate and are judged, and these universities, together, make a dominant contribution to scholarship and to the standards of what is known as excellent.

A great public university is different from, and can be more than a great private university. We can map out, for illustration, the several points of commitment of institutional aims and program for this sort of university, in Figure 6. Are these commitments compatible with each other? If there are some incompatibilities or conflicts among aims, what strategies can a university use to embrace them all? Or must it consider giving up some of them? Where the university's aims include several points along the same value dimension, these may be complementary and reinforcing or they may be independent of each other, but they are rarely in direct conflict as basic aims. The issue of competition generally arises when it is necessary to allocate scarce resources to programs that are, inescapably, in competition for institutional funds, space, and the attention of faculty and staff.

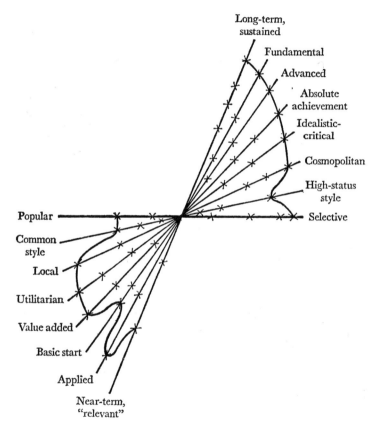

FIGURE 6. A major public university.

Complementarity can be illustrated by the conduct of fundamental research in a discipline as against problem-centered research, where the problem——in a field of technology or of social policy—does not depend neatly on a single background discipline. The best problem-centered research is done with the guidance of powerful theory and sound research methodology—both drawn from the several disciplines that may be pertinent to the problem. At the same time, those engaged in problem-centered research may (and often do) uncover evidence that poses new questions for fundamental research; and they may have to develop methods of measurement, techniques of computation, and other methodology that can then be used in basic scientific investigation. These complementarities have frequently occurred between biological science and applied agricultural research; between physics and several branches of engineering; between economics and business administration; and between pure mathematics and the users of mathematics.

To achieve organizational focus and to assure that resources will not be misapplied to one task when they are dedicated to another, it is often wise to arrange some separation between the fundamental and the applied work, and to give each group some shelter from the immediate pressures faced by the other. But some traffic between them is often fruitful, and when this is true, the two kinds of commitment are complementary.

Elements of complementarity and jointness in the operation of educational programs have already been discussed. Let us now consider a possible case of conflict in aims by supposing that a university commits itself to both open admission in some areas and selective admission in others, and that it attempts to emphasize both a large improvement of learning for students (large educational value-added) and high absolute achievement. Suppose that the broadly selected students are put into the same courses and programs with the highly selected, and suppose also that the standard accepted by students and faculty is one of high absolute achievement (enforced by a high minimum passing standard and by special recognition for those who excel). The highly qualified students will for the most part do well, and they will set the pace of achievement. Some of the less qualified students will also excel, and more, by struggling hard, will meet the acceptable minimum standard of performance. But in the conventional organization of instruction, a much larger fraction of the less qualified students than of the more qualified ones will have academic difficulties.

Some strong public universities have operated in this way. A broad spectrum of students is eligible to enroll and to try, but the attrition rate for academic reasons is very high among those not well prepared or strongly motivated. Inflicting failure on a large number (and percentage) of students imposes heavy and often very damaging burdens on them, and this policy is criticized increasingly, in this egalitarian age, as unacceptable. If the odds are well known to prospective students, those not prepared for the high risks may self-select away from such an institution.

There are, however, several ways to design the organization of instruction to reduce the incidence of failures. One is to separate the streams of students, both by areas of motivation and interest and according to initial level of mastery. The students who need more initial help can then get it, at the appropriate pace, while those of exceptional preparation and ability progress more rapidly toward advanced courses. A second approach is to individuate the learning process, putting each student in a situation in which individual guidance and development are facilitated by competent and patient faculty. This approach is far more expensive in faculty time than the first. It also reduces the stimulus that other students would otherwise get from those who excel. A third approach is the most difficult to bring off. It entails keeping a broad spectrum of students together, using the example of the superior performers to stimulate, and using their talents to help less qualified students meet the standard of acceptability.

These three approaches can be labeled *separation and stratification, individuation,* and *mutuality.* All three are employed to some extent in public universities. But the second requires much more budget per student than public universities have been permitted to have, and the third requires organizational inventions that we have not as yet been able to devise and apply widely.

The public university has interesting problems of educational organization to meet its institutional aims. These are far more complicated than the design of institutions that are settled at one end of the spectrum or the other. However, the educational setting of the strong public university offers the excellent student far more challenge and access to learning at the frontier than could be provided in a purely local and popular institution, because it gains complementarities between its superstructure of graduate education and research and its undergraduate programs. The public university, by the devices just discussed, can also meet the needs of a broader spectrum of students than the purely elite institution, but there are still educational designs and approaches to mutuality of learning to be worked out.

As for the question of constituency support, it is essential to state first that public universities are infused with commitments to the deepest, and often controversial, questions of philosophical and social values but are not in a politically partisan business. Furthermore, public universities need all the friends they can win and keep on terms that are compatible with right reason. Ideally, each public university should be capable of engendering the support and loyalty —in different aspects of its operations—of interests in the community ranging from the conservative to the left-of-center. Because each university has some essential institutional principles of operation, however, none is likely to be fully acceptable to any one interest bloc unless it both throws away those of its commitments and standards that are found repugnant and abandons its defense of some of its autonomous philosophical commitments. No university should give up its essential mandate, and none should give up the attempt to harmonize, where it can, divergent social interests and support. Thus, the public university must always be in a state of tension with the coalitions of support that it tries to build.

A public university's institutional aims, commitments, and approaches to constituency support may seem to lack the easy coherence that is possessed by an institution designed conclusively at one end of the value spectrum or the other. But this concept of a public university is based on a view of what a democratic society is like and ought to be like—not choosing between social justice and excellence, but regarding both aims as essential and compatible. Whether the great public university will continue to be viable depends essentially on whether the general society continues to embrace this double commitment.

The many friends a public university has among the establishmentarians are friends it needs, and this point needs to be emphasized both to the establishmentarians themselves (who occasionally may doubt the need of the public university for them and their need for it) and to the egalitarians, who have many differences of views with the establishmentarians. As I have argued earlier, the university needs to serve as a meeting point for the major interests and themes of society, which would be badly off indeed if it became so polarized that every significant institution had to be exclusively in one camp or the other.

Specifically, the establishmentarians are needed by the public university because they are sources of much of the power and influence in the great corporations, the leading professions, the trade unions, and organized agriculture. To a considerable extent, the public university serves these interests, especially if one is able to take the long view instead of the short, for it contributes to the vitality of technology, the economy, and social process.

But the establishmentarians are also a major support and audience for high culture. They control the mass media, which tell us all that it is fitting for us to know about ourselves. In the major professions—law, especially, but also the health professions and the administrative professions—they supply leadership and thoughtful action. Not only does the public university help to train the new recruits into these professions; it also depends on the perspective they bring to their leadership role.

Finally, there is financial support. The establishmentarians control the great foundations, and the great foundations are important indeed to universities because (when they are doing as they should) they provide much seed funding for experiments and ideas that can qualify for major governmental support only after they have been worked up to the point of at least significant promise.

Also, the rich among the establishmentarians (they are not all rich, only highly influential) have given heavily to universities, including public universities. The major private universities have always relied on major private donors, but public universities have a good case for similar benefactions to assist in providing a margin of excellence, and they welcome this support.

Universities must depend substantially on other sources of funds. The establishmentarians are important here too through their influence in state capitols and in Washington. The egalitarian political leader works for various changes in the established order and especially toward redistributions in favor of the poor, the young, the old, and the wage worker—in other words, most of the people. For obvious reasons, this power base is not as solid as that of the establishmentarians, even though it is much more numerous in people and potential votes.

We can hope that the egalitarians will appreciate the reasons why the public university is in touch with and asks the support of the establishmentarians. It can also be hoped that establishmentarians in their turn will understand that the public university has to explain itself to, cultivate, and respond to egalitarian interests. Thus, the public university must defend the philosophical basis of an institution committed to learning and academic excellence, and it also has to argue to all of its constituencies for the right to do so under conditions of autonomy and self-regulation.

Egalitarian concerns to which the public university can properly respond include the removal of financial barriers to educational opportunity, provision of a wide diversity of offerings of instruction, and expansion of the graduate professions in areas of prime social need. Public universities are also strongly accountable now for their performance in attracting minority students and women to their programs and to their faculty and staff. The public university in a state is part of a spectrum of institutions, and it therefore has to contribute to the overall educational capability of the state system in numerous ways. Finally, the public university has to respond positively to demands for applied research of a problem-solving nature, and it is obliged to offer a wide range of public services to government and the community.

Thus, we end as we began. The significant universities of the western world vary greatly in age, size, legal form of organization, institutional style, and mode of financing. Yet they have in common the coupling of teaching and research, the offering of a diversity of programs up to the most advanced stages of systematic learning, and the implicit commitment to humane ideals and scholarly interests that cross the boundaries of governments.

If this book has clarified the ways in which universities have to function, warrant support, and can be guided to fulfill their aims, it has accomplished its purpose.

Let me end, then, on a note of faith. Universities will survive in the service of a good society, for despite their crankiness and their unsettling qualities, they are essential to it. They operate by internal processes that require high personal motivation on the part of scholar and student and confer a great deal of individual latitude. This gives them a character that may be a hopeful portent for other kinds of organizations of the postindustrial society.

Checklists for Academic Quality Assessment and Program Evaluation

Chapter Six discusses several types of evidence that a university can obtain about its general position in the markets for enrollment, faculty, and academic reputation. The checklists here can be used to facilitate quality assessment and program evaluation, both of which are important issues for the institutional leadership of universities.

Assessment of Academic Quality

I. Criteria for and indicators of academic quality in conventional scholarly disciplines
1. Student input quality: ability of incoming students (minimum, median, or average, and proportion of students of superior potential, based on test scores)

283

2. Student academic achievement during university career
   a. Absolute achievement of individual student
      (1) on generalized measures (e.g., GRE)
      (2) on judgments of scholarly promise
   b. Absolute achievement: minimum passing standard
   c. Achievement relative to initial status
      (1) for each student, ratio of GRE score on completion to CEEB achievement scores or SAT at initial stage
      (2) for a population or cohort of students, rate of persistence relative to initial ability distribution and given passing standard
3. Student maturation and capacity for responsibility in career and in society
   a. Value transformations
   b. Rounded experience
   c. Career persistence and success: student "destinations" initially and after five, ten, twenty years
4. Institutional capability in field
   a. Total size of faculty cadre
   b. Borrowing of strengths from related groups
   c. Specializations
   d. Quality of faculty
      (1) stars
      (2) solid journeymen
      (3) senior unknowns (deadwood ratio)
      (4) vital younger members
   e. Achievement in research
   f. Availability of critical resources
      (1) extramural research funding
      (2) pertinent library, computer, and other basic resources
      (3) specialized resources: laboratories, building space, support personnel
5. Faculty vigor and quality
   a. Major publications—amounts and perceived quality and usage (citation indices)
   b. Success rate in obtaining peer-judged research grants
   c. Generalized opinion ranking (Cartter and Roose-Andersen ratings)
   d. Officers, editors, members of editorial boards of scholarly societies and journals
   e. Members of evaluation panels in research funding organizations
   f. Entering graduate students receiving competitive national fellowships

  g. Applicants of high quality for postdoctoral study and research intervals

  h. Honorific appointments (measures of conventional distinction)—Guggenheim, NAS, Nobel, others

 6. Faculty and program cohesion, relative to the tradition in the field

  a. Joint papers and research

  b. Other team efforts, including:

   (1) organized research

   (2) departmental committee structure and operation

 7. Progressiveness in graduate training and research

  a. Research effort and achievement focused upon major frontier issues in the discipline

  b. Closeness of theses projects and graduate courses and seminars to frontier issues

  c. Availability and use of instrumentation and methodology in frontier issues

  d. Rankings over time on opinion and reputation indices

 8. Mechanisms for imputing academic quality

  a. Use of above indicators

  b. Visiting committees of prominent scholars to evaluate department

  c. Reading of a national sample of doctoral dissertations in field to see whether outstanding ones come from department or outside reading of all accepted dissertations for a year in department

II. Criteria for and indicators of academic quality in graduate professions

 1. For academic reputation, use I

 2. Market rating of graduates at time of degree completion

  a. Starting salaries in first jobs

  b. Recruiter interviews of pending graduates

  c. Judgments of a sample of prominent professionals of the promise of graduates

 3. Early success of graduates

  a. E.g., in law schools, law-clerk appointments with prominent judges

  b. Early professional leadership

   (1) membership in professional organizations and societies

   (2) involvement in community organizations, politics, other "action" spheres

  c. Career location after five, ten, twenty years

   (1) working in same field

   (2) independently established .

   (3) dropouts and disappearances

   (4) advancement: salary, title, etc,

4. Institutional and faculty relations with practitioner communities
   a. Use of faculty members as advisors by practitioner enterprises, professional groups, Federal agencies, other agencies
   b. Generalized opinion ranking by prominent practitioners (analogous to Cartter and Roose-Andersen ratings—usually not available but can be obtained by setting up surveys)
   c. Faculty involvement in practitioner and professional societies
   d. Reformist impact on practitioner outlook and standards
   e. Origination of journals by faculty; reputation and role of such journals
5. Areas of distinction nationally
   a. Coupling of instruction and a research program in a prominent area of concern
   b. Approbation by scholars in basic disciplines
      (1) collaborative efforts with basic-discipline scholars
      (2) judgments of scholarly reputation of professional school faculty in special areas
6. *Strength of image:* distinguishing characterization by other professional schools in field, practitioner communities, prospective students

Overall Evaluation of Academic Programs

Assessment of the current quality of an academic program (using indicators of the sort described in the previous section) is important, but it is only one ingredient in decisions about the future of an academic program—decisions which involve funding, enrollment, allocations of faculty positions, and, on occasion, phasing out a program.

Eight criteria for program evaluation were enunciated by the priorities committee at Princeton University (Bowen, 1972) and were quoted and discussed in Chapter Five. The following checklist includes these and other considerations.

1. Significance of scholarship and findings in the field to the quality of culture, the future of science, or long-range issues of public policy
   a. External priority: interest in funding shown by foundations, research agencies, other agencies of the Federal and state governments, and private donors
   b. Judgments of importance by national policy-study commissions or other bodies and by leading scholars within university
2. Manpower considerations: long-range forecasts of academic and other employment of recipients of advanced degrees

   a. Employment prospects relative to current size of all programs in field
   b. Enrollment of highly qualified students and employment of those earning degrees from program
3. Importance of program to students and faculty in related fields at university
   a. Choice of this program as part of curriculum of students in other programs
   b. Multidisciplinary research and other outside involvements
4. Resources employed in program at current level
   a. Direct operating budget allocations
   b. Extramural research and training funds attracted by faculty
   c. Requirements of program
      (1) building space and major equipment
      (2) support services
      (3) library support
      (4) other significant induced costs
   d. Projections of future resource costs to maintain current level
5. Unit costs and efficiency
   a. Services provided to other programs and departments
   b. Estimates of cost per student year and cost per degree granted
6. Requirements for improving quality or expanding program beyond current level
   a. Institutionally budgeted resources: faculty positions, support, space, equipment
   b. Faculty and administrative leadership
   c. Special efforts and costs to attract outstanding students and to attract greater total enrollment
7. Effects of withdrawing resources if there are negative indications concerning current quality of the program and importance of the field to the university
   a. Direct reductions of expenditures for each of several years after a decision to reduce or terminate
   b. Reductions or increases of costs by related departments
   c. Reductions of revenue directly attributable to the program for each of several years after a decision to reduce or terminate
   d. Adverse constituency responses to a termination decision (considering all affected constituencies, external and internal)

Reports of the Ford Foundation Program for Research in University Administration

68-3: OLIVER, R. M. *Models for Predicting Gross Enrollments at the University of California.* (August 1968.)

69-1: MARSHALL, K., AND OLIVER, R. M. *A Constant Work Model for Student Attendance and Enrollment.* (February 1969.)

69-4: BRENEMAN, D. W. *The Stability of Faculty Input Coefficients in Linear Workload Models of the University of California* (April 1969.)

69-10: OLIVER, R. M. *An Equilibrium Model of Faculty Appointments, Promotions, and Quota Restrictions.* (March 1969.)

P-1: LEIMKUHLER, F., AND COOPER, M. *Analytical Planning for University Libraries.* (January 1970.)

P-2: LEIMKUHLER, F., AND COOPER, M. *Cost Accounting and Analysis for University Libraries.* (January 1970.)

P-3: SANDERSON, R. D. *The Expansion of University Facilities to Accommodate Increasing Enrollments.* (November 1969.)

P-4:   BARTHOLOMEW, D. J. *A Mathematical Analysis of Structural Control in a Graded Manpower System.* (December 1969.)

P-5:   BALDERSTON, F. E. *Thinking About the Outputs of Higher Education.* (May 1970.)

P-6:   WEATHERSBY, G. B. *Educational Planning and Decision Making: The Use of Decision and Control Analysis.* (May 1970.)

P-7:   KELLER, J. E. *Higher Education Objectives: Measures of Performance and Effectiveness.* (May 1970.)

P-8:   BRENEMAN, D. W. *An Economic Theory of Ph.D. Production.* (June 1970.)

P-9:   WINSLOW, F. D. *The Capital Costs of a University.* (January 1971.)

P-10: HALPERN, J. *Bounds for New Faculty Positions in a Budget Plan.* (May 1970.)

P-11: ROWE, S., WAGNER, W. G., AND WEATHERSBY, G. B. *A Control Theory Solution to Optimal Faculty Staffing.* (November 1970.)

P-12: WEATHERSBY, G. B., AND WEINSTEIN, M. C. *A Structural Comparison of Analytical Models.* (August 1970.)

P-13: PUGLIARESI, L. S. *Inquiries into a New Degree: The Candidate in Philosophy.* (November 1970.)

P-14: ADAMS, R. F., AND MICHAELSEN, J. B. *Assessing the Benefits of Collegiate Structure: The Case at Santa Cruz.* (February 1971.)

P-15: BALDERSTON, F. E. *The Repayment Period for Loan-Financed College Education.* (January 1971.)

P-16: BRENEMAN, D. W. *The Ph.D. Production Function: The Case at Berkeley.* (December 1970.)

P-17: BRENEMAN, D. W. *The Ph.D. Degree at Berkeley: Interviews, Placement, and Recommendations.* (January 1971.)

P-18: LLUBIA, L. *An Analysis of the Schools of Business Administration at the University of California, Berkeley.* (December 1971.)

P-19: WING, P. *Costs of Medical Education.* (September 1971.)

P-20: KREPLIN, H. S. *Credit by Examination: A Review and Analysis of the Literature.* (July 1971.)

P-21: PERL, L. J. *Graduation, Graduate School Attendance, and Investments in College Training.* (July 1971.)

P-22: WAGNER, W. G., AND WEATHERSBY, G. B. *Optimality in College Planning: A Control Theoretic Approach.* (December 1971.)

P-23: JEWETT, J. E. *College Admissions Planning: Use of a Student Segmentation Model.* (November 1971.)

P-24: BRENEMAN, D. W. (Ed.) *Internal Pricing Within the University—A Conference Report.* (December 1971.)

P-25: GEOFFRION, A. M., DYER, J. S., AND FEINBERG, A. *Academic Departmental Management: An Application of an Interactive Multi-Criterion Optimization Approach.* (October 1971.)

P-26: BALDERSTON, F. E., AND RADNER, R. *Academic Demand for New Ph.D.'s, 1970–90: Its Sensitivity to Alternative Policies.* (December 1971.)

P-27: MORRIS, J. *Educational Training and Careers of Ph.D. Holders: An Exploratory Empirical Study.* (January 1972.)

P-28: WING, P. *Planning and Decision Making for Medical Education: An Analysis of Costs and Benefits.* (January 1972.)

P-29: BALDERSTON, F. E. *Varieties of Financial Crisis.* (March 1972.)

P-30: WEATHERSBY, G. B. *Structural Issues in the Supply and Demand for Scientific Manpower: Implications for National Manpower Policy.* (May 1972.)

P-31: WEATHERSBY, G. B., AND BALDERSTON, F. E. *PPBS in Higher Education Planning and Management.* (May 1972.)

P-32: BALDERSTON, F. E. *Financing Postsecondary Education—Statement to the Joint Committee on the Master Plan for Higher Education of the California Legislature, April 12, 1972* (July 1972.)

P-33: BALDERSTON, F. E. *Cost Analysis in Higher Education.* (July 1972.)

P-34: SMITH, D. E., AND WAGNER, W. G. *SPACE: Space Planning and Cost Estimating Model for Higher Education.* (July 1972.)

P-35: HELD, P. *The Migration of the 1955–1965 Graduates of American Medical Schools.* (January 1973.)

P-36: CARLSON, D. E. *The Production and Cost Behavior of Higher Education Institutions.* (December 1972.)

P-37: WISE, D. A. *Academic Achievement and Job Performance: Earnings and Promotions.* (January 1973.)

P-38: MAC LACHLAN, J. *A Plan for a Publication Network for Rapid Dissemination of Technical Information.* (June 1973.)

P-39: BALDERSTON, F. E. *Complementarity, Independence and Substitution in University Resource Allocation and Operation.* (August 1973.)

P-40: WINKLER, D. R. *The Social Benefits of Higher Education: Implications for Regional Finance.* (July 1973.)

P-41: KREPLIN, H. S., AND BOLCE, J. W. *Interinstitutional Cooperation in Higher Education: An Analysis and Critique.* (October 1973.)

P-42: SCHMIDTLEIN, F. A. *The Selection of Decision Process Paradigms in Higher Education: Can We Make the Right Decision or Must We Make the Decision Right?* (October 1973.)

These reports may be ordered from the Center for Research in Management Science, 26 Barrows Hall, University of California, Berkeley, Calif. 94720.

References

ADAMS, R. F., AND MICHAELSEN, J. B. *Assessing the Benefits of Collegiate Structure: The Case at Santa Cruz.* Berkeley: Ford Foundation Program for Research in University Administration, Report P-14, 1971.

AMERICAN ASSOCIATION OF UNIVERSITY PROFESSORS (AAUP). *At the Brink: Preliminary Report on the Economic Status of the Profession, 1970–1971.* Washington, D.C.: 1971.

BALDERSTON, F. E. *Thinking about the Outputs of Higher Education.* Berkeley: Ford Foundation Program for Research in University Administration, Report P-5, 1970.

BALDERSTON, F. E. *Financing Postsecondary Education—Statement to the Joint Commitee on the Master Plan for Higher Education of the California Legislature.* Berkeley: Ford Foundation Program for Research in University Administration, Report P-32, 1972a.

BALDERSTON, F. E. *Varieties of Financial Crisis.* Berkeley: Ford Foundation Program for Research in University Administration, Report P-29, 1972b.

BALDERSTON, F. E. *Complementarity, Independence, and Substitution in University Resource Allocation and Operation.* Berkeley: Ford Foundation Program for Research in University Administration, Report P-39, 1973.

BALDERSTON, F. E., AND RADNER, R. *Academic Demand for New PhDs, 1970–1999: Its Sensitivity to Alternative Policies.* Berkeley:

293

Ford Foundation Program for Research in University Administration, Report P-26, 1971.

BALDERSTON, F. E., AND WALSH, T. "Comment." *Minerva,* July 1971, *9* (3), 414–417.

BARTHOLOMEW, D. J. *A Mathematical Analysis of Structural Control in a Graded Manpower System.* Berkeley: Ford Foundation Program for Research in University Administration, Report P-4, 1969.

BARNARD, C. I. *Functions of the Executive.* Cambridge, Mass.: Harvard University Press, 1938.

BECKER, G. *Human Capital.* New York: National Bureau of Economic Research, 1964.

BOWEN, H. (Ed.) *Evaluation and Accountability.* Special issue of *Journal of Institutional Research.* San Francisco: Jossey-Bass, 1974.

BOWEN, H., AND DOUGLASS, G. *Efficiency in Liberal Education.* Berkeley: Carnegie Commission on Higher Education, 1973.

BOWEN, W. G. *The Economics of the Major Private Universities.* New York: McGraw-Hill, 1968.

BOWEN, W. G. "Economic Pressures on the Major Private Universities." In Government Printing Office (Ed.), *The Economics and Financing of Higher Education to the United States: A Compendium of Papers Submitted to the Joint Economic Committee, Congress of the United States.* Washington, D.C.: 1969.

BOWEN, W. G., AND OTHERS. *Budgeting and Resource Allocation at Princeton University.* Princeton, N.J.: Princeton University Press, 1972.

BRENEMAN, D. W. *The PhD Production Function: The Case at Berkeley.* Berkeley: Ford Foundation Program for Research in University Administration, Report P-16, 1970.

BRENEMAN, D. W. *An Economic Theory of PhD Production.* Berkeley: Ford Foundation Program for Research in University Administration, Report P-8, 1971a.

BRENEMAN, D. W. *The PhD Degree at Berkeley: Interviews, Placement, and Recommendations.* Berkeley: Ford Foundation Program for Research in University Administration, Report P-17, 1971b.

BRENEMAN, D. W. (Ed.) *Internal Pricing Within the University—A Conference Report.* Berkeley: Ford Foundation Program for Research in University Administration, Report P-24, 1972.

CALIFORNIA, UNIVERSITY OF. VICE-PRESIDENT–PLANNING AND ANALYSIS. *Faculty Effort and Output.* Report to the Regents of the University of California. Berkeley, 1970.

California Legislature, Joint Committee on Higher Education. *The Challenge of Achievement*. Sacramento, 1969.

CAPLOW, T., AND MC GEE, R. J. *The Academic Marketplace*. New York: Basic Books, 1958.

CARLSON, D. E. *The Production and Cost Behavior of Higher Education Institutions*. Berkeley: Ford Foundation Program for Research in University Administration, 1972.

CARNEGIE COMMISSION ON HIGHER EDUCATION. *Dissent and Disruption*. New York: McGraw-Hill, 1971a.

CARNEGIE COMMISSION ON HIGHER EDUCATION. *Less Time, More Options*. New York: McGraw-Hill, 1971b.

CARNEGIE COMMISSION ON HIGHER EDUCATION. *Quality and Equality*. New York: McGraw-Hill, 1971.

CARNEGIE COMMISSION ON HIGHER EDUCATION. *More Effective Use of Resources*. New York: McGraw-Hill, 1972.

CARTTER, A. M. *An Assessment of Quality in Graduate Education: A Comparative Study of Graduate Departments in Twenty-Nine Academic Disciplines*. Washington, D.C.: American Council on Education, 1966.

CARTTER, A. M. "Supply and Demand for Ph.D.'s" *Science*, 1971, *172*.

CARTTER, A. M. *The Academic Labor Market*. In M. S. Gordon (Ed.), *Higher Education and the Labor Market*. New York: McGraw-Hill, 1974.

CHEIT, E. *The New Depression in Higher Education*, New York: McGraw-Hill, 1971a.

CHEIT, E. Testimony before the Special Subcommittee on Education, Committee on Education and Labor, U.S. House of Representatives, Washington, D.C., March 29, 1971b.

CHEIT, E. *The Management Systems Challenge: How to Be Academic Though Systematic*. Speech given at the annual meeting of the American Council on Education. Washington, D.C., Fall 1973a.

CHEIT, E. *The New Depression: Two Years Later*. Berkeley: Carnegie Commission on Higher Education, 1973b.

COHEN, M. D., AND MARCH, J. G. *Leadership and Ambiguity: The American College President*. New York: McGraw-Hill, 1974.

COMMITTEE FOR ECONOMIC DEVELOPMENT (CED). *Management and Financing of Colleges*. New York, 1973.

COORDINATING COUNCIL FOR HIGHER EDUCATION. SELECT COMMITTEE ON THE MASTER PLAN. *The California Master Plan for Higher Education in the Seventies and Beyond*. Sacramento, 1972.

CORNELL UNIVERSITY. *Study of Rising Costs at Ten Universities*. Ithaca, N.Y.: 1967.

Daedalus. The Embattled University. Winter 1970.

DRESCH, S. P. *Perspectives on the Evolution and Financing of Graduate Education.* Paper prepared for the National Board on Graduate Education. Washington, D.C.: 1973.

DRESSEL, P., JOHNSON, F. C., AND MARCUS, P. M. *The Confidence Crisis.* San Francisco: Jossey-Bass, 1970.

ECKAUS, R. *Estimating the Returns to Education, a Disaggregated Approach.* Berkeley: Carnegie Commission on Higher Education, 1973.

GARBARINO, J. W. "Creeping Unionism in the Faculty Labor Market." In M. S. Gordon (Ed.), *Higher Education and the Labor Market.* New York: McGraw-Hill, 1974a.

GARBARINO, J. W. *Statement, Hearings on Collective Negotiation in Higher Education.* California Legislature, Joint Committee on Postsecondary Education, April 19, 1974b.

GEOFFRION, A. M., DYER, D. S., AND FEINBERG, A. *Academic Departmental Management: An Application of an Interactive Multicriterion Optimization Approach.* Berkeley: Ford Foundation Program for Research in University Administration, Report P-25, 1972.

GRINOLD, R. C., AND STANFORD, R. E. *Optimal Control of a Graded Manpower System.* Berkeley: Operations Research Center, University of California, 1973.

HELD, P. J. *The Migration of the 1955–1965 Graduates of American Medical Schools.* Berkeley: Ford Foundation Program for Research in University Administration, 1973.

HOFSTADTER, R. *Anti-Intellectualism in American Life.* New York: Knopf, 1963.

HUMPHREY, D. Letter to the editor. *The Chronicle of Higher Education,* January 31, 1972.

JENNY, H. H., AND WYNN, G. R. *The Golden Years: A Study of Income and Expenditure Growth and Distribution of Forty-Eight Private Four-Year Liberal Arts Colleges, 1960–1968.* Wooster, Ohio: College of Wooster, 1971.

JENNY, H. H., AND WYNN, G. R. *After the Golden Years.* Wooster, Ohio: College of Wooster, 1972a.

JENNY, H. H., AND WYNN, R. *The Turning Point.* Wooster, Ohio: College of Wooster, 1972b.

JEWETT, J. E. *College Admissions Planning: Use of a Student Segmentation Model.* Berkeley: Ford Foundation Program for Research in University Administration, Report P-23, 1971.

KALUDIS, G. "Emerging Principles for Budgeting." In G. Kaludis (Ed.),

Strategies for Budgeting (New Directions for Higher Education, No. 2). San Francisco: Jossey-Bass, 1973.

KERR, C. *The Uses of the University.* Cambridge, Mass.: Harvard University Press, 1963.

KERSHAW, J. Discussion of "Varieties of Financial Crisis." In L. Wilson and O. Mills (Eds.), *Universal Higher Education.* Washington, D.C.: American Council on Education, 1972.

KREPLIN, H. S., AND BOLCE, J. W. *Interinstitutional Cooperation in Higher Education: An Analysis and Critique.* Berkeley: Ford Foundation Program for Research in University Administration, Report P-41, 1973.

LEE, E. C., AND BOWEN, F. M. *The Multicampus University: A Study of Academic Governance.* Berkeley: Carnegie Commission on Higher Education, 1971.

LEIMKUHLER, F. F., AND COOPER, M. D. *Analytical Planning for University Libraries.* Berkeley: Ford Foundation Program for Research in University Administration, 1970a.

LEIMKUHLER, F. F., AND COOPER, M. D. *Cost Accounting and Analysis for University Libraries.* Berkeley: Ford Foundation Program for Research in University Administration, 1970b.

LIPSET, S. M. "The Politics of Academia." In D. E. Nichols (Ed.), *Perspectives on Campus Tensions.* Washington, D.C.: American Council on Education, 1970.

MC CARTHY, J. L., AND DEENER, D. R. *The Costs and Benefits of Graduate Education: Commentary with Recommendations.* Washington, D.C.: Council of Graduate Schools, 1972.

MORSE, P. M. *Library Effectiveness: A Systems Approach.* Cambridge, Mass.: M.I.T. Press, 1968.

NATIONAL BOARD ON GRADUATE EDUCATION. *Doctorate Manpower and Policy Problems.* Washington, D.C.: 1973a.

NATIONAL BOARD ON GRADUATE EDUCATION. *Doctorate Manpower Forecasts and Policy.* Washington, D.C.: 1973b.

NATIONAL BOARD ON GRADUATE EDUCATION. *Federal Policy Alternatives Toward Graduate Education and Research.* Washington, D.C.: 1974.

NATIONAL CENTER FOR HIGHER EDUCATION MANAGEMENT SYSTEMS (NCHEMS). *Cost-Finding Principles and Procedures.* Boulder, 1972.

NATIONAL CENTER FOR HIGHER EDUCATION MANAGEMENT SYSTEMS (NCHEMS). *Introduction to the Resource Requirements Prediction Model 1.6,* Technical Report 34A. Boulder, 1973a.

NATIONAL CENTER FOR HIGHER EDUCATION MANAGEMENT SYSTEMS
(NCHEMS). *Resource Requirement Prediction Model 1.6 Reports*, Technical Report 34B. Boulder, 1973b.

OFFICE OF THE VICE PRESIDENT—PLANNING AND ANALYSIS. *Faculty Effort and Output*, Report to the Regents of the University of California. Berkeley: January, 1970.

OLIVER, R. M. *An Equilibrium Model of Faculty Appointments, Promotions, and Quota Restrictions.* Berkeley: Ford Foundation Program for Research in University Administration, Report 69-10, 1969.

O'NEILL, J. *Resource Use in Higher Education: Trends in Outputs and Inputs, 1930-1967.* Berkeley: Carnegie Commission on Higher Education, 1971.

POWEL, J. H., AND LAMSON, R. D. *Elements Related to the Determination of Costs and Benefits of Graduate Education.* Washington, D.C.: Council of Graduate Schools, 1972.

RADNER, R., AND MILLER, L. S. "Demand and Supply in U.S. Higher Education: A Progress Report." *American Economic Review,* May 1970, 328-329.

RIVLIN, A. *Toward a Long-Range Plan for Federal Financial Support for Higher Education: A Report to the President.* Washington, D.C.: U.S. Department of Health, Education, and Welfare, Assistant Secretary for Planning and Evaluation, 1969.

RIVLIN, A. Testimony, Special Subcommittee on Education, Committee on Education and Labor, U.S. House of Representatives, Apr. 1971.

ROOSE, K. D., AND ANDERSEN, C. J. *A Rating of Graduate Programs.* Washington, D.C.: American Council on Education, 1970.

SANDERSON, R. D. *The Expansion of University Facilities to Accommodate Increasing Enrollments.* Berkeley: Ford Foundation Program for Research in University Administration, Report P-3, 1969.

SCHULTZ, T. W. *The Economic Value of Education.* New York: Columbia University Press, 1963.

SCHULTZ, T. W. "Resources for Higher Education." In M. D. Orwig (Ed.), *Financing Higher Education: Alternatives for the Federal Government.* Iowa City: The American College Testing Program, 1971.

SCHULTZ, T. W. (Ed.) *Investment in Education.* Special issue of *The Journal of Political Economy,* May/June 1972, *80* (3), Part II.

SEARLE, J. *The Campus War.* New York: World, 1971.

SIMON, H. A. *Administrative Behavior.* New York: Macmillan, 1947.

SMITH, D., AND WAGNER, W. G. *SPACE: Space Planning and Cost Estimating Model for Higher Education.* Berkeley: Ford Foundation Program for Research in University Administration, Report P-34, 1972.

SMITH, V. "Institutional Economies." In American Council on Education (Ed.), *Universal Higher Education.* Washington, D.C.: 1972.

STADTMAN, V. A. *The University of California, 1886–1968.* New York: McGraw-Hill, 1970.

SYSTEMS RESEARCH GROUP, INC. *Campus VII, College and University Planning Model.* Toronto, 1972.

TUTTLE, H. W., BROWN, N. B., AND HUFF, W. H. "Price Indexes for 1970, and U.S. Periodicals and Services." *Library Journal,* July 1970, 2427–2429.

WEATHERSBY, G. B., AND BALDERSTON, F. E. *PPBS in Higher Education Planning and Management.* Berkeley: Ford Foundation Program for Research in University Administration, Report P-31, 1972.

WESTERN INTERSTATE COMMISSION ON HIGHER EDUCATION (WICHE). *The Outputs of Higher Education.* Boulder, 1970.

WESTERN INTERSTATE COMMISSION ON HIGHER EDUCATION (WICHE). *Higher Education Facilities Planning and Management Manual.* Boulder, 1971.

WILLIAMS, G. L., BLACKSTONE, T., AND METCALF, D. *An Academic Labor Market.* Amsterdam: Elsevier, in preparation.

WILSON, L., AND MILLS, O. (Eds.) *Universal Higher Education.* Washington, D.C.: American Council on Education, 1972.

WOLFLE, D., AND KIDD, C. V. "Demand and Supply for PhDs." *Science,* 1971, *173,* 784–793.

Index